69

WRITING STRATEGIES

FOR
ESL STUDENTS

JUDITH ANNE JOHNSON
Eastern Michigan University

MACMILLAN PUBLISHING CO., INC.
New York

COLLIER MACMILLAN PUBLISHERS
London

Macmillan Publishing Co., Inc.
866 Third Avenue, New York, New York 10022

Collier Macmillan Canada, Inc.

Library of Congress Cataloging in Publication Data

Johnson, Judith Anne.
  Writing strategies for ESL students.

  Bibliography: p.
  Includes index.
  1. English language — Text-books for foreigners.
2. English language — Rhetoric. I. Title
PE1128.J584   808'.042   82-15276
ISBN 0-02-361020-4

Printing: 4 5 6 7 8   Year: 7 8 9 0

ISBN 0-02-361020-4

Preface

This book is for those highly intelligent, highly motivated, incredibly hard working students from many countries around the world to whose older brothers and sisters I have had the privilege and pleasure of teaching freshman composition for several years. These students could have passed a regular course in composition; their ability to compose their thoughts in correct written English frequently proved to be superior to the ability of native speakers: they rarely used "who" when "whom" was required; they did not express themselves in tired cliches; their modifiers rarely dangled; and they had a gift for simile and metaphor that could put some poets to the blush. However, because they had frequent problems with things like English determiners, verb forms, and punctuation and with the cultural assumptions of the usual essay anthologies used in the usual English composition courses, they enrolled in the special sections of freshman composition which I taught for non-native speakers of English.

Failing to find the textbooks I wanted for those students, I used a lot of handouts. Eventually, those handouts evolved into this book, which is intended for advanced ESL students or non-native speakers of English in special sections of regular English composition courses.

Section One reviews those aspects of written English that are likely to elicit red ink from a composition teacher's pen: mechanics, punctuation, grammar, and sentence structure. This review section comes first because a relatively quick review of basic composition error areas helps the instructor determine which students have problems with which areas, and it provides the students, at the beginning of the course, with a reference to consult when such problems occur after they start writing paragraphs and themes. There is a potential fault with having the review at the beginning: an instructor can unwittingly spend too much time on the error areas and the exercises and consequently leave too little time for the real subject matter of the book, the composition of well-organized, well-developed paragraphs and themes. But if the review section is used *only* to determine individual students' problems and for reference as needed throughout the term, unnecessary time will not be spent on it.

Section Two is the heart of the book. A student who can write a thoughtfully limited, well-organized, well-developed paragraph has all the skills necessary to write a thorough, informative, and well-focused letter, report, examination, summary, or article. Various methods of organizing the various kinds of evidence demanded by native speakers of English (and of many other Western European languages) are presented with numerous example compositions. These are followed by composition exercises that require using the organizational models just illustrated in the examples. Paragraph revision is presented in a separate chapter which points out the specific problems of a sample paragraph — mechanics, grammar, punctuation, sentence structure, vocabulary, and transitions — and shows how to correct those problems one by one. The emphasis is on "how to."

Section Three concerns multi-paragraph compositions — themes. Like paragraphs, themes are discussed in terms of modes of organizing and developing ideas. The numerous examples chosen to illustrate the modes of organization and development are a deliberate departure from the usual literary essays assigned for composition courses. Students from non-Western cultures often possess good English language skills, but are at a disadvantage when a reading assignment demands native-speaker awareness of myriad aspects of Western culture. Success in an American college or university does not depend on a thorough understanding of American culture and history. Rather, it depends on a general understanding of the disciplines that constitute the basic courses required for graduation and a thorough understanding of one's chosen major and minor fields. All students, native speaker or not, must be able to read, comprehend, and write about language, literature, art, music, chemistry, philosophy, biology, economics, history, mathematics, psychology, management, marketing, computer science, and numerous other fields of study.

Thus, the "themes" in Section Three have been taken primarily from college textbooks in required courses and themes written by my students for class assignments, which they have generously given me permission to use. All selections are not for all students; students majoring in mathematics, computer science, engineering, or one of the laboratory sciences will probably find the essay "The Primes" (pages 233–235) more interesting and intelligible than the one on "The Poets of World War I" (pages 187–188). Students majoring in history, humanities, or literature will probably react to these two essays in exactly the opposite way. It will not hurt either group to read and try to understand both essays. A discussion of both could include a discussion of the specialized vocabularies of different academic fields. The exercises in this section require written compositions on a variety of subjects, with an emphasis on organization and development of ideas.

A chapter on theme revision is included to show how two students altered, added to, and subtracted from rough drafts to produce final papers. This section should not be used alone. Paragraph revision is an integral part of the process of theme revision; the two processes of revision should interact to produce a polished final paper. The chapter on theme revision assumes the simultaneous use of Chapter 10, on paragraph revision.

Section Four, the final section of the book, explains the fundamental skills needed to write research papers and includes footnote and bibliography writing exercises. If a student can write a paragraph that makes good use of an appropriate quotation or an idea that is not the student's own, and if he or she can properly document the original source of that quotation or idea, that student has the ability to write a research report, a term paper, and even (given the right subject matter and background knowledge from the appropriate sequence of courses) a dissertation.

This book is dedicated to my students in the special sections of English composition — special in more ways than one. If I had not met them, this book would never have been written. They taught me as much as I taught them.

My special thanks to Cheryll Conklin, who not only typed the original manuscript and all the necessary revisions, but who also cheered me on each time she handed me a new pile of crisp, typed pages with the words, "I understood it — I even found it interesting."

J. A. J.

Contents

SECTION FOUR:
CITING AUTHORITY   261

SECTION ONE

REVIEW

CHAPTER 1

Review of
Mechanics

Organizing ideas into paragraphs and organizing paragraphs into compositions are the concerns of later chapters. This chapter is a review of mechanics — writing rules that have nothing to do with what is said, but have a lot to do with making it easier for a reader to follow what is said.

INDENTING PARAGRAPHS

The first thing a reader sees after opening a letter, a composition, a magazine, a newspaper, or a book is a page full of writing or type. The writer's continual responsibility is to help the reader understand that page. One of the ways this is done is by indenting paragraphs, which means starting the first line of each paragraph five typewriter spaces or about an inch (2.5 cm) to the right of the left-hand margin. The sentences within a paragraph should immediately follow one another. Each sentence should not begin a new line. This paragraph contains six sentences, but most of them begin in the middle of a line.

This paragraph begins with an indentation; the writer is signalling to the readers that there is a slight change of subject. In many cultures, calligraphy — the art of handwriting — is important, and the writer tries to produce a page of writing that is beautiful. In some cultures, this may involve starting each sentence on a separate line. Writers of English are more concerned with getting a lot of information onto each page. They try to write legibly, but most are not concerned with aesthetics. This is perhaps regrettable, but it is a characteristic of writing in English.

In addition to indenting the first line of each paragraph, a writer is expected to leave a margin on each side of a written page. Most notebook paper of the kind usually used for compositions has a margin line down the left-hand side, but does not have one on the right-hand side of the page. This often leads students to write to the edge of the page, squeezing words and punctuation marks into too little space. Leaving a margin an inch (2.5 cm) wide on the right-hand side of the paper as well as on the left makes a neater, more easily read composition.

ABBREVIATIONS AND NUMERALS

The general rule about using abbreviations or numerals in a composition is *don't.* There are six types of exceptions. Abbreviations *are* used in:

1. A few titles: *Mr.* Sim, *Mrs.* Comacho, *Ms.* Jacob, *Dr.* Chung, and *St.* John. Other titles should be written out: *Professor* Lang, not Prof. Lang, and *Senator* Smith, not Sen. Smith.
2. Degrees and family designations preceded by names: Howard Rubin, *M.D.*, Janet Sugihara, *Ph.D.*, Robert Nissle, *D.D.S.*, Henry Ford, *Jr.* ("Junior" is used to specify the son of a family in which both the father and son have the same name. If a third generation carries the same name, Roman numerals are used: John Jones, III, is the grandson of John Jones and the son of John Jones, Jr.)
3. Initial letters of words in phrases naming organizations, places, and long technical terms: "UNESCO," "NATO," "the U.S.A.," and "CAT scanner." (See Chapter 2 for the use of periods.) Unless the abbreviation is generally known and used, write the word or phrase in its complete form the first time, followed by the abbreviation in parentheses:

    The National Organization of Women (NOW) supports the
    Equal Rights Amendment (ERA).

    The chemical elements and most compounds should not be abbreviated by the designations they have in the chemistry laboratory. You can talk about your "chem lab," but don't write this in a formal paper. In a composition, it should be "oxygen," not "O," and "water," not "H_2O." Your chemistry laboratory professor may not require formal writing in your laboratory reports, but your composition professor (please, not "comp prof") expects it in your themes. There are a few exceptions: "DDT" is preferable to "dichlorodiphenyltrichloroethane"; everyone knows what DDT is, although many people do not know what words the three letters abbreviate.
4. Time designations, when used with specific numbers: 349 B.C., A.D. 1066, 6:00 a.m., 6:00 p.m. (but not "yesterday p.m.").
5. Dollars and cents together, or dollars alone, but not cents alone: $32.67, $30.00, seventy-four cents.
6. Numbers longer than two words: 127, 1980, one hundred. Avoid beginning a sentence with an Arabic numeral; either spell the number out or put it elsewhere:

    Two hundred and thirty-seven people were there.
    There were 237 people there.

7. Abbreviations for words referring to portions of addresses (the names of streets, avenues, boulevards, etc. and of states, provinces, counties, etc.) are correct only when they appear in addresses on envelopes or letter headings:

> Dr. A. N. Chandler
> 1234 Main St. N.W.
> Any Town, Yorks, G.B.

Many words in footnotes and bibliographic entries are abbreviated. (See Chapter 14). Most abbreviations, however, belong only on personal notes, shopping lists, and other types of writing intended for private use. The written phrase "10 lbs. flour" is fine on a grocery list, but in a composition it should be "ten pounds of flour."

CAPITAL LETTERS

There are four functions of capital letters:

1. To mark the beginning of a sentence.
2. To mark the major words in titles of themes, articles, essays, and art works (including books, plays, paintings, musical compositions, etc). Determiners, prepositions, and conjunctions of less than five letters are not capitalized unless they begin their titles.
3. The first person pronoun, "I," and the poetic exclamation "O" (but not the common exclamation "oh!").
4. Proper nouns and adjectives derived from them. Words like "street," "avenue," "university," "doctor," and "professor," are capitalized only if they are used as part of a proper noun. Compare the following pairs of nouns, in which the proper noun names a specific person, course, or place and the corresponding common noun does not refer to a specific person, course, or place:

PROPER NOUNS	COMMON NOUNS
They met Dr. Ahmed Madavi.	They met the doctor.
They met Professor Andrews.	They met the professor.
They met President Reagan.	They met the president.
He is taking Biology 101, History 205, Economics 110, and English 221.	He is taking biology, history, economics, and English.
She is a student at Colorado State University.	She is a student at the university.
He toured the South during the summer.	He went south this summer.
MIT's College of Engineering has a fine reputation.	He went to college to study engineering.

EXERCISE

1. The following paragraph contains some incorrectly used abbreviations and numerals; it does not contain any capital letters. Rewrite it, using capitals where they are necessary, and correcting the errors of abbreviations and numerals.

prof. gonzalez teaches math. 503, a new course in basic mathematics for students who do not intend to major in science or math. central state college is one of the 1st in the u.s. to offer such a course. it should appeal to english majors, artists, musicians, and people in the social sciences. the course is affectionately known as "numbers for ninnies," although its official title is "fundamental concepts of mathematics." doctor gonzalez is well qualified to teach the course; for his 1st 3 yrs. as an undergrad., he majored in french and minored in poli. sci. then he switched to english lit. not until he became a grad. student did he get interested in math. he went to a univ. in the s.w. which offered 7 interdisciplinary courses in science, math, and humanities, and he realized that one could combine a love for lit. and lang. with computational skills.

END-OF-LINE PUNCTUATION AND SYLLABLE STRUCTURE

Only three marks of punctuation may begin a line of writing: an open *quotation mark* ☐ at the beginning of a quotation, an open *parenthesis* ☐ at the beginning of a parenthetical expression, and a *dash* ☐. None of the others may begin a line; their proper place is in the middle or at the end of a line. (An inch-wide margin on the right-hand side ensures room for punctuation marks.)

A hyphen (a short dash) is used at the end of a line to indicate that the word is incomplete and that the missing portion appears at the beginning of the next line. There is a restriction on splitting a word at the end of a line: the split can occur only between syllables. The word "education" could be written with "ed-," "edu-," or "educa-," at the end of a line, because it contains the syllables "ed," "u," "ca," and "tion." The word "chairs" cannot be split, because it contains only one syllable. Dictionary entries indicate the syllable structures of words, as the following example from *Webster's New Ideal Dictionary* shows:

oc·cu·pa·tion /ˌäk-yə-ˈpā-shən/ 1: an activity in which one engages; esp : one's business or vocation 2 a: the taking possession of property : occupancy b: the taking possession or holding and controlling of an area by a foreign military force — **oc·cu·pa·tion·al** / -shnəl, -shən-əl/ *adj* — **oc·cu·pa·tion·al·ly**/ -ē/ *adv*

CHAPTER 2

Review of Punctuation

The purpose of writing is to communicate with someone when speech is not possible or practical. In speech, there are signals that inform a listener when the speaker has finished expressing one idea and is about to start another: pauses, lowering the voice, raising the voice, stressing a word, and so on. Punctuation serves the same purpose in written communication. It helps the reader follow the author's ideas without becoming confused, or misinterpreting what the author is saying.

THE COMMA $\boxed{,}$

No punctuation mark causes as many problems to writers and produces as much red ink from composition teachers as the comma. The comma has eight separate functions; it is not surprising that inexperienced writers tend either to omit it when it is required or to give it extra functions that are inappropriate. Commas are used for the following reasons:

1. They separate items in a series, as in
   a. Hedeel, Khadiga, and Hansoon are planning a trip to Kentucky, Tennessee, and Florida.
   b. Tareq has classes every morning, three afternoons, and one evening.
   c. That tall, dark, elegantly dressed man is the ambassador.
   d. Resa went to class, lost his book, broke his glasses, and wished he had stayed home.
2. They set off a word, phrase, or clause that introduces the main idea of a sentence, as in
   a. No, Carlos has not registered yet.
   b. Obviously, Aurelio is not used to cold weather.

6

    c. Hoping for a letter from home, Un Ha anxiously awaited the postman.

    d. Because his parents were coming for a visit, Vincent wanted to take the test early.

3. They separate two sentences which are joined by a coordinating conjunction (and, but, or, nor, yet, so, for), as in

    a. Miss Cisneros plans a career in biochemistry, and Miss Mejia intends to be a teacher.

    b. Mr. Zhixing will spend the summer with his family, but Mr. Wong will continue taking courses at the university.

    c. Miss Serrano could spend the holidays with her sister in Chicago, or she could join a tour group going to New York.

    d. Mr. Mohtadi does not enjoy basketball, nor is he keen on baseball.

    e. Mr. Lee has received his visa, yet his plans are indefinite.

    f. Susanna needs a winter coat, so she has gone shopping.

    g. Azin studied all night, for she knew the examination would be difficult.

4. They set off sentence "interruptors": words, phrases, or clauses that interrupt or add a final note to the main structure of the sentence without adding essential information, as in

    a. Would you, Tina, put the example on the board?

    b. Johnson, who studied English for six years in Nigeria, speaks very fluently.

    c. The statistics course, offered every semester, is required on the education major.

    d. Ramin has started to diet, having gained ten pounds last month.

    e. Some students find chemistry easy, of course.

5. They set off phrases that provide a contrast to the main idea; these phrases often begin with "not," or "but," as in

    a. It was Jamal, not Javad, who won the scholarship.

    b. There are not three choices, but two.

6. They set off parts of dates, addresses and place names, and numbers, as in

    a. On July, 1776, America won its independence.

    b. Senab lives at 1234 Main Street, Fargo, North Dakota.

    c. There are 1,547,632 subscribers to that newspaper.

7. A comma sets off a quotation from the remainder of the sentence in which it occurs. Commas go outside opening quotation marks and inside closing ones, as in

    a. Ahmed announced, "The bus will leave for the airport in five minutes."

    b. "Hand in your themes," the teacher requested.

    c. "When, "asked Pouran," is the term paper due?"

8. Commas are used to avoid confusing a reader, as in the following sentence, which sounds incomplete:

    a. Students who can go home for the holidays.

The addition of a comma clarifies the meaning:

    b. Students who can, go home for the holidays.

If the meaning of a sentence is clear without the addition of one or more commas and if none of the seven basic rules for comma usage applies, do not add commas simply because a person reading the sentence aloud would pause to take breath at certain points. On the other hand, if the average reader would have trouble understanding the sentence, check to see that all required commas are present and that where confusion might occur a comma has been added.

EXERCISES

1. The following paragraph is missing some required commas, and it contains some commas which do not belong. Rewrite the paragraph, adding commas where they are needed and deleting them where they are not wanted. Be prepared to discuss your decisions.

Linguistically the American population never became the kind of sedentary long-settled group, that is described in most of the works, on language history. In order to understand the development of American English we cannot limit ourselves, to the British-derived Americans as though they were alone, and worked out their own language development, with only minor influences, from elsewhere.

Conventional histories, in their concern, with the claims, and counterclaims, of the European nations, to the "new" continent find it all too easy to overlook the fact, that two of the most prominent groups, with which the "white" europeans came into contact, were the American Indians and the West-Africa-derived slaves.[1]

2. Take a paragraph or two from one of your textbooks and rewrite it, omitting all commas. Then read through your written version, putting in the missing commas. Check your revision against the original paragraph(s), carefully noting the location of each comma. If you have more commas than the original, determine why some are not necessary. If the original has commas where your revision does not, determine why those in the original are necessary.

THE PERIOD ⊡

Much less apt to be misused than a comma, a period has three primary functions.

---

[1] J. L. Dillard, *All-American English: A History of the English Language In America*, Chap. 4. (New York: Random House, Vintage Books, 1975), p. 117. The published text has been revised, with dreadful misuse, to illustrate the point of this portion of the punctuation review. The correct version is printed in the Teacher's Manual.

1. It signals the end of a statement or command-request, as in
   a. Pouran rides a bicycle to class.
   b. Turn in your themes.
2. It signals the end of a statement containing an indirect question, as in
   a. Moise asked where he could meet us.
   b. Bjorn wondered what he should read.

Compare the second example with the following, which is a statement containing a direct question:

   c. Bjorn wondered, "What should I read?"
3. It signals that a word or phrase has been abbreviated, as in
   a. Mr. Ogbonna's daughter earned her Ph.D. from M.I.T.

Periods are not always used for abbreviations of organizations or institutions, especially when three or more words are abbreviated, as in "AAUP" (The American Association of University Professors). Periods are never used for *acronyms*, abbreviations which can be pronounced as words, such as "NATO" and "UNESCO."

NOTE: Using a comma rather than a period at the end of a statement produces a major error, a *comma splice*. Using nothing produces another major error, a *fused sentence*. Using a period at the end of a structure which is not a complete statement produces a third major error, a *sentence fragment*. (For further discussion of these, see chapters 6 and 7.)

EXERCISES

1. Some of the periods in the following paragraph are correctly used; some are incorrectly used; and some are missing. Add periods where they are needed, and remove those which do not belong.

   The blizzard of March, 1965, disrupted many people's lives thousands of households were without power for hours. And, in some cases, days. Children could not get to their schools, and adults either could not get to their jobs. Or could not get home. From their jobs. Motorists were stranded on snow-blocked roads. And highways. And the motels in a three-state area were filled to capacity it took road crews and power company crews three weeks to undo. What the three-day blizzard had done.

2. Copy a paragraph from one of your textbooks, omitting all periods and all capital letters which begin sentences. Without looking at the book, try to punctuate the paragraph correctly, capitalizing words as needed. Check your corrected paragraph with the original, noting particularly where your version and the book's version differ.

THE QUESTION MARK ⸂?⸃

A question mark has one primary function: to signal the end of a *direct question*, as in:

1. Has Zairo received her visa yet**?**
2. Will Wolfgang be able to go home this summer**?**
3. Did Zeinab take the TOEFL examination**?**

When a quoted questions occurs within a statement, the question mark goes inside the quotation marks, with no period, as in

4. Ahmed asked Ali, "Where can I buy some saffron**?**"

When a quoted statement occurs at the end of a question, the question mark goes outside the quotation marks, with no period, as in

5. Did Parvin really tell Demetrios, "You look like an American teenager"**?**

When a quoted question occurs at the end of a question, only one question mark is used, inside the quotation marks, as in

6. Should I ask my professor, "When is the research paper due**?**"

As we observed above, an indirect question should not be marked with a question mark. Compare the three sentences at the beginning of this section with the following:

7. I wonder if Zairo has received her visa yet.
8. I wonder if Wolfgang will be able to go home this summer.
9. I wonder if Zeinab took the TOEFL examination.

EXERCISE

1. In the following paragraph, some question marks are correctly used, some are incorrectly used, and some are missing. Add question marks where they are needed, and remove those which do not belong.

> Have you ever considered a career as a taster. Many companies employ tasters to determine whether their product can successfully compete with the competitor's. A taster must first ask him or herself, "Is the flavor of this product appealing"? He or she must also decide whether the texture of the product is pleasing. If the taster's assessment proves to be wrong, what are the consequences. Suppose a taster decides that a new kind of bread is the best he has ever tasted, and urges his company to market a large quantity of it? If shoppers do not agree with the taster, they will not buy the product. If they will not buy it, how will the company make money?

QUOTATION MARKS "

Quotation marks have two main uses and one minor one.

1. They signal direct quotations, usually words written or spoken by someone other than the writer, as in
   a. Eugenia announced, "I plan to become a physician."
   b. Anton suggested to his roommate, "Let's get an apartment next year."
   c. As a famous poet once wrote, "Life's but a passing shadow."

NOTE: Indirect quotations are statements that give the ideas of another person, but not in that person's exact words, as in

   d. Eugenia announced that she planned to become a physician.
   e. Anton suggested to his roommate that they should consider getting an apartment for the following year.
   f. A famous poet once remarked that life does not last very long.

Indirect quotations, as in (d), (e), and (f), should *not* be punctuated with quotation marks.

2. Quotation marks signal the title of a story, an article, an essay, a song, a short poem, a radio or television program, or a chapter or section of a book, as in
   a. Have you read the story "The Ransom of Red Chief"?
   b. This month's alumni magazine contains the article "Graduates are Turning Grey."
   c. The national anthem of the U.S.A. is "The Star Spangled Banner."
   d. Hannah enjoys watching "Mork and Mindy."
   e. You should review the section "Selecting Details" from this book.
3. They also denote a special use of a word, as in
   a. The word "turkey" can refer to either a bird or a person.
   b. Linguists refer to the order of words in sentences as "syntax."

Italics (see below) are sometimes also used for this purpose. The reason for marking a word in such a sentence is clarity. Without the quotation marks around "turkey," an unsuspecting reader might ask, "What is a word turkey?"

ITALICS

Italics are a slanted alphabet *that looks like this*. They are indicated in a handwritten or typed paper by underlining. Italics are used for three reasons:

1. They mark titles of books, long poems, newspapers, magazines, and journals, as in
   a. Have you read *The Lord of the Rings?*
   b. Tennyson's *In Memoriam* was written to honor a friend.
   c. *The New York Times* is a highly respected newspaper.

    d. The recent issue of *Equus* has an excellent article on taming wild mustangs.

    e. Sonja's article on Chaucer's puns will appear in *Speculum.*

2. They mark a word being defined, named, or used in a special way (see also paragraph 3 above), as in

    a. *Phonology* is the study of speech sounds.

    b. "Smog" was formed by merging parts of two words, "smoke" and "fog." This process of word formation is called *blending.*

    c. The *however* is used incorrectly in that sentence.

3. Italics mark a word or phrase from another language which does not have widespread use in English, as in

    a. The *pièce de resistance* of the meal was the desert.

    b. Jules suffered from an attack of *mal de mer* (seasickness).

EXERCISES

Add the needed quotation marks or italics (underlining) to each of the following sentences.

1. Felicia finds zoris more comfortable than shoes.
2. Ismail's spelling of psyche is incorrect, but phonetically accurate.
3. The Sword in the Stone is one part of the book, The Once and Future King.
4. The theme song of the University of Michigan is The Victors.
5. Valence is a chemical term.
6. Sophia lent Tomas an excellent book, The Study of Islam.
7. Deciding What Ideas to Include is the ninth chapter in Writing Strategies.

THE EXCLAMATION POINT   !

The exclamation point is well named. It should be used only when the writer wishes to express in written form what would be shouted or exclaimed in speech, as in

1. Look out! (You are about to get run over by a cyclist.)
2. Help! (I am in twelve feet of water with no boat, and I cannot swim.)
3. Ouch!
4. Phone the police!
5. The house is on fire!

Exclamation points (and underlines, too) should not be used as a substitute for precise vocabulary choices. Examples 6 and 7 below are preferable to examples 8 and 9.

6. Indira was ecstatic about winning the scholarship.

7. Sean was furious/enraged about the robbery.
8. Indira was really <u>happy</u> about winning the scholarship!
9. Sean was really <u>mad</u> (or worse, "real mad") about the robbery!

THE SEMICOLON   [;]

Semicolons have three main functions:

1. Normally, a semicolon can be used only where a period would also be correct, between two independent clauses. A semicolon is preferable to a period when the ideas in one sentence are closely linked to the ideas in the sentence that precedes it, as in
   a. George enjoys tinkering with engines. He plans to become an auto mechanic.

These two sentences are closely related, so a semicolon is appropriate:

   b. George enjoys tinkering with engines; he plans to become an auto mechanic.

Example (d) below links the two ideas more clearly than (c) does:

   c. Azin was seriously injured last Monday. She fell out of a third-story window.
   d. Azin was seriously injured last Monday; she fell out of a third-story window.

When the second of a pair of clauses has a connection to the first which is specified in a transition word like "therefore," "however," or "thus," these words function as introductory phrases and must be followed by commas, as in

   e. Sol had to get to New York in a hurry. Therefore, he took a plane.

or

   f. Sol had to get to New York in a hurry; therefore, he took a plane.
   g. Rachel wanted to prepare a special meal. However, she could not find the necessary ingredients.

or

   h. Rachel wanted to prepare a special meal; however, she could not find the necessary ingredients.

Incorrect use of a semicolon, like incorrect use of a period, may produce one of the three major errors, a *comma splice*, *fused sentence*, or *sentence fragment*. Using a comma where a semicolon or period is required produces a *comma splice*. Using no punctuation mark where a semicolon or period is required produces a *fused sentence*. Using a semicolon or period at the end of a structure which is not a complete sentence produces a *sentence fragment*.

These three errors are both punctuation errors and sentence structure errors. They are discussed further in Chapters 6 and 7.

2. Two sentences joined with a coordinating conjunction such as "and," "but," "or," "nor," "yet," "so," or "for" usually require only a comma before the conjunction. (See page 7, #3). However, if one or both of the sentences thus joined contain other commas, a semicolon before the conjunction is more helpful to a reader than a comma. The following sentence is potentially confusing:

    a. Freshman English, which is a required course in most universities, should be taken during a student's first year, but some students, hoping for easier courses at the beginning of their programs, delay taking it, sometimes until the semester before graduation.

Using a semicolon before "but" makes it clear where one main idea ends and the next one begins:

    b. Freshman English, which is a required course in most universities, should be taken during a student's first year; but some students, hoping for easier courses at the beginning of their programs, delay taking it, sometimes until the semester before graduation.

3. Occasionally, a writer produces a series composed of structures which need internal commas. If a writer wanted to say that she had visited Caracas, Venezuela, and Dallas, Texas, and Provo, Utah, and Anchorage, Alaska, she would have a problem. Some readers might not know that Caracas, Dallas, Provo, and Anchorage are cities in the country of Venezuela and the states of Texas, Utah, and Alaska, respectively. To make it clear that each unit of city and state or country is one place, the writer should use semicolons:

    a. We visited Caracas, Venezuela; Dallas, Texas; Provo, Utah; and Anchorage, Alaska.

The following sentence contains a series of three nouns, each modified by a descriptive phrase. To make it clear that three, not six people were invited, the author has used semicolons:

    b. To her party, Carmen invited a doctor, a friend from Spain; a lawyer, a neightbor of her sister's; and a salesman, the fiance of her roommate.

THE COLON :

A colon has one major function: to signal that what follows it is an explanation, clarification, or specification of the statement preceding it. Like a period or semicolon, the colon appears only at the end of a complete statement. Unlike a period or a semicolon, a colon may be followed by a structure that is not a complete sentence:

1. Tareq is depressed today. He got a D on his mathematics test.
2. Tareq is depressed today; he got a D on his mathematics test.

3. Tareq is depressed today: he got a D on his mathematics test.
4. Tareq got a poor grade on his mathematics test: a D.

A frequent mistake of student writers is putting a colon in front of a list of explanatory items, as in

5. *Some varieties of fruit trees are: apple, cherry, plum, and pear.

The asterisk (*) marks the sentence as incorrect. The correct version would omit the colon, since it does not come at the end of a complete sentence:

6. Some varieties of fruit trees are apple, cherry, plum, and pear.

A common error is the use of a colon after the words "for example," as in

7. *There are several types of fruit trees, for example: apple, cherry, plum, and pear.

A correct form of this sentence would have a comma in place of the colon. A better sentence would either leave out the words "for example," putting the colon after "trees," as in 8 or substitute a word like "including" for "for example" and omitting the colon, as in 9.

8. There are several types of fruit trees: apple, cherry, plum, and pear.
9. There are several types of fruit trees, including apple, cherry, plum, and pear.

EXERCISE

Correct the punctuation in the following sentences, in which colons and semicolons have been omitted or misused:

1. Students come to the university from many countries, Japan, Korea, China, Thailand, Iran, Saudi Arabia, Egypt, Yemen, and Nigeria.
2. The most popular courses of study are: engineering, business, biology, and computer science.
3. An engineering degree can prepare students for several careers; consulting, contracting, doing research, or teaching.
4. Computer science is popular for one main reason. Jobs.
5. Students take linguistics for one of three reasons, to prepare for graduate school, to teach, or to improve their understanding of languages.
6. Business graduates have no problems finding jobs, for example: Nicole was offered five jobs the day she graduated.
7. The following courses are required of all students in the university English, history, laboratory science, humanities, and physical education.
8. The least popular course in the university is: freshman English.
9. There are two excellent laboratory instructors in the physics department, Professor Thabet and Professor Mukbell.
10. Cutting classes can have a serious result flunking.

THE DASH   [—]

Some writers use the dash as an all-purpose punctuation mark that can substitute for a comma, a period, a semicolon, or a colon. In personal letters, some people use nothing but dashes. If the recipients of the letters can clearly understand the contents, there are no problems. However, for an editorial, essay, report, short story, or any other piece of informal or formal writing intended for an audience consisting at least in part of readers whom the writer does not know, the dash alone is not enough.

Some writers never use dashes, being convinced that the dash is not allowed in any form of writing except possibly a note to the milkman. These writers are unnecessarily depriving themselves of a useful punctuation mark.

Although the dash cannot substitute for a period or semicolon, it can substitute — and very effectively — for a comma or a colon. The important question is this: When is a dash clearer or more effective than a comma or colon?

There are two major functions of the dash.

1. It is used to avoid confusion, as in sentences like this:
   a. The works of four modern literary artists, two novelists, one poet, and one dramatist, will be covered in the course.

A reader might wonder whether the works of four writers or eight are going to be assigned. Compare the sentence above with the following:

   b. The works of four modern literary artists—two novelists, one poet, and one dramatist—will be covered in the course.

When a sentence needs commas to set off items in a series, also using commas to set off an interruptor that contains those items in series is confusing. Dashes are a better choice.

If the subject of a sentence contains numerous phrases and clauses, some of which are set off by commas, an author may use a dash to mark the end of the subject and continue the sentence with a pronoun and the predicate, as in this example:

   c. Spending too little time studying and too much time socializing, sleeping too few hours, eating improperly and irregularly, and skipping class too often—these can lead to academic problems.

2. It emphasizes a sentence interruptor or add-on:
   a. The hitchhiker Miguel picked up last Wednesday—dressed in raggedy jeans and dirty T-shirt—turned out to be a famous novelist.
   b. Copies of the final examination had been stolen from the secretary's office, but they were returned—at the end of the year.

PARENTHESES   [( )]

Parentheses have three uses.

1. They de-emphasize a sentence interruptor or add-on, as in

a. The birthday party we had for Sharon (who was twenty-five years old) was a great success; she was not expecting many people to remember it.

Here, the interruptor contains relatively unimportant informatin. The difference among commas, dashes, and parentheses when they are used to set off interruptors is the difference in speech among normal tone of voice, slightly raised tone of voice, and a near-whisper. Compare these sentences:

b. The football coach, a former quarterback for the University of Michigan Wolverines, has a winning team.
c. The football coach—a former quaterback for the Minnesota Vikings — has a winning team.
d. The football coach (a former quarterback for Central High School) has a winning team.

In the first sentence, the information between the commas is mildly interesting. In the second it is noteworthy. In the third, it is of little interest to the average reader.

When a parenthetical expression comes at the end of a sentence, the period to end the sentence goes outside the closing parenthesis:

e. Manuel's uncle was a colonel during World War II (1941–1945).

When a parenthetical expression comes at the end of an introductory phrase or clause, or at the end of the first clause in a coordinated pair, the comma to set off the introductory material comes at the end of the closing parenthesis:

f. When Jamal bought his car (in 1975), he expected to trade it in four years later (in 1979), but he was so shocked at the prices of new cars that he decided to continue driving the old one for another four years.

2. Parentheses set off numbers and letters enumerating items in a series incorporated into a paragraph, or referring to a previously designated reference, as in

a. The committee hopes to accomplish three goals: (1) to raise enough money for a trip to the art museum, (2) to host a workshop for promising young artists, and (3) to hire a well-known artist for a lecture series.
b. As example (a) indicates, faulty punctuation can lead to misunderstanding.

3. They also set off publication information in a footnote. See Chapter 14.

THE APOSTROPHE 　❵

The apostrophe has three main functions.

1. It indicates that one or more letters have been omitted from a word or phrase, resulting in a contraction, as in

can not = can't

do not = don't

it is = it's (Note that this word is not a possessive pronoun.)

2. To signal the possessive form of a noun, as in

the book belonging to Youseff = Youseff's book
the books belonging to the students = the students' books
the pet belonging to the children = the children's pet
the dedication shown by Monique = Monique's dedication
the behavior of the musicians = the musicians' behavior

For a singular noun or a plural noun which ends in something other than *s*, the possessive is formed by adding *'s* (the student's book, the children's pet); for a plural noun that ends in *s*, the possessive is formed by adding just the apostrophe (the students' books, the musicians' behavior).

For a compound word or phrase, the possessive is formed by adding the appropriate marker to the last word, as in

my brother-in-law's car
my brother-in-laws' cars
the Queen of England's grandson
the president of the United States' wife

For conjoined nouns, the possessive marker should be added to each individual noun to show individual possession; but only to the last one to show joint possession:

Maria's and Jose's bicycles (Maria and Jose each have a bicycle.)
Maria and Jose's bicycle (Maria and Jose share a bicycle.)

3. To signal the plural of letters, numerals, and words, as in

Shakiba got three A's and two B's.
In the 1980's, cars will get smaller and more expensive.
Your *yes*'s sound like *no*'s.

EXERCISE

Add the missing apostrophes to the following paragraph:

Fatimas note to the babysitter warned her to ignore the two-year-olds demands for a drink of water and to listen for the babys cry for food. The babysitter didnt remember the instructions. When the mother returned, the baby had not been fed, and its shrieks echoed throughout the house. The two-year-old, on the other hand, had soaked the babysitters skirt with two glasses of water. Fatimas reaction wasnt an angry one; she just said, "Ill leave written instructions in the future. Its easier."

SUMMARY

With practice, one can learn to hear some punctuation marks:

Sound Effect	Punctuation Mark	Example
1. voice lowers and stops	? or . or ; or :	Who said that? People are funny. People are funny; relatives are weird. People are funny: strangers, relatives, friends, enemies, spouses, lovers, and children.
2. voice raises and stops	?	Are you ready?
3. voice stays level, but pauses briefly	,	When they arrived, we were relieved. The party, which was a very lavish affair, went on until midnight. They served oysters, shrimp, escargots, and lobsters.
4. voice stays level, but pauses rather dramatically	—	The doctor — famous for cancer research — has written a book.
5. voice pauses briefly, and then continues very quietly	( )	His aunt (the one from New York) is a lawyer.

Whether one learns to "hear" punctuation marks or memorizes their various functions is not important. What is important is the correct use of each mark of punctuation. The omission or faulty use of periods, commas, colons, semicolons, etc. can confuse a reader and cause a potentially good composition to be a poor one. Correct punctuation can make a good composition seem even better.

EXERCISES

1. Choose the correct punctuation mark from each of the bracketed pairs in the paragraph below.

The vocabulary of English contains many words borrowed from other languages [./,] [M/m] any words referring to [:/ø] food [,/ø] music [,/ø] and mathematics [,/ø] come from other languages [./,] German is the source [ø/,] of the names [,/ø] hamburger [ø/,] frankfurter [,/ø] and sauerkraut. Other food names are Italian [./:] [P/p] izza, lasagna, ravioli, spaghetti. Saute [,/ø] braise [ø/,] and roast are French words referring to cooking methods [;/.] Oriental and African languages have also provided English with words related to food.

2. The following paragraph contains no punctuation and no capital letters. Add the necessary punctuation marks and capital letters and be prepared to explain each one.

The storm of july 1980 was awesome a group of students from yemen had been in their english class for half an hour the sky was overcast that morning so classroom lights were needed all over the university even in rooms with windows by 8:30 the students could see the black storm clouds approaching suddenly the sky turned dark green then black as night only when the lightning flashed could they see the trees whipping in the gale force winds then the rain began pounding against the windows the light went out then flickered on again the professor told the students to go into the hallway and to stay away from the windows until the storm ended two minutes later a large tree limb wrenched off by the violent wind crashed through the window of the now empty classroom.

3. The following paragraph contains numerous punctuation errors. Correct the errors, by changing the punctuation or, in some cases, by combining sentences.

Students have many worries. Studying long hours sometimes getting low grades. Not having enough money. Being homesick. I studied hard for a test last week, I thought I had done very well but when the test was returned the grade was a C so I felt depressed. Therefore I wanted to forget all about it I wanted to go out to have dinner and enjoy a relaxing evening with some friends only I did not have enough money even for a hamburger. Although, I could not afford to pay the prevous months phone bill. I made a long distance call to my family that did not make me feel any better in spite of the fact that, my father said he could send me some money, I got homesick when I heard my mother and fathers voices.

4. Write a theme of about two pages about your feelings about being far away from home. Read it aloud carefully, and correct any punctuation errors you find. Then exchange papers with a friend and check his or her punctuation while he or she is checking yours. When you get your composition back, consider each suggested correction. If there are some suggestions you disagree with, discuss them with your friend.

CHAPTER 3

Review of Determiners and Numbers

There are four kinds of determiners: possessive nouns and pronouns, articles (a, an, the), demonstrative pronouns (this, that, these, those), and quantifiers (any, each, every, all, some, much, most, many, a few, several.) Numbers sometimes function as determiners, so they will also be discussed in this chapter. The rules for determiner use are directly related to the meanings of the nouns they accompany, in the contexts in which the nouns occur. Thus, the rules are complex. There is one general rule, to which there are few exceptions: a determiner must be used with the singular form of a noun, if that noun can be pluralized. The rules for using determiners with plural nouns are less general.

POSSESSIVE NOUNS AND PRONOUNS

Possessive nouns and pronouns are used in place of other determiners to express ownership, inherent feature, or action:

Kelly's chair	The children's toys
His bicycle	Their behavior
Her appearance	My house
Its disappearance	Our pets

Two pitfalls await the unwary writer in the choice of possessive pronouns:

1. The possessive pronoun "its" is never spelled with an apostrophe. None of the possessive pronouns contains an apostrophe. Only possessive *nouns* have apostrophes. ("It's" is a contraction of "it is": the apostrophe is inserted

where the *i* of "is" is deleted.) The misspelling of the possessive pronoun "its" is one of the most frequent errors committed by native speakers of English.

2. The correct choice of a possessive pronoun depends on the number (singular or plural) and, in three cases, the gender of its antecedent. There is no problem with the gender-neutral forms "my," "your," "our," and "their"; there is no problem with the neuter pronoun "its." Nor is there a problem with "his" or "her" if the antecedent is clearly masculine or feminine. The problem arises when the antecedent is human (so "its" cannot be used) but not gender-specific (a person, a human being, everyone, someone, everybody, somebody). Until recently, grammar books taught that the correct pronoun to use was the masculine singular one:

   a. *Each student* was asked to bring *his* book to class.

However, several generations of speakers of English were aware that not all human beings are masculine, so in informal conversation, people favored an ungrammatical, but gender-neutral, plural pronoun (they, them, their) to follow a singular antecedent in such cases:

   b. *Each student* was asked to bring *their* book to class.

Current practice favors a grammatically correct, although rather awkward, double form, at least for formal writing:

   c. *Each student* was asked to bring *his or her* book to class.

In time, English may devlop a set of a pronouns for human gender-neutral reference. Or *their* may become acceptable as a singular as well as a plural. That happened to *your*, after all.

ARTICLES

The Definite Article

The articles occur more frequently than the other determiners, and, since the indefinite article *a(n)* occurs only with singular nouns, the definite article *the* is most common. In fact, *the* is the most frequently used word in the English language.

The Definite Article with Plural Nouns

Most nouns in English refer to things that can be counted. In their plural forms, count nouns sometimes require determiners, but not always. When a plural noun means "all" or "in general," no determiner (except "all") is used:

1. *Textbooks* are expensive. (*All textbooks* are expensive.)

2. *Laboratories* require expensive equipment.
3. *Students* often do not get enough sleep.

When a plural noun means "a limited number, amount, or kind," the definite article (or another determiner) is necessary:

4. *The textbooks* for science are expensive. (Not all textbooks are expensive.)
5. The SSU budget is very high: *the laboratories* require expensive equipment. (Not all laboratories — only those at SSU — are considered.)
6. *The stereos* and *(the) radios* in my dorm blare all night, so *the students* often do not get enough sleep. (*Note:* When two or more nouns occur in a series, only the first one requires a determiner.)

EXERCISE

Decide which of the following blanks need a definite article or possessive pronoun and which do not, and discuss your choices in class. (In some cases, either choice may be correct.)

_____ sports are enjoyed all over the world. During each of _____ seasons of the year, _____ men, _____ women, and _____ children take advantage of _____ days off, _____ weekends, and _____ holidays to enjoy _____ sports that are favored in _____ respective countries. In _____ winter, _____ skiers and _____ ice skaters of _____ snowy countries cover _____ hills and _____ ponds with _____ brightly colored sportswear. In _____ summer, _____ lakes, _____ ponds, and _____ pools of every country are invaded by_____ swimmers, _____ boaters, _____ fishermen, and _____ waterskiers. _____ sports fans also enjoy _____ spectator sports that are most popular in _____ countries. _____ games of soccer, rugby, football, basketball, cricket, and baseball excite _____ thousands of people in _____ nations of the world.

The Definite Article with Non-count Nouns

The mass or non-count nouns of English have singular forms and, when functioning as subjects, require singular verbs, but they carry plural meaning, so the indefinite article is never used with them. The rules for using the definite article with non-count nouns are the same as the rules for plural nouns:

a non-count noun used to denote "all" or "in general" does not take any determiner (except "all"):

1. *Rice* can be cooked in many ways.
2. *Equipment* is necessary for most sports.
3. *Weather* cannot be controlled.
4. [All] Travel is broadening.

But when the meaning of the noun is "a limited amount or kind," the definite article (or another determiner) is used:

5. Dinner will be ready soon; *the rice* is not quite done.
6. *The equipment* needed for skating is inexpensive.
7. *The weather* ruined many children's Christmas plans.

Some non-count nouns also have plural forms. When these occur, they refer to subtypes or subspecies of a more general class or group:

8. Leonard is studying *the cereals* of the Plains states.
9. That specialty shop carries *the teas* of a dozen countries.

The Definite Article with Abstract Nouns

Abstract nouns behave like non-count nouns (although they do not carry plural meaning). When an abstract noun is used in the sense of "in general," no determiner is used:

1. *Liberty* is desired by all people, but enjoyed by few.
2. The judge recommended *mercy.*
3. It has been said that *love* conquers all.
4. *Equality* under the law promises *justice* to all.

When an abstract or non-count noun denotes a definite act, event, or kind, a determiner is used (and the noun may be pluralized):

5. *The liberties* guaranteed in the U.S. Constitution include freedom of speech.
6. The prisoner was grateful for *the many mercies* shown him by his captors.
7. *The love* of a mother for her child is beautiful.

EXERCISE

Decide which of the following blanks need an article and which do not, and discuss your choices in class. (In some cases, either choice may be correct.)

_____ rice can be served in many ways, as an accompaniment for a wide variety of main dishes. _____ rice preferred by many Americans is a long-grained variety, which does not turn as sticky as _____ regular rice. One of the most popular ways to serve _____ rice is with _____ salt, _____ pepper, and _____ butter. Some people prefer spicier seasonings, such as _____ saffron, parsley, _____ sage, _____ thyme, or _____ curry powder. When cooking _____ rice that is to be added to a casserole and baked, the chef should avoid letting it cook too much. _____ rice should be simmered, not boiled. Like _____ spaghetti or _____ macaroni, _____ rice will get glutinous if it is boiled or overcooked. To cook one cup of _____ rice, two and one half cups of _____ water is the recommended amount. _____ water should be brought to a full, rolling boil before _____ rice is added, and then lowered immediately to a gentle simmer. When _____ rice is done, strain it and then rinse it with _____ hot water, to ensure that _____ rice is fluffy and light.

The Definite Article with Singular Nouns—The Exceptions

With a few exceptions, all singular nouns require determiners. The exceptions are singular nouns that have no plural forms: proper nouns, titles used with proper nouns, the names of specific bodies of knowledge (often, school subjects), and the names of sports or games. None of these occurs with a determiner:

1. *Jorge* is comparing the soil of *North Dakota* and *Egypt*.
2. *Professor Jones* visited *Dr. Smith*.
3. Marla is stydying *English, history, mathematics,* and *botany*.
4. *Football, rugby* and *soccer* are similar games.

The following sentences seem to contradict the rule just stated, but they don't.

5. *The Jorge* that I met spent the summer in *the Dakotas*. (There is more than one person named Jorge, and there are two Dakotas, North Dakota and South Dakota.)
6. *The professor* at the conference is *the doctor* Sam met. (Titles are proper nouns only when they occur with a name. There is more than one professor and more than one doctor.)
7. *The histories* of England are numerous. (The word "history" may mean "a book," as it does in this example, or "a chronology of events and personalities," or "a body of knowledge." When the word carries the second meaning, it is a non-count noun, so it does not take a determiner unless it refers to a specific kind of history, as in (9):

8. History is full of contradictions.
9. The history of Scotland is full of contradictions.

Many proper nouns function as modifiers of other nouns. When this is the case, the noun being modified or named usually requires an article, which remains even if the noun is omitted:

1. *Mississippi* is a southern state. (but)
1a. *The Mississippi* [*River*] flows through *Mississippi*.
2. *English* is an interesting language. (but)
2a. *The English language* is interesting.
3. *The English people* enjoy rugby. (and)
3a. *The English* enjoy rugby.

The names of most countries occur without articles, because they are truly names. There are a few exceptions — "*the* U.S.A." and "*the* U.S.S.R." — that are not really names. They are descriptive phrases, similar to phrases like "the Dominion of Canada" (usually known as just "Canada") and "the Republic of China" ("China"). The term "the U.S.A." describes both "the United States of America" (sometimes called just "America") and "the Union of South Africa." "The U.S.S.R." is better known as "Russia," but the initials spell "the Union of Soviet Socialist Republics."

One last problem set needs mention: the names of meals. In the singular they rarely take articles:

1. Breakfast (lunch, dinner) is served.
2. Have you finished supper?

Usually, an article is used only when one is talking about a specific meal served in the past, or about a formal meal to which numerous guests are invited (at which point the informal word "lunch" becomes the formal word "luncheon").

3. The dinner Sally cooked Saturday was superb.
4. Tomas is going to the dinner for the governor tomorrow.
5. Suzanne has invited twelve people to the luncheon. (but)
5a. Suzanne has invited twelve people to lunch.
6. The lunch Carlos ate yesterday gave him indigestion.

In the plural, the names of meals are like all other plural nouns: the definite article (or another determiner) is used if the reference is to some number less than "all."

The definite article is sometimes used with a singular noun that names all of a species or set. When this is the case, the noun could be changed to a plural (using either "all" or no determiner), with no change of meaning:

1. *The lion* belongs to the cat family. ([All] lions belong . . .)
2. *The car* has changed America's social structure. (Cars in general)

There is one exception to this *generic* use of the definite article; the word "man," without a definite article, may mean "all people" or "mankind in general":

3. The evolution of *man* is a continuing process.
   (*Compare:* The evolution of *the horse* is a continuing process.)

The Definite Article: The General Rule

The exceptions to the general rule that singular nouns require a definite article (or another determiner) need careful discussion and illustration, but they are few in number and limited in scope. The general rule is valid 95 per cent of the time: a determiner is required with the singular form of a count noun. The definite article is used with a singular noun when that noun is a definite or specific one:

1. *The house* Micah bought last year is a good investment. (Other houses may be poor investments.)
2. Micah bought a house last year; *the house* is on a lakeshore. (The house he bought is on a lakeshore.)
3. Bob saw *the house* he likes. (He has seen it before and has liked it for some time.)

EXERCISE

Decide which blanks in the following sentence need definite articles, and discuss your choices in class:

_____ history of _____ U.S. in _____ twentieth century will include many diverse discoveries, inventions, and events: _____ penicillin and _____ sulfa, _____ radio and _____ television, _____ election of several presidents and resignation of one, _____ atomic bomb and _____ nuclear power, _____ car and _____ airplane, _____ walk on _____ moon and _____ discovery of another of Jupiter's moons, _____ Camp David agreement and _____ takeover of an embassy.

The Indefinite Article

The two words "a" and "an" are actually variant forms of the same word, deriving from the old English word for "one." Several centuries ago, the n was dropped if the following word began with a consonant sound, so the two forms we now use came into being. Usually, the indefinite articles still mean "one," in the sense of "one among many, not particularized":

1. Fred bought *a house* last year. (one house)

Occasionally, the indefinite article may mean "any one," in which case the sentence could be rephrased by substituting a plural noun (with either "all" or no determiner) for the singular one:

2. *A house* is a good investment. ([All] houses are good investments.)

EXERCISES

1. In the following sentences, which indefinite articles mean "any" and which mean "one"?
   a. A basic studies course is a course required for graduation.
   b. Robert is taking a math course.
   c. Although yesterday was a raw and windy day, a skater was on the lake, trying out a new pair of skates.
   d. A car is a necessity for a commuter who lives a long distance from his job.

2. Decide whether each slot in the following paragraphs needs a definite or indefinite article, or a possessive pronoun, and be ready to explain your decision.

   a. _____ fisherman, patiently casting _____ rod in _____ hope of attracting _____ fish, realized that _____ bobber on one of _____ trolling lines had disappeared. He quickly reached for _____ rod, set _____ hook, and began carefully reeling in _____ fish he knew was on _____ other end of _____ line.

   b. _____ English language got _____ name from _____ tribe of _____ hired Germanic soldiers who settled in _____ British Isles around 500 A.D. _____ new settlers came from several tribes, including _____ Angles, whose dialect of _____ Germanic language was soon renamed _____ Angle-isch. _____ speaker of that language would not be understood by _____English speakers today, because _____ languages change over _____ period of _____ time, and _____ English is not _____exception. Some words have been lost and many others have been borrowed from _____ languages that _____ English-speaking explorers have encountered in _____ travels.

THE DEMONSTRATIVE PRONOUNS

The demonstrative pronouns "this" and "that" (used with both singular and non-count nouns) and "these" and "those" (used with plural nouns) are used instead of the definite article when the writer wants to refer unambiguously to an earlier term:

1. Much research is being done on solar energy. *This* source of energy differs from traditional sources.

In this example, the phrase "this source of energy" refers to "solar energy," not some other source. Had the definite article been used, a reader might momentarily think that some other source was about to be discussed. Consider what potential difference of meaning would result if the definite article were substituted for the demonstrative pronouns in each of the following examples:

2. The risks taken by the boat people were unbelievable, but *these* people were desperate.
3. The first presidential primary is in New Hampshire. *That* primary often results in a surprise victory for a little-known candidate.
4. Three of Kevin's five courses last semester were in literature. *Those* courses required a lot of reading.

The difference between "this" and "that" and between "these" and "those" is sometimes subjective. Generally, "this" and "these" are used when the reference is relatively close in time, space, or consciousness; "that" and "those" are used for more distant references. In the examples above, the relative closeness or distance is not apparent, and each sentence would be equally correct if the other demonstrative pronoun were used. The difference between "*this* year" and "*that* year" or "*these* days" and "*those* days" is clearer: "that year" and "those days" can only refer to some time in the past or future.

EXERCISE

Fill in the blanks in the following paragraph with the appropriate definite article, indefinite article, or demonstrative pronoun.

_____ U.S. economy is in _____ recession. _____ fact has caused _____ slowest Christmas shopping season in years. _____ year, _____ department store that normally shows _____ large profit and _____ high turnover of merchandise during _____ months of November and December had its worst season since 1974. _____ store, like many others, reported _____ decline in _____ number of shoppers and in _____ amount spent by each shopper. Only _____ toy department enjoyed _____ expected seasonal increase. _____computer games were _____ big attraction _____ season, and _____ large profits of _____ toy departments were due to _____ fact that _____ games are expensive. _____ parents who would have preferred spending _____modest ten dollars for their child's Christmas gift had to spend — or charge — between twenty and forty dollars for one of _____ wonders of modern technology.

QUANTIFIERS

Quantifiers with Non-count Nouns

Since most of the quantifiers are associated with number, either singular or plural, most of them do not occur with non-count nouns. Four exceptions — "all," "most," "some," and "any" — can occur with non-count nouns as well as others:

1. *All* coffee contains some caffeine.
2. *Most* tea contains some caffeine.
3. *Some* pop contains caffeine.
4. *Any* cola contains caffeine.

Much

The quantifier "much" occurs only with non-count nouns, and even then only in negative statements and questions, as a rule. In affirmative statements, a phrase like "a lot of" or "lots of" usually substitutes:

5. Is there *much* water in your basement?
6. No, there isn't *much* water in my basement.
7. Yes, there is *a lot of* water in my basement.

Quantifiers with Plural Nouns

The quantifiers which occur with plural nouns range in meaning from "all" to "none":

1. *All* cars require gas.
2. *Most* cars require sparkplugs. (A few of them don't.)
3. *Many* cars require unleaded gas. (Not all, or most, do.)
4. *Some* cars get twenty miles to a gallon of gas. (Not many.)
5. *Several* cars get twenty five miles to a gallon. (Less than some.)
6. *A few* cars get thirty miles to a gallon. (Maybe five percent.)
7. *Few* cars get forty miles to a gallon. (Almost none.)
8. *No* cars get a hundred miles to a gallon.
9. There aren't *any* cars that get a hundred miles to a gallon.

Any

The word "any" is odd. Usually, it is used in questions and negative statements, in place of quantifiers "some" and "no," which appear in affirmative statements. In a negative statement or negative question, "any" must be used in place of "no," to avoid a double negative:

1. Bob has bought *some* books.
2. Bob has bought *no* books.
3. Bob hasn't bought *any* books.
4. *Bob hasn't bought *no* books. (An ungrammatical double negative.)
5. Has Bob bought *some* books? (The assumption is that he has.)
6. Has Bob bought *any* books? (The assumption is that he has not.)
7. Has Bob bought *no* books? (Formal, expressing surprise and assuming that he has not.)
8. Hasn't Bob bought *any* books? (Informal, expressing surprise and assuming that he has not.)

"Any" is also used with a noun whose meaning is restricted, to give more emphasis than an indefinite article would give:

9. *A* student who frequently cuts class is apt to get poor grades.
10. *Any* student who frequently cuts class is apt to get poor grades.
11. *A* well-constructed exam is a learning experience.
12. *Any* well-constructed exam is a learning experience.

Used with a non-count noun, the word "any" means "all of the subtypes or subcategories of the whole." The earlier example, "Any cola contains caffeine," means "Any one of the several types of cola contains caffeine," or "All varieties of cola contain caffeine."

Quantifiers with Singular Nouns

With one exception, the quantifiers used with a singular noun make that noun into a representative of its entire class:

1. *Each* plane was carefully inspected. (All of the class of planes, in single sequence.)
2. *Every* plane was carefully inspected. (All of the class, as a whole.)
3. He can fly *any* plane. (All of the class, with no exceptions.)
4. *Any* plane that came in for a safety check was carefully inspected. (All of the limited class of those planes which came in.)
5. *Any* plane should be carefully inspected. (All of the class, but see discussion below.)

Any and *Some*

Again "any" differs from the other quantifiers. It is used in an affirmative statement if its noun is either restricted in meaning or means "all, without a single exception," or if the verbal action is conditional, not actual.

Unlike "each," "even," and "any," the quantifier "some," when used with singular nouns, means simply "one" or "a certain one." Its use is often frowned upon, because it is frequently heard in informal, colloquial speech as a substitute for the indefinite article:

6. *Some guy* was at the door, selling encyclopedias.
   (*Formal: A man* was at the door, selling encyclopedias.)

"Some" is also used, with no frowns from critical readers, to provide a compromise between the indefinite nouns "someone" and "somebody" and a more specific noun with an indefinite article:

Someone
A student   has forgotten to take his/her briefcase.
Some student

7. "Any" is also used with singular nouns, as with plural and non-count nouns, as a substitute for "no" in negative statements and in questions:
   a. The mechanics inspected *no* plane.
   b. The mechanics did *not* inspect *any* plane.
   c. Did the mechanics inspect *any* plane?
   d. Did*n't* the mechanics inspect *any* plane?

EXERCISE

Fill in the slots in the following paragraph with appropriate determiners, using quantifiers as frequently as possible.

_____ people are born to be diplomats; _____ people will start _____ fight at _____ opportunity. _____ successful diplomats have _____ ability to consider _____ side of _____ question, and to persuade, not force, _____ adversaries that _____ courses of action are worth _____ consideration. _____ great diplomats are _____ rare human beings who can convince _____ adversary that his point of view is the one they have adopted.

NUMBERS

A number sometimes functions as a determiner. At other times, a number is only a modifier of a noun that requires a regular determiner, in addition to the number.

One

A singular noun may be preceded by the cardinal number "one" functioning as a determiner:

1. *One* student was standing in the hall.

This sentence implies that, although there are other students, either only one of them is standing or only one of them is doing his standing in the hall.
The number "one" may also function as a modifier, meaning "single" or "only," in which case a determiner precedes it:

1. *The one* book Shirin wanted was unavailable. (the only one)
2. *That one* course nearly ended Matthew's career as a student. (that single one)
3. *Her one* asset was a lovely smile. (her only one)
4. *No one* television show appeals to everyone. (no single one)

Ordinals

Singular nouns may also be preceded by the ordinal numbers "first, second, third," etc. Unlike the cardinal numbers, the ordinals always need a determiner in front of them, because they are always modifiers.

1. *The first* batter came to the plate.
2. *The second* exam is difficult.
3. *A third* game should have been played.
4. *Every fourth* news article is tragic.

Plurals

Plural nouns may be specified by a cardinal number alone, functioning as a determiner and implying that the group specified is only a part of a larger group:

1. *Ten* troopers followed the cyclist. (other troopers did not)
2. *Six hundred* soldiers slept soundly. (others did not)

Or plural nouns may be specified by a cardinal number functioning as a modifier and accompanied by a true determiner, implying that the group is a complete whole:

1. Into the valley of death rode *the six hundred* horsemen.
2. *Those four* cats in my house are not related.
3. *His twenty* grandchildren are all boys.
4. *All twenty-two* members of the team respect the coach.
5. *No three* people could perform her job.

A plural noun may also be modified by an ordinal and a cardinal number together, denoting one specific portion of a larger group.

1. *The first three* men were redheads.
2. *His second five* grades were *A*'s.

Cardinal numbers, ordinal numbers, and quantifiers may be linked together in pairs by the preposition "of" denoting one part of a finite group:

1. *Each of the six* fishermen caught a huge salmon.
2. *All of the fifty-six* employees were fired.
3. *Several of the many* candidates were well qualified.
4. The decline in auto sales was *the first of many* indications that a recession had begun.
5. *Three of (the) twelve* salesmen resigned.

Plural nouns may also be preceded by the idioms "lots of" and "a lot of," which are structurally parallel to "few of" and "a few of," although they are the informal synonyms of "many" or "much." However, "lots" and "a lot" never appear without the preposition "of," and they are used with both plural and non-count nouns:

1. [Few/a few/many] students enjoy examinations.
2. [Few of/a few of/a lot of] my students enjoy examinations.
3. [Much/lots of/a lot of] information can be found in a good encyclopedia.

| **EXERCISE** |

Underline the appropriate word or phrase of the pair in parentheses in each of the following sentences.

1. Luis bought (first/the first) car he saw.
2. (Thirty, those thirty) hours are required for a major.
3. Mario bought (a lot/a lot of) groceries.
4. (First two/the first two) months away from home are the loneliest.
5. Riad liked (all/all of) six people he met.
6. (One/first) course Sima took was calculus.

CHAPTER 4

Review of
English Clause
Structure

BASIC PATTERNS

English sentences can be simple or complex, but whatever their nature, they are made up of clauses. Clauses are the building blocks that make up all English writing, from notes on postcards to chapters in textbooks and novels. Most writing requires careful editing and revising before it can be submitted to a reader. Much editing and revising involves correcting and improving clauses. So although this book is primarily concerned with compositions of various kinds, a brief review of clause structure is important.

Each English sentence must contain an *independent clause:* a structure with a subject and a predicate that could stand alone as a sentence.[1] A structure that does not contain both of these elements is a sentence fragment, which will be discussed in more detail later.

English clauses follow one of three patterns.

Pattern A

The simplest sentence in English has only one clause, and its predicate consists only of an *intransitive verb* (a verb which needs only the subject to complete the meaning). Thus, a sentence may be only two or three words long:

SUBJECT	PREDICATE: INTRANSITIVE VERB
1. The goat	coughed.
2. The train	arrived.

[1]Command-request sentences are an exception to the rule about clause structure. The subject of such a sentence is an unstated "you," as in "Turn in your themes" ("[You] turn in your themes").

3. Charles   laughed.
4. Jean   cried.
5. The children   slept.

These examples could be expanded by adding to the predicate one or more verb modifiers — words or phrases specifying time, place, or manner. These modifiers are optional, not required, elements of Pattern A:

SUBJECT	PREDICATE: VERB	PLUS OPTIONAL MODIFIER
1a. The goat	coughed	loudly/yesterday/in the garden.
2a. The train	arrived	at the station/promptly/at noon.
3a. Charles	laughed	up oariously. / on Saturday. / at the play.
4a. Jean	cried	Wednesday night. / at the movie.
5a. The children	slept	soundly. / through the night. / in the car.

We will look at modifiers in more detail in the next chapter; for now, our concern is with the required elements of clauses, not with the optional ones.

Pattern B

In some English sentences, the subject is followed by a predicate which contains a "linking" verb and something else. These sentences can be further classified according to the nature of the "something else": it may be a noun, an adjective, or an adverbial denoting location or time.

In sentences with a noun as the second element in the predicate, the linking verb is like an equals sign, equating the subject with the predicate noun:

SUBJECT	PREDICATE: LINKING VERB	PLUS NOUN
1. Newfi	is	a pet. / my dog.
2. Dylan	was	a Welshman. / a genius. / a poet.
3. Paul	became	a scholar. / a writer.
4. Socrates	was	a Greek. / a philosopher.

In sentences with an adjective as the second element in the predicate, the adjective describes the subject:

	PREDICATE:	
SUBJECT	LINKING VERB	PLUS ADJECTIVE
5. The milk	is/was turned smelled	sour.
6. Jess	was turned became looked seemed	silly.

In sentences with a linking verb followed by an adverbial specifying location, the various forms of the verb "be" mean "be located or situated":

	PREDICATE:	
SUBJECT	LINKING VERB	LOCATION
7. Sam	was	upstairs
8. Tess	is	in the kitchen.
9. The book	could not have been	there.

In sentences with a linking verb followed by an adverbial specifying time, the various forms of the verb "be" mean "happen, occur, take place, begin":

	PREDICATE:	
SUBJECT	LINKING VERB	TIME
10. The accident	was	in the morning.
11. The picnic	will be	on Sunday.
12. The meeting	is	at 7 p.m.

The examples of Pattern B could all be expanded, like the examples of Pattern A, by adding verb modifiers of manner, time, location, etc., but, as with Pattern A, such additions to Pattern B are optional, not required, elements of the basic structure.

EXERCISES

1. Create a sentence with each of the following verbs, following either Pattern A (subject plus intransitive verb) or Pattern B (subject plus something else: noun, adjective, or adverbial of time or location):

    a. screamed   d. appeared
    b. looked   e. yawned
    c. giggled   f. began

2. Some verbs may function either as intrasitive verbs or linking verbs: "appear" is one such verb. Compare the following examples, and discuss the two meanings of "appeared."

a. Hassan appeared sleepy.

b. Hassan appeared in the doorway.

3. The verb "look" is also ambiguous (that is, it has more than one meaning). Discuss the possible meanings of the sentence "Maria looked hard."

Pattern C

In some English sentences, the subject is followed by a predicate containing a verb that requires a *direct object* (a noun that is affected by the verbal action). Verbs that require direct objects are called *transitive* verbs, because the action *transits* (moves across) from the subject to the direct object.

1. Sally kicked the wall.
2. Jim is studying calculus.
3. Louis wanted a book.

The verbs in Pattern C sentences are verbs of action. The subject is an actor, a doer, and the direct object answers the question, "What (or who) was affected by the verb?" In the first example above, Sally is doing something: she is kicking. The wall is receiving the kicking action; it is being kicked. The examples below are Pattern C sentences.

SUBJECT	PREDICATE: TRANSITIVE VERB	PLUS DIRECT OBJECT
4. Congress	passed	a law.
(What was passed?	a law.)	
5. The President	vetoed	the bill.
(What was vetoed?	the bill.)	

EXERCISES

1. Create Pattern C sentences by inserting a direct object after each verb.

a.   Khalil is studying _____ .

b.   He wants _____ .

c.   He has recently bought _____ .

2. Create Pattern C sentences using these verbs:

a. drove   d. planted
b. washed   e. attacked
c. moved

3. Create Pattern A, B, and/or C sentences using these verbs:

a. destroyed   d. plays
b. smokes   e. became
c. turned

(*Note:* some verbs are intransitive in some sentences, but transitive in others: "Jose reads" vs. "Jose reads *Newsweek.*")

4. Describe the structure of each of your sentences (subject plus what else?)

Indirect Objects in Pattern C Sentences

Some verbs that require direct objects also require indirect objects. Generally, *an indirect object* is a person or animal that receives or benefits from the verbal action. When the direct object immediately follows the verb, the indirect object is easy to identify; it is preceded by a preposition, usually "to" or "for":

1. The noise gave a headache *to Julie.*
2. Ramon sent a letter *to his friend.*
3. Gertraud bought a book *for her roommate.*
4. Chris showed movies *to/for his friends.*

However, these sentences may be slightly restructured: the indirect object may precede the direct object. When it does, the preposition drops out:

1a. The noise gave *Julie* a headache.
2a. Ramon sent *his friend* a letter.
3a. Gertraud bought *her roommate* a book.
4a. Chris showed *his friends* movies.

The decision to put an indirect object before or after the direct object usually depends on the emphasis desired by the writer. If the writer wants to emphasize the direct object, he or she puts it after the indirect object. If one of the two objects has already been mentioned in a previous sentence, the writer would emphasize the other one, because it is new information. Example 1a above would probably follow sentences that mention both Julie and the noise; it adds the new information that Julie has a headache to the reader's previous awareness that Julie was in a noisy place.

EXERCISES

1. Rephrase each of the following sentences so that the indirect object precedes the direct object.

a. The employer gave layoff notices to 125 employees.
b. Jordan drove his car to the garage.

c. The university awarded a scholarship to José.
d. Mrs. Smith bought a coat for her daughter.
e. Javad told a lie to the dean.

(*Note:* one of these sentences contains no indirect object, only a direct object. How does it differ from the other sentences?)

2. Rephrase each of the following sentences so that the direct object precedes the indirect object:

a. Dr. Wu promised Bill a job.
b. Stanislaw sent the company an application.
c. Barbara showed her roomate the menu.
d. Ahmed considered Karim a genius.
e. Johan told the doctor his symptoms.

(*Note:* one of these sentences contains no indirect object, only a complex direct object. How does it differ from the other sentences?)

3. Create at least one sentence for each of the following verbs. What structure does each of your sentences follow?

a. annoyed   f. charged
b. smelled   g. gave
c. intended   h. played
d. mailed   i. pledged
e. told   j. sent

PASSIVE SENTENCES

Pattern C sentences, sentences containing transitive verbs with objects, differ from sentences with intransitive verbs or linking verbs in an important way: the word order of the major elements can be changed, without changing the meaning:

1. Lightning struck the house.
1a. The house was struck by lightning.

In the second sentence above, the subject and direct object of the first sentence have switched positions. Also, two additions appear in the second sentence, the words "by" and "was." This type of sentence is a *passive sentence,* a sentence in which the passive nondoer (a former object) becomes the grammatical subject of the sentence; the "agent," the active doer (the former subject), is either given a less important position at the end of the sentence (preceded by a preposition like "by") or is omitted entirely:

2. Something startled Simin. (Active sentence)

2a. Simin was startled by something. (Passive sentence with agent)
2b. Simin was startled. (Passive sentence without agent)

The word "by" appears in a passive sentence only if the agent also appears. The word "was" or some other form of the verb "be" is always present, immediately before the main verb of the sentence:

3. A scholarship has *been* awarded to Karim.
4. He *was* pleased *by* the award.
5. His high school teachers should *be* gratified.

EXERCISE

Change each of the following sentences into passives:

1. The international situation concerns many people.
2. Militants have captured an embassy.
3. Foreign troops have invaded three countries.
4. Rebels have overthrown two governments.
5. Dictators have become presidents in two countries.
6. All of these events worry people.

(*Note:* One of these sentences does not contain a transitive verb and cannot, therefore, be made into a passive sentence.)

When a writer chooses a passive sentence, rather than an active one, it is usually for one of two general reasons.

1. The passive is used when the agent is either unknown or so obvious that including it in a sentence would be repetitious. In this case, the agent is usually not expressed at all:

   a. Rudy's grandfather was killed in World War II (by someone/something unknown).
   b. Prices are expected (by almost everyone) to continue to rise.
   c. Most children have been inoculated against polio (by thousands of doctors and nurses).
   d. A new moon has recently been discovered revolving around Jupiter.

The last sentence might appear in an article explaining what was revealed in films taken by a spaceship orbiting Jupiter. The scientists interpreting the films would be the discoverers, but an article in which numerous sentences began with the words "The scientists discovered . . ." would be repetitious. Most scientific articles and books contain numerous passive sentences, for this reason.

2. The passive is also used when the agent is less important to the meaning of the sentence than what would, in an active sentence, be the direct or indirect object. The major focus of a sentence, the center of interest, comes at the beginning, so usually, the subject of the sentence is the focus. In a paragraph discussing computers, for example, the word "computers" would be the preferred subject of many sentences, which would cause a writer to change some active sentences to passive ones:

   a. Computers used to be too complex and expensive for widespread sales. Today, computers *are purchased* by businesses, schools, homes, and even churches. (Rather than, "Today, businesses, schools, homes and even churches purchase computers.")

Another example:

   b. Insulin injections allow many diabetics to lead normal lives and to enjoy a normal life expectancy. Insulin injections *were* first *administered* in 1921, by Drs. Bunting and Best.

Active sentences containing indirect objects always contain direct objects as well. Thus, such sentences can be turned into passives. In fact, there are two possible passive sentences (as well as two active ones) for an idea involving both a direct object and an indirect object; either object may become the subject of a passive sentence:

1. The driver gave a credit card to the attendant. (Active)
2. The driver gave the attendant a credit card. (Active)
3. A credit card was given to the attendant by the driver. (Passive)
4. The attendant was given a credit card by the driver. (Passive)

EXERCISE

In the following sentences, the focus shifts back and forth from the British (sentences 1, 2, 3, 6, and 8) and to the colonists/the colonies (4, 5, and 7). Rewrite the sentences as a paragraph, changing some sentences into passive ones with the colonists as subjects, so that the focus of each sentence is on the colonists.

1. In the eighteenth century, the British governed the U.S.
2. They did not allow the American colonists to explain their problems and needs.
3. They were shipping large quantities of unwanted tea to the colonists and making them pay heavy taxes on it.
4. The colonists promised retaliation to the British.
5. They dumped the tea into Boston Harbor.
6. The British challenged the colonists.

7. The colonists accepted the challenge and confronted the British on the battlefield.
8. Finally, the British granted independence to the American colonies.

SUBJECT-VERB AGREEMENT

Most of the verbs in the examples discussed so far have been past tense forms. Except for the verb "be," there is only one past tense form for each English verb, regardless of its subject. The verb "be" has two past tense forms.

1. "Was" is used with the subjects "I, she, he, it" and any singular noun.
2. "Were" is used with the subjects "we, you, they" and any plural noun.

Except for the verb "be," English verbs have two present tense forms.

1. The stem form alone, used with the pronoun "I" and with plural subjects: "we, you, they" and any plural noun;
2. A singular form consisting of the verb stem and an "-(e)s" suffix, used with the singular subjects "he, she it" and any singular noun.

The verb "be" is an exception: it has three present tense forms, none of which uses the stem "be":

1. I   *am*
2. he, she it   *is*
   the student
3. we, you they   *are*
   the students

In any English clause, the subject and the present tense verb must "agree"; that is, if the subject is plural, the verb cannot have the singular suffix. Through historical coincidence, the plural form of most nouns in English became stem-plus-"s" (or "es") and so did the singular form of present tense verbs. Thus, if the subject of a clause is "I, you, they" or a plural noun (usually signalled by an "s"), the verb *cannot* have an "s" suffix. Conversely, if the subject is "he, she, it" or a singular or non-count noun, the present tense verb form *must* have an "s" suffix.

EXERCISES

1. In the following paragraph, underline each of the subjects and their verbs, and discuss the agreement between them.

Many foreign students have never seen an American football game, although most are familiar with soccer, which is sometimes called football. One of the differences involves the players' use of their hands. Kicking rules in football are unlike those in soccer, and scoring differs, too. But there is one important similarity: thousands of people enjoy watching both games.

2. Choose the correct verb form from each pair in the following paragraph.

The first exams in a school term [make/makes] many students nervous. There [is/are] many reasons for this. Some professors ask questions about material in the textbook which [has/have] not been discussed in class, so students [wonder/wonders] if they [has/have] [study/studied] the right things. Some professors [ask/asks] questions which [requires/require] essay answers; others [prefer/prefers] multiple-choice or short-answer questions. One of the students in a literature course [has/have] failed an exam because the professor [expect/expects] a detailed explanation of "yes-no" answers.

3. The following paragraph contains several examples of faulty agreement between subject and verb. Rewrite the paragraph, correcting the errors.

Roses needs special care if one expect them to live through a Canadian winter. A heavy covering of snow help insulate their roots so they aren't kill by frost. In areas where the snow blow away and leave the root unprotect, they will survives if there is dirt and leaves covering them. One of the easiest ways to keep the cover in place are to put a small fence around each bush.

4. For each sentence in the following paragraph, change the subject and verb to plural forms.

A student who wants to graduate within four years normally takes a full course load during the regular academic year and usually registers for at least one summer term as well. She probably needs to work other summers at a job which provides enough money for college expenses, since there is no better way to pay for tuition, room and board, and books, as well as incidentals.

5. For each sentence in the following paragraph, change the subject and verb (and other forms as necessary) to singular forms.

Paintings tell a lot about people. People whose favorite paintings are of rural landscapes like natural, uncrowded lives. Others, who prefer modern abstractions, probably want orderly, well planned lives. Those who collect portraits need busy social lives and enjoy meeting other people. Psychiatrists learn a great deal about patients' personalities if they ask about their patients' artistic preferences.

AUXILIARIES

Agreement Between Subject and Auxiliary

A predicate may contain more than one verb; in addition to the main verb, the one which carries the basic meaning of the clause, there may be *auxiliary* verbs. *Auxiliaries* are verb forms that do not affect the basic meaning of a clause, but that do provide a time frame for that meaning. The subject of a clause must agree with the first verb form in the predicate.

Progressive tenses: The predicate consists of a form of "be" as an auxiliary and the present participle (-ing) form of the main verb. The agreement is between the subject and "be."

Present progressive: Describes action beginning in the past and continuing in the present.

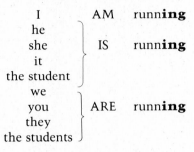

Past progressive: Describes action beginning in the past and ending before the immediate present.

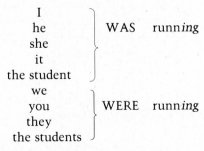

Perfect tenses: The predicate consists of a present or past tense form of "have" as an auxiliary and the past participle form (-en, -ed) of the main verb.
The agreement is between the subject and "have."

Present perfect: Describes action completed in the past, but unlike simple past tense, the present perfect often implies that the action was performed more than once and may be performed again in the future.

He
She } HAS   seen the car frequently and may see it again.
It   HAS   walked home several times and may do so again.
The student

I
You } HAVE   seen the car frequently and may see it again.
We   HAVE   walked home several times and may do so again.
They
The students

Past perfect: Describes action completed in the past, before or after a change of some kind occurred, or during a period of time.

I, He, She, It, We, You, They, The   ⌈ HAD   walked   home   before/after
student, The students   lunch.
                                         ⌊ HAD   seen the car every day that
                                            week.

Perfect progressive tenses: Describe continuing action, begun in the past. The predicate consists of both perfective and progressive auxiliaries: a present or past tense form of "have," the past participle form of "be" ("been"), and the present participle form of the main verb (verb stem plus "-ing"). The agreement is between the subject and "have."

Present perfect progressive: Describes continuing action, begun in the past, which may continue in the future

He, She, It, The student   HAS   BEEN walking.
I, We, You, They, The students   HAVE BEEN walking.

Past perfect progressive: Describes continuing action, begun in the past and ended in the past.

(all subjects) HAD BEEN walking.

EXERCISES

A. In the following paragraph, underline each subject and its auxiliaries and main verb, and discuss the agreement between them.

Thanksgiving has been a traditional American holiday since the early settlers of the U.S.A. first invited their Indian neighbors to dinner to celebrate the successful harvest they had had. People have been preparing turkey dinners with cranberry sauce and pumpkin pie for decades, and their families and friends have been invited to share the feast. Raising turkeys for Thanksgiving dinners has turned into a highly profitable business. If the early settlers had guessed that their harvest celebration would become a national holiday, they might have stopped raising chickens and switched to turkeys.

B. Choose the correct verb form from each pair in the following paragraph.

Although most juniors [have/has] [finish/finished] their basic graduation requirements, a few [has/have] [waited/wait], hoping that the requirements [will have/would have/have] changed by the time they [are/were] ready to graduate. One of my classmates [have/has] [took/taken] none of the required English courses, because he [had/has] been [telling/told] that one of them might be [drop/dropped]. He [has/have] been [attend/attending] university for seven years and [have/has] [acquire/acquired] two hundred credits.

C. The following paragraph contains several examples of faulty agreement between subject and verb and between auxiliary and another verb. Rewrite the paragraph, correcting the errors.

Many people has decide that dormitory are cheaper to live in than apartment. They have learn that paying rent is only one expense in an apartment. There is also groceries which has to be payed for, and furniture which have to be rent or bought. Many people have been move out of their apartments because the cost of utilities have increasing too fast.

D. In each of the following sentences, change the subject and predicate to plural forms.

A friend of mine has been anxiously waiting for winter to begin because he has recently discovered the pleasure of ice fishing. Until last year, he had never been ice fishing, but one day he was persuaded to join a friend who was a keen fisherman. He had beginner's luck: three hours after they started, he was the proud possessor of five large pike. He has told everyone that this winter will be the best one ever.

E. Change each of the following sentences into

    a) a present progressive ("be" and "ing")
    b) a past progressive ("be" and "ing")
    c) a present perfect ("have" and "en/ed")
    d) a past perfect ("have" and "en/ed")

e) a present perfect progressive ("have" plus "been" and "ing")
f) a past perfect progressive ("have" plus "been" and "ing")

1. Jorge drove the car.
2. He listened to the radio.
3. He started to tap his feet in time with the music.
4. He stomped his foot on the accelerator.
5. The accelerator began to stick.
6. Jorge hoped to avoid an accident.

F. Discuss the differences in the implied time for each set of sentences in Exercise E.

Modal Auxiliaries

The modal auxiliaries have nonvarying forms; there is no difference between the form used with a singular subject like "the student" and the form used with a plural one like "the students." Furthermore, these auxiliaries do not have past tense forms. Their meanings are not directly related to specific time references, but they do express other meanings, such as condition, ability, permission, obligation, intention, and probability.

She *may* visit her sister.	is permitted to is possibly going to
She *can* visit her sister.	is able to
She *should* visit her sister.	is moderately obliged to
She *ought to* visit her sister.	is obliged to
She *will* visit her sister.	intends to, is going to
He *would* study astronomy if he had time.	is not going to, due to a condition or circumstance
He *could* study astronomy if he had time.	is able to, but prevented by a condition or circumstance
He *might* study astronomy.	possibly is going to
He *must* study astronomy.	is strongly obliged to very probably does

With one exception, the modals can occur with the progressive and/or perfective auxiliaries, as well as with just the main verb. When a modal is used, the stem form of an auxiliary or verb follows it. Modals are never followed by tense-marked verb forms.

1. He *may* talk.   (modal and main verb stem)
2. She *could* be talking.   (modal, "be" stem, and present participle form of main verb)
3. He *must* have talked.   (modal, "have" stem, and past participle form of main verb)

4. She *might* have been talking.   (modal, "have" stem, "been," and present participle form of main verb)

The modal "can" does not combine well with the perfective or progressive. When a speaker/writer wishes to express the idea of ability to do something in the past, he or she uses "could."

5. She can read a book or write a letter now/tomorrow.
6. She could have read a book or written a letter yesterday.
7. She could have been reading a book or writing a letter.

| **EXERCISE** |

Using the main verbs "read" and "write," create four sentences for each of the modal auxiliaries except "can," one with just the main verb and the modal, one with the modal and progressive, one with the modal and perfective, and one with the modal, progressive, and perfective.

QUESTIONS

So far, our examples have all been statements. Questions are also clauses, having the same basic structure as statements. The word order for most questions is somewhat different than for a statement. For a yes-no question, the subject does not come first, a verb form does. If the statement form contains one or more auxiliaries, the corresponding question form begins with the first auxiliary, followed by the subject:

1a. The student is studying.
1b. Is the student studying?

2a. The student had studied.
2b. Had the student studied?

3a. The student has been studying.
3b. Has the student been studying?

4a. The student should study.
4b. Should the student study?

5a. The student should be studying.
5b. Should the student be studying?

6a. The student should have studied.
6b. Should the student have studied?

7a. The student should have been studying.
7b. Should the student have been studying?

If the statement form contains only the verb "be," the be-form comes first in a question:

8a. Jamal is a student.
8b. Is Jamal a student?
9a. The students were serious.
9b. Were the students serious?

If the statement form does not contain the verb "be" and it has no auxiliary, the corresponding question form begins with a form of "do," which takes its tense from the verb in the statement, leaving that verb in its stem form:

10a. The student studi*es*. ⎫
10b. Do*es* the student *study*? ⎬ present tense
11a. The student studi*ed*. ⎫
11b. *Did* the student *study*? ⎬ past tense

WH- questions differ slightly from yes-no questions. They begin with an interrogative pronoun (who, whom, what, where, why, how). If the interrogative pronoun is the subject of the clause, the question follows regular statement word order:

12a. The student studies English.
12b. Who studies English?

All other WH- questions follow the question word order, with an auxiliary (or "be") preceding the subject:

13a. The student studies English.
13b. What does the student study?
14a. The student had studied in the library.
14b. Where had the student studied?
15a. The student has been studying on weekends.
15b. When has the student been studying?

EXERCISES

1. Turn each of the following statements into yes-no questions:

    a. Afshin can swim.
    b. He is very athletic.
    c. He has won many trophies.
    d. The university awarded him an athletic scholarship last year.

2. Turn each of the statements in Exercise 1 into a Wh- question, substituting "who" for the subjects.

3. Turn statements (c) and (d) in Exercise 1 into Wh- questions, substituting "what" for the direct object of each.

4. Turn statement (d) in Exercise 1 into a Wh- question, substituting "whom" for the indirect object.

Questions are frequently used in letters, for the same reason they are used in conversation: to elicit a response from the person being addressed (How's mother? Are you enjoying your classes? What has the weather been like? Where did you go last weekend?) Questions are rarely used in compositions. When one does occur, it is for one of two reasons:

The writer wants to *quote* a question asked by someone else:

> The owner of the hotel that burned, killing dozens of people, kept asking, "Why didn't the alarm system work?"

The writer may want to make the reader think about an idea, before giving his own views, by asking a *rhetorical* questions:

> Many students will be visiting the travel agency this week to make reservations for trips home for Christmas vacation. Will they all be successful? That depends on the outcome of contract negotiations between the airlines and the Airline Pilots' Association (APA). If no agreement is reached by December 1, the pilots will strike, and many flights will be cancelled.

SENTENCE FRAGMENTS AGAIN (*Frag*)

Casual conversation with friends differs in numerous ways from written communication with strangers. Basic sentence structure is essential to written communication; it is relatively unimportant among friends, as the following sample conversation indicates:

Sancho: "Coke?"
Ahmed: "Sure."
Sancho: "Union?"
Ahmed: "O.K."
Sancho: "Half an hour?"
Ahmed: "Fine. Pass your test?"
Sancho: "B. Which pleased me."
Ahmed: "Good. See you at 2:30."

All of the quoted dialogue above consists of sentence fragments, structures that are not complete sentences, punctuated as if they were. Sentence fragments should not be used in written English unless the writer is recording or creating spoken conversation or has consciously decided, in the writing of a short story or something similar, that a conversational tone is appropriate. Sentence fragments do not belong in the kind of writing students are usually asked to do in their various classes.

EXERCISE

Rewrite the sentence fragments in the dialogue above as complete sentences.

CHAPTER 5

Review of
Simple Modifiers

Simple modifiers modify nouns by describing qualities or attributes; they modify verbs by describing when, where, how, why, or by what means the action was done; and they modify adjectives and adverbs by describing their extent. Simple modifiers are so necessary to clear, interesting writing that it is difficult to write even basic clauses without them.

SIMPLE NOUN MODIFIERS

Nouns can be modified by adjectives — words like "tall" to which the suffixes "-er" and "-est" can be added to express a comparative degree (taller) or a superlative degree (tallest). One-syllable adjectives, like "tall," are inflected by adding the suffixes "-er" and "-est." Three-syllable adjectives, like "intelligent," are inflected by using "more" and "most" (more intelligent, most intelligent). The two-syllable adjectives are the problem ones. Those which end in "-y," like "lovely" and "ugly," generally use "er/est" (lovelier, ugliest); other two-syllable adjectives generally use "more/most" (more subtle, most vicious).

Nouns can also be modified by verb participles, as in the phrases "the sleeping puppy" and "the hidden treasure." The participles function just like adjectives, except that they have no comparative or superlative forms.

Nouns can also be modified by other nouns, which may describe the material from which the noun is made, as in "the stone wall" or "the silk dress," or may describe the location, origin, or destination of the noun, as in "the London train" or "the city dwellers."

Nouns can also be modified by possessive nouns, as we noted in Chapter 3. When the name of a country is used as a modifier, either the adjective form or one of two possessive forms may be used: "Canada's people," "the people of

Canada," or "the Canadian people." However, the name of the country is never used alone as a modifier. It is incorrect to say *"the Canada people."

Nouns can also be modified by prepositional phrases describing location, time, or attire:

> The man *in the red velvet suit* attended the meeting *in Chicago*
> *on Monday* with the woman *in the grey flannel dress.*

Everyone uses noun modifiers, almost unconsciously. The key to using them effectively is choosing them with care. One of the most overworked adjectives in American English is "nice." Vocal intonation can give it meaning when it is spoken, but the written phrase "a nice girl" can mean anything from "a well-mannered girl" to " a plain, dull girl." Obviously, the phrase needs a more descriptive word than "nice" to convey a clear meaning.

EXERCISES

1. Substitute two or three different words for the words in parentheses in each of the following sentences.

   a. It was the (darkest), (dreariest) night (of the year).
   b. The (ruined) castle looked (ominous).
   c. The (rumbling) thunder drowned out all the (peaceful) sounds of the (normally) (quiet) valley.
   d. Suddenly, we heard a (piercing) shriek, and we all started to run toward the (distant) car.
   e. The (terrifying) noise, we soon discovered, came from a (lovesick) tomcat, in pursuit of a (haughty) Siamese.

2. Discuss the meaning differences resulting from use of different modifiers in Exercise 1.

SIMPLE VERB MODIFIERS

Simple verb modifiers are of two kinds: manner adverbs, which describe *how*, or *in what manner*, the verbal action was done; and adverbial phrases and words describing *when, why, where*, or *by what means* the verbal action was done. Most manner adverbs are words formed by adding *-ly* to an adjective.

  1. Carlos walked *in a slow manner.*
1a. Carlos walked *slowly.*

  2. He was looking at the sidewalk *in an intent manner.*
2a. He was looking at the sidewalk *intently.*

  3. The day before, he had dropped his wallet *in a careless manner.*
3a. The day before, he had dropped his wallet *carelessly.*

4. *In a joyful manner*, he began to smile.
4a. *Joyfully*, he began to smile.
5. Reaching down to a sidewalk grating, he picked up the wallet *in a careful manner*.
5a. Reaching down to a sidewalk grating, he picked up the wallet *carefully*.

Manner adverbs have considerable freedom of movement within their clauses.

1b. Slowly, Carlos walked.
1c. Carlos slowly walked.

2b. He was looking intently at the sidewalk.
2c. He was intently looking at the sidewalk.
2d. Intently, he was looking at the sidewalk.

3b. The day before, he had carelessly dropped his wallet.
3c. The day before, he carelessly had dropped his wallet.
3d. The day before, carelessly he had dropped his wallet.

4b. He joyfully began to smile.
4c. He began joyfully to smile.
4d. He began to smile joyfully.

5b. Reaching down to a sidewalk grating, he carefully picked up the wallet.
5c. Reaching down to a sidewalk grating, carefully he picked up the wallet.

Verbs may also be modified by adverbial words or phrases denoting the time, location, duration, etc., as in the following examples:

6. We are going to the lecture at one o'clock.   TIME
                                now.
                                tomorrow.
                                (on) Saturday.
                                immediately.
7. Jane is meeting Sue in the lobby.   LOCATION
                                here.
                                there.
8. We looked for a parking place for twenty minutes.   DURATION
                                during lunch hour.
9. We hurried toward the building.   DIRECTION
                                to the auditorium.
10. The scientist illustrated his lecture with slides.   INSTRUMENT
11. The audience were fascinated by the lecture.   AGENT (see pps. 41–42)
12. Several students discussed the subject with their professors.   ACCOMPANIMENT

Like manner adverbs, adverbial phrases and words have some freedom of movement within their clauses:

13. At one o'clock, we are going to the lecture.

As with noun modifiers, verb modifiers can help to create interesting, well-structured, clear, and pleasing sentences, if they are used with care. A few well-chosen, well-placed ones make the difference between average writing and good writing. Too many modifiers, carelessly selected and carelessly placed, will cause problems; too few will produce dull prose.

EXERCISES

1. Discuss the effectiveness of each of the italicized modifiers in the following paragraph. Considering each one in turn, what would the paragraph lose if it were omitted? If a different word were substituted?

Previous theories about the *extremely complex* makeup of Saturn's *unique* rings have *recently* proved to be totally inaccurate. *Incredible* photographs of Saturn's system, relayed from the *exploratory* rocket launched into space *months ago*, reveal *puzzling, unexplainable* facts. A *braided* ring is *impossible*, according to *current* laws of physics. But Saturn has one. Our *present* theories of *biological* evolution conclude that Saturn is *too cold* for *carbon-based* life forms to exist. But the *basic* materials of *such* life forms exist on a moon of this *distant, enigmatic* planet. *Highly respected* scientists are *ruefully* admitting that they are *temporarily* baffled by the *indisputable* evidence from the *far-away* cameras.

2. In the following paragraph, the underlined modifiers are either uninteresting, uninformative, or misleading. Rewrite the paragraph, substituting better modifiers. Be prepared to discuss your substitutions.

A while ago, some nice people *from near here nicely* invited a group of *sad* foreign students to a *special* dinner at *their pretty* home. The *happy* students were *sort of quiet at first,* but the *easy* friendliness of their *Yankee* hosts *soon* had the *dumbest* student talking *wildly.*

3. Write a paragraph about a hobby or sport you enjoy. Then rewrite it, after carefully considering whether each sentence could be made clearer and/or more interesting to the reader if more modifiers were added, some were changed, or some were omitted.

MODIFIERS OF MODIFIERS: INTENSIVE ADVERBS

Simple noun and verb modifiers may, themselves, be modified or qualified by "intensive" adverbs—manner adverbs or words like "very," "too," "rather," "quite," etc. Frequently, intensives are virtually meaningless, except in their emphasis. A person who is "awfully intelligent" is not "awful" in any sense of the word; he or she is just "very" intelligent. Too often, an intensive adverb is used because the writer did not choose the word it modifies with sufficient care; rather than saying that someone is "awfully fat," why not use the word "obese"? The intensive adverbs do have their uses, when used deliberately and thoughtfully. Compare the different meanings of the following sentences:

The dog next door is
{ very
extremely
incredibly
rather
quite }
annoying.

Sally drives
{ very
extremely
frighteningly
alarmingly
incredibly
rather
quite }
fast.

EXERCISES

---

1. Fill in each slot in the following sentences with an appropriate noun or verb modifier, qualified by an intensive adverb. Then discuss whether the sentence sounds better with the intensive adverb or without it. If you omit most of them, the one or two which remain will provide emphasis for the most important ideas in the paragraph.

   a. Suzanne waited for the _____ _____ results of the _____ exam.

   b. If she passed it with a _____ _____ score, she could begin classes _____ _____.

   c. She had studied _____ _____, and her parents had sacrificed __ _____ so that she could become a _____ _____ doctor.

   d. She saw the mailman trotting _____ _____ toward her house, with a _____ _____ smile on his _____ _____ face.

   e. She knew that her _____ _____ dream had come true.

2. Combine each of the following sets of sentences by reducing the sentences containing potential modifiers and making them part of the first sentence.

Example: The soccer player scored a goal. He did it at the last second.
               He was happy. The goal was the winning one of the game.
Revision: The happy soccer player scored the winning goal of the game at the last second.

a. The hound sniffed at the footprint. It was nearly obliterated. The hound was eager. Her manner was intent.
b. Five days before, it happened. A girl accepted a car ride. Her manner was willing. She was lonely. She was little. The ride was with a stranger. He was smiling.
c. Her parents had looked for her. They had been everywhere. They were frantic.
d. They had offered a reward for her return. The reward was substantial. Her return would have to be safe.
e. The hound was their hope. She had a keen nose. The hope was their last one. (*Suggestion:* "had a keen nose" could become a modifier, "keen-nosed.")

3. Underline the simple modifiers in the following selection and discuss what each one contributes to the passage.

READING SELECTION

"THE STORM"

It is a hot afternoon in July. Thunderheads pile high in the west, building, building. Whipped-cream white on top, the storm is dirty gray on its underside, and ominously yellow-gray green in its boiling midsection. An audible threat is the almost continuous rumble from within.

In a small village directly in its path, townsfolk gather in small groups in their front yards, looking at the awesome sight. All are quiet, wide-eyed, alert. So far, not a breath of air movement.

One woman, suddenly remembering, hurries to her backyard to remove a few things from her clothesline.

Pink flashes blush in repetitious sequences deep in the folds of the mass. The storm grows frighteningly fast as the churning clouds keep boiling up and out. Now sharp-edged thunder follows each sequence of flashes.

Finally the creamy top hides the sun. The opaqueness of the clouds is felt at once as solid shade quickly drops the temperature a few degrees. The first air movement rustles a few leaves, then hesitates.

The menacing rumbles grow louder.

The edge of the wind, the front, a tight, horizontal rolling cloud almost white against the dark blue-gray base of the storm above and behind it, has been flying low, sneaking up on the town, hidden by a forested hill. Now, just before it strikes, the people can see it coming over the treetops. They scurry onto porches or into their homes.

There are thumps of slamming windows around the town. A car races down a street; the hardware store owner has remembered that his wife is out, so he scoots home to shut up the house.

Les Blacklock, *Meet My Psychiatrist* (Bloomington, MN: Voyageur Press, 1977), pp. 90-91.

Review of Simple Modifiers

CHAPTER 6

Review of Coordination and Parallel Structure

INTRODUCTION

A person writing two sentences whose ideas are closely linked may commit one of two errors: a comma splice (FS) or a fused sentence (CS). These errors have already been discussed in Chapter 2, but they are sufficiently serious to warrant further comment. A comma splice or fused sentence can be corrected by adding the correct punctuation mark, which is why they are discussed in the chapter on punctuation. However, they are errors of sentence structure as well as punctuation, and like other sentence structure errors, they can cause a reader to misunderstand or even totally fail to understand the meaning of a sentence. When two sentences contain closely linked ideas, they cannot simply be joined by a comma or by zero punctuation.

Using only a comma creates a comma splice:

CS

People are worried about the future (,) they are especially concerned about the economy.

Using no mark of punctuation at all creates a fused sentence:

FS

People are worried about the future () they are especially concerned about the economy.

As we observed in Chapter 2, a period or semicolon is needed between these two independent clauses.

There is a third possibility for the writer who consciously decides to show the close connection between the ideas of the two clauses: coordinate them. This chapter concerns the coordination of independent clauses as well as numerous other structures.

CHAPTER 7

Review of
Complex Sentence
Structure

Stating the most important idea of a paragraph in a short, simple sentence is a very effective way of emphasizing that idea. However, if all the other sentences in the paragraph are also simple sentences, following basic clause structure, the main idea may be difficult for a reader to determine. One way to combine sentences that contain less important ideas is to coordinate them, as we have already seen. Coordination serves to emphasize a close relationship between two or more ideas that are of equal importance. If the ideas are not equally important, the less important one(s) can usually be subordinated. Subordinating a clause involves slightly changing its structure and making it part of another sentence. A sentence composed of an independent clause and a subordinate clause is called a complex sentence.

ADVERBIAL CLAUSES

Like other adverbs, adverbial clauses modify verbs, supplying additional information about *when, why,* or *how* the verbal action was done. An adverbial clause is similar to an independent clause, an ordinary sentence, in that it contains a subject and a predicate. However, it is not an independent clause, so it cannot be punctuated with a period. It is a dependent, subordinate clause, because it begins with a *subordinating conjunction* (so, because, since, if, although, when, before, after, while). A clause that begins with a subordinating conjunction depends on another clause, an independent one, for its full meaning. Punctuating a subordinate clause with a period creates a *sentence fragment*, which is a serious fault because it ignores the meaning of the sentence. In the following example, two independent clauses have been coordinated.

1. José is studying calculus, and he wants to be an engineer.

Either of the two independent clauses could be subordinated to the other to emphasize it:

1a. José is studying calculus, because he wants to be an engineer.
1b. José wants to be an engineer, so he is studying calculus.

In example 1a, the main idea is "José is studying calculus." The adverbial "because" clause gives additional, less important information. In example 1b, the main idea is "José wants to be an engineer," and the subordinate clause gives additional information about what he is doing to achieve his goal.

The subordinating conjunctions in examples 1a and 1b also provide something that is missing from example 1: each one establishes a relationship of cause and effect between the main idea and the subordinate clause. That relationship is missing from example 1. In each of the following sentences, various relationships between the main idea and the subordinate one are clarified by the subordinating conjunctions:

2. José will get a scholarship, *if* he receives all A's this year. (conditional relationship)
3. He needs a scholarship, *although* his parents are wealthy. (resolution of apparent contradiction)
4. He had excellent grades *before* he transferred to this college. (time relationship)
5. He plans to attend MIT *after* he has graduated. (time)
6. He will eventually return home, *since* his country needs engineers. (reason)
7. His mother has not seen him *since* he left home. (time)
8. She intends to visit him *when/while* he is in graduate school. (time)
9. José wants to be a good student, *so (that)* his mother will be proud of him. (reason)

With the exception of the "so" clause in example (1b), all of these subordinate clauses could precede their independent clauses:

1c. Because José wants to be an engineer, he is studying calculus.
1d. *So he is studying calculus, José wants to be an engineer. (Why doesn't this work? Compare it with examples 9 and 9a).
2a. If he receives all A's this year, José will get a scholarship.
3a. Although his parents are wealthy, he needs a scholarship.
4a. Before he transferred to this college, he had excellent grades.
5a. After he has graduated, he plans to attend MIT.
6a. Since his country needs engineers, he will eventually return home.
7a. Since he left home, his mother has not seen him.
8a. When/While he is in graduate school, she intends to visit him.
9a. So (that) his mother will be proud of him, José wants to be a good student.

Example 10, below, contains several independent clauses simply strung together with coordinating conjunctions. In example 10a some of those clauses have been subordinated, and the result is both clearer and smoother.

10. Many gardeners have stopped using chemical sprays and fertilizers and these substances are harmful to birds and insects but some insects and most birds are beneficial to gardens and they prey on harmful insects and a gardener uses a spray to kill harmful cutworms but he may also kill helpful lady bugs and earthworms and he uses a spray to kill fruit tree parasites and the chemical may be swallowed by a bird and the bird may lay eggs and the chemical can cause the egg shells to be brittle and they break and the baby birds have no chance to hatch.

10a. Many gardeners have stopped using chemical sprays and fertilizers, because those substances are harmful to birds and insects. Some insects and birds are beneficial to gardens, because they prey on harmful insects. If a gardener uses a spray to kill harmful cutworms, he may also kill helpful lady bugs and earthworms. If he uses a spray to kill fruit tree parasites, the chemical may be swallowed by a bird before the bird lays its eggs. The chemical can cause the egg shells to be brittle, so that they break before the baby birds have a chance to hatch.

EXERCISES

1. Combine the following sets of sentences, using various subordinating conjunctions and varying the sequence of the main idea and subordinate clauses. Punctuate carefully, avoiding sentence fragments. Consider the difference in focus and meaning of each of your rewritten versions:

Example: Sam is not afraid of being drafted. He has been accepted for medical school.

1. Sam is not afraid of being drafted, $\left\{ \begin{array}{l} \text{although} \\ \text{because} \\ \text{since} \end{array} \right\}$ he has been accepted for medical school.

2. $\left\{ \begin{array}{l} \text{Because} \\ \text{Although} \\ \text{Since} \end{array} \right\}$ he has been accepted for medical school, Sam is not afraid of being drafted.

3. Sam has been accepted for medical school, so he is not afraid of being drafted.

4. Sam has been accepted for medical school because he is not afraid of being drafted.

5. Sam has been accepted for medical school since he is not afraid of being drafted.

6. Although he is not afraid of being drafted, Sam has been accepted for medical school.
7. Because he is not afraid of being drafted, Sam has been accepted for medical school.
8. Since he is not afraid of being drafted, Sam has been accepted for medical school.
   a. Twentieth-century Americans depend on automobiles. Their ancestors managed to cross the continent with horses.
   b. In the 1880s, travel across North America was an adventure. One might encounter Indians, tornadoes, floods, or other wagon trains.
   c. People knew the trip would take months. They forced themselves to be patient.
   d. The wagon trains stopped at night. The people could cook a meal and have a comfortable rest.
   e. Most of the western United States was settled by people who disliked the East. It was getting crowded.

2. Underline the adverbial clauses in the following passage and discuss how they contribute to the reader's understanding of the subject:

If somebody showed us a document which he said was an unpublished letter of Dr. [Samuel] Johnson's, and [if] on reading it through we came across the word "telephone," we should be fairly justified in sending him about his business. The fact that there was no such thing as a telephone until many years after Johnson's death would leave no doubt whatever in our minds that the letter was not written by him. If we cared to go farther, we could say with equal certainty that the letter was written since the beginning of the nineteenth century, when the telephone was invented.[1]

MODIFIERS OF NOUNS—RELATIVE CLAUSES

A writer with two or more sentences that contain the same noun might wish to subordinate all but one of them, by creating relative clauses. This is accomplished by substituting a relative pronoun ("who," "that," or "which") for a noun in the sentence to be subordinated, and by moving the resulting relative clause so it immediately follows the noun it modifies. The pairs of examples below show how two basic sentences are converted into one sentence with two clauses: an independent clause containing the main idea and a dependent, relative clause.

[1]Owen Barfield. *History in English Words* (London: Faber and Faber, Ltd., 1953), p. 11.

1. Medicine has become a science. It was a guessing game in the middle ages.
1a. Medicine, which was a guessing game in the middle ages, has become a science.
2. The doctor was an undergraduate physics major. He lives next door.
2a. The doctor who lives next door was an undergraduate physics major.
3. His field of specialization is medical physics. It is relatively new.
3a. His field of specialization, which is relatively new, is medical physics.

Note that "who" refers to people and "which" to other nouns. Many people also refer to their pets as "who."

EXERCISE

Combine each of the following pairs of sentences by turning one of the pair into a relative clause. Punctuate carefully to avoid sentence fragments.

1. Many women are becoming executives. They once worked as secretaries.
2. Women are becoming aware of their abilities. They were told they were inferior to men.
3. Many men find it pleasant to work for women. These men are not insecure.
4. The Equal Rights Amendment is not yet law. It would eliminate sex discrimination.

So far we have been working only with those relative clauses in which the relative pronoun is the subject of its own clause. There are other kinds. Any noun in a clause may be replaced by a relative pronoun if there is a noun or pronoun identical to it in a preceding clause. Whether its function, however — direct object, indirect object, place or time reference, or whatever — the relative pronoun (with its preposition, for formal writing) must be the first element in its clause.

4. The play had an all-star cast. Julio saw *the play*.
4a. The play *that* Julio saw had an all-star cast.
5. Parvin enjoyed the play. Julio gave a ticket *to Parvin*.
5a. Parvin, *to whom* Julio gave a ticket, enjoyed the play. (formal)
5b. Parvin, *whom* Julio gave a ticket *to*, enjoyed the play. (informal)

It is a common mistake to treat the relative pronoun as if it were a subordinating conjunction, adding it to an otherwise complete clause, and keeping the noun (or a pronoun) for which it substitutes.

6. *The play that Jorge acted in *it* was a comedy.

The correct structure would be:

6a. The play that Jorge acted in was a comedy.

Relative pronouns also appear in clauses describing *place* and *time*. The preposition in such clauses may either precede the relative pronoun or be left behind:

7. The resort was in Manitoba. We stayed *in the resort* last summer.
7a. The resort *in which* we stayed last summer was in Manitoba.
7b. The resort *that* we stayed *in* last summer was in Manitoba.

(*Note:* not "The resort that we stayed in *it* last summer was in Manitoba.")

Where

Another relative pronoun, "where," whose use is restricted to place, or location, phrases, may be used instead of the phrases "in/at/on which":

7c. The resort *where* we stayed last summer was in Manitoba.

Another relative pronoun, "when," may be substituted for time phrases such as "on which," "at which," "during which," etc.

8. Our vacation was in June. We had some free time *in June.*
8a. Our vacation was in June, *in which* we had some free time.
8b. Our vacation was in June, *when* we had some free time.

EXERCISES

1. Combine the following pairs of sentences by turning one of them into a relative clause. Punctuate carefully, to avoid sentence fragments.

    a. The trip to Argentina was exciting. We took the trip last summer.
    b. The plane left from Chicago. We travelled on the plane.
    c. The guide laughed at our Spanish. We hired the guide to show us the museums.
    d. The hotels were called "pensions." We stayed in the hotels.
    e. We particularly enjoyed the food. After we returned home, we tried cooking some of the food.

2. Combine the sentences above by creating a relative clause out of each of the sentences you used as the main clause in Exercise 1.

3. Compare each of the preceding pairs of sentences (1a and 2a, 1b and 2b, etc.) and discuss how the main idea of each (a) sentence becomes the less important idea in the corresponding (b) sentence.

RESTRICTIVE VS. NONRESTRICTIVE RELATIVE CLAUSES

Non-restrictive Relative Clauses

A nonrestrictive relative clause simply gives additional information about a noun whose meaning is specific. When this is the case, a speaker pauses between the noun and the relative pronoun, and a writer puts a comma between them:

1. Students, who often get too little sleep, catch frequent colds. (The noun "students" is specific, in that it refers to all students.)
2. Geology 101, *which* students are required to take, involves laboratory work. (The noun "Geology 101" specifically names a particular course.)

Restrictive Relative Clauses

A restrictive relative clause, on the other hand, limits or restricts an otherwise nonspecific noun. When this is the case, the clause is introduced by "who" or "that" (in place of the "which" of non-restrictive relative clauses), no commas are used, and a speaker does not pause:

1. Students who get too little sleep catch frequent colds. (The noun "students," in this sentence, does not refer to all students.)
2. The geology course that Jamal took was easy. (There are several geology courses; Jamal took one of them.)

In restrictive relative clauses, "that" can substitute for "who(m)" and should, in American usage, replace "which." The relative pronoun "that" is never preceded by a comma.

1a. Students *that* get too little sleep catch frequent colds.
2a. The geology course *that* Jamal took was easy.

EXERCISES

1. In the following sentences, distinguish between the restrictive and non-restrictive relative clauses by supplying the appropriate relative pronouns and any necessary commas.

    a. One course _____ Ernestine took last year was American Literature.

    b. This course _____ is required of all students proved to be very difficult for her.

    c. Literature _____ is unlike most other academic subjects depends on an understanding of the culture _____ produces it.

d. After only six months in the United States, Ernestine was still discovering aspects of American culture _____ puzzled her.

e. In many countries, young people respect their parents _____ are not only older but also wiser than they are.

f. Several of the assignments in Ernestine's literature class concerned young people _____ seemed to scorn their parents.

g. It was hard for Ernestine to understand the emotions of American literary characters _____ behavior would be unthinkable in her culture.

2. Write a restrictive or non-restrictive relative clause to modify the subject noun in each of the following sentences, being careful to punctuate correctly.

a. The dormitory _____ has a dining room.

b. Students _____ can eat a well-balanced diet at a reasonable price.

c. However, the food _____ is not very interesting.

d. The cooks _____ use very few spices.

e. Hamburger _____ appears on the menu with monotonous regularity.

f. The chili _____ contains very little meat.

g. Many students _____ sorely miss their mothers' cooking.

Like other modifiers, relative clauses can be coordinated. In the following example, three relative clauses provide a good example of parallel structure:

The Governor, who was concerned about the state's ecology, who deplored the contamination of the state's lakes, and to whom the DNR had appealed for help, advocated tighter controls on industrial waste disposal.

MORE MODIFIERS OF NOUNS—APPOSITIVES

Appositives are similar to relative clauses, but they do not contain relative pronouns. A relative clause which seems unnecessarily wordy and which slows down a lively sentence often sounds better as an appositive:

1. The graduation ceremonies, which were scheduled to begin at 10 a.m., have been delayed.

1a. The graduation ceremonies, scheduled to begin at 10 a.m., have been delayed.

2. The electrician who was hired to hook up the spotlights came down with mumps.
2a. The electrician hired to hook up the spotlights came down with mumps.

As the examples indicate, appositives can also be restrictive or nonrestrictive.

EXERCISE

Combine the sentences in the following sets by creating relative clauses from one or two of them. Then turn the relative clause into an appositive. Which version is clearer? More concise?

1. One design for homes uses solar energy as a heat source. The design is not dependent upon conventional fuels.
2. Windows direct sunlight onto the floor. The windows are carefully placed to admit winter sun. The floor is made of brick.
3. At night, the bricks give off heat from the sunlight. The sunlight is absorbed during the day.

Sometimes an unnecessarily wordy relative clause does not sound much better as an appositive; it may even be worse. Often the important word in a relative clause can be used as a simple noun modifier, without the complex structure necessary for a relative clause:

4. A soprano who was highly praised sang the title role in "Aida."
4a. A soprano highly praised sang the title role in "Aida."
4b. A highly-praised soprano sang the title role in "Aida."

5. The tenor, who was off-key and inexperienced, spoiled the performance.
5a. The tenor, off key and inexperienced, spoiled the performance.
5b. The off key, inexperienced tenor spoiled the performance.

An appositive that consists of a verb participle and a manner adverb can be converted into a simple noun modifier only if the order of the two elements is reversed:

6. A dog, *barking loudly*, warned people of the fire.
6a. A *loudly barking* dog warned people of the fire.

EXERCISES

Rewrite each of the following sentences by turning the relative clauses into appositives. Then turn the appositives into simple noun modifiers, if possible. Discuss the effectiveness of each of the three versions of each sentence.

1. Laura enjoyed listening to the birds, which were chirping joyfully.
2. She had neither seen nor heard any birds during the winter, which had been unusually severe.
3. Now that weather which was warmer had returned, so had the robins, which were seeking worms in her flower beds.
4. Their chirping sounded like a chorus which was operatic, which was demanding rain.

Underline each relative clause, appositive, and simple modifier in the following selection, and discuss their effectiveness in making the main idea interesting.

The man who sat on the ground in his tipi meditating on life and its meaning, accepting the kinship of all creatures, and acknowledging unity with the universe of things was infusing into his being the true essence of civilization. And when native man left off this form of development, his humanization was retarded in growth.[2]

MODIFIERS OF NOUNS—INTRODUCTORY ADJECTIVAL AND PARTICIPIAL PHRASES

To give more emphasis to the modifier of a noun which is the subject of a sentence, a writer may decide to put the modifier at the beginning of the sentence, as an introductory phrase. Examples 4 and 5 on page 73 could be rephrased as follows:

1. Off-key and inexperienced, the tenor spoiled the performance.
2. Barking loudly, a dog warned people of the fire.

EXERCISE

Rewrite the relative clauses in the following sentences as appositives. Then rewrite the appositives as introductory modifiers. Discuss the effectiveness of each of the three versions of each sentence.

1. Bernard, who was driving too fast, lost control of the car.
2. The car, which was weaving all over the road, finally rolled over in the ditch.
3. Bernard, who was bruised and bleeding, crawled out of the window.

[2]Chief Luther Standing Bear, quoted in *Touch the Earth: A Self-Portrait of Indian Existence*, compiled by T. C. McLuhan (New York: Outerbridge and Dienstfrey, 1971), p. 99.

4. A passerby, who was afraid the car might explode, grabbed his arm and helped him walk down the road.
5. Bernard, who was contrite, apologized for his carelessness.

Misplaced and Dangling Modifiers

The requirement of introductory adjectival and participial modifiers is that they be immediately followed by the noun they modify. This is what many writers forget, with rather odd or confusing results:

1. Cooled by a tray of ice cubes, Clare enjoyed the iced tea. (Presumably, the tea was cooled by the ice cubes, but the sentence implies that Clare was.)
2. Strolling down the street, the buildings provided shade for us. (Buildings do not stroll.)
3. Lost in the mail, Tomas never received the letter. (Normally, the postal service loses letters, not people.)

If the number of noun modifiers in a sentence is not excessive, and if each modifier is immediately before or behind the noun it modifies, the meaning of the sentence will be clear. Confusion results from disregard of those two "ifs." In examples 4–7, the modifiers are too far from the words they are apparently intended to modify; that is, the modifiers are *misplaced*. Example 4 seems to imply that it is George who would not start, and there are similar problems in the other examples.

4. The car annoyed George that wouldn't start.
5. The monkeys amused the people in cages at the zoo. (Who were in cages?)
6. A shark may attack a man that is hungry. (Who is hungry?)
7. A mysterious man entered the hotel, carrying a raincoat. (Who was carrying a raincoat?)

Confusion and ambiguity will also result if the word being modified is not in the sentence. The modifier in the following example has been left dangling:

8. Scuba diving in Florida, sharks are a potential danger. (Sharks do not go scuba diving in Florida or anywhere else.)

EXERCISE

Rewrite each of the following sentences to clarify the ambiguities and avoid confusion.

1. The playwright enjoyed coffee that arose at dawn.
2. The puppy wagged its tail at the lady, chewing a slipper.
3. Troubled by a defective battery, Carlos took the car to the garage.

4. Lions are not a danger to people in enclosures at the nature preserve.
5. People should not sit near electrical appliances in the bathtub.

EXERCISES — REVIEW OF MODIFIERS

A. The following paragraph is dull. Turn some of its sentences into noun modifiers and others into verb modifiers, and then add a few other carefully chosen modifiers to give it more life.

We were sitting on the riverbank. We were fishing. A snake appeared. It was green. It had stripes. It was ugly. It crawled toward us. Jane does not like snakes. She screamed. She got up. She started to back away. She fell in the river. She looked a mess. She was green. She had stripes. She was not pretty. She crawled toward me. I laughed.

B. Paragraphs 1 and 2 below are composed of grammatically correct sentences, but they need considerable revision to become examples of good writing. Paragraphs 1a, 1b, and 1c are revisions of paragraph 1. Compare each of them with the original version, and then write two or three revisions of paragraph 2, using the same techniques of turning less important sentences into modifiers.

1. President Carter was in an interview. The interview was released on Saturday. He said that the U.S. had been keeping China informed. The U.S. has informed China about its positions. They are basic. They have been discussed in talks. The talks were with the Soviet Union. The talks were about arms control.

   1a. In an interview released Saturday, President Carter said that the U.S. has been keeping China informed about its basic positions, which have been discussed in talks with the Soviet Union, about arms control.

   1b. President Carter said, in an interview released Saturday, that the U.S. has been keeping China informed about its basic positions, discussed in arms control talks with the Soviet Union.

   1c. The U.S. has been keeping China informed about the basic positions discussed in arms control talks with the Soviet Union, President Carter said in an interview released Saturday.[3]

2. Andrew Young made a statement. He was the U.N. Ambassador. It was controversial. Cuban troops were in Angola. Young said that the troops "stabilized the situation" in Angola. President Carter wanted Cuba to withdraw the troops. Carter said that he agreed with Young's statement.

[3]1c is an actual paragraph from *The Detroit News*, April 17, 1977, p. 1A.

(*Note:* a carefully inserted "although" will neutralize the apparent contradiction between the last two sentences.)

C. Underline the noun and verb modifiers in the following passage. What would the passage lose if the modifiers were omitted?

> Early morning in the wilderness is the time for smells. Before senses have become contaminated with common odors, while they are still aware and receptive, is the time to go hunting. Winnow the morning air before it is adulterated with the winds and the full blaze of sunlight, and, no matter where you happen to be, you will find something worth remembering.
>
> One morning not long ago I walked down the lake trail, listening to the sounds of spring: the flowing of water and its trickling from the rocks, the oozing, sodden sounds of newly thawing earth. Redwings were calling from the cattails, killdeer keening over the meadows, but more than the sounds that May morning were the smells of wet earth and the opening of a billion buds. More alive and vibrant, more penetrating than all the rest was the heady pungence of balm of Gilead, whose great buds, filled with sticky resin, were just beginning to burst their hard encasing scales, releasing odors that enriched the air for a mile around.[4]

COMPLEX DIRECT OBJECTS AND COMPLEX SUBJECTS

In Chapter 4, we discussed sentences with simple direct objects (Pattern C). But a direct object is not always a single word; it may be an entire phrase or clause which functions as a single word. In the following examples, both the direct objects answer the questions "What was anticipated?" However, the direct object in the second example is not just one word; it is the entire clause "that the vaccine would work."

	PREDICATE:	
SUBJECT	TRANSITIVE VERB	PLUS DIRECT OBJECT
1. John	anticipated	the result.
2. John	anticipated	that the vaccine would work.

The most common type of complex direct object is a "that" clause. The word "that" in such clauses is not a relative pronoun. It is a word with no meaning that is added to a complex direct object clause as a marker. It does not replace a noun, as does a relative pronoun. If it is omitted, a complete clause remains:

3a. Fariba said *that she would take calculus.*
3b. Fariba said *she would take calculus.*

---

[4]Sigurd F. Olson, *The Singing Wilderness* (New York: Alfred A. Knopf, 1973), pp. 54–55.

A Pattern C sentence may contain both a noun as the simple direct object and a "that" clause which clarifies the meaning of the noun:

4. John anticipated *the result that the vaccine would work.*

Direct quotations and "if/whether" clauses also function as complex direct objects:

5. John said, "The vaccine will work."
6. John wondered if/whether the vaccine would work.

When the direct object is a noun, many verbs use a two-word verb (a verb plus an adverbial particle, such as "for" and "in"), but not when the direct object is a clause:

7. Maria hoped *for* a vacation.
8. Maria hoped that she could take a vacation.
9. Ali believed *in* hard work.
10. Ali believed that hard work was necessary.

EXERCISES

Create at least one sentence from each of the following verbs. For each verb that requires a direct object, try to use a noun as direct object in one sentence, and a clause as direct object in a second one.

1. thought (of)   2. promised   3. turned   4. announced

There are other complex direct object structures:

1. The ambassador asked *why his office had not been informed of the situation.* (Indirect question. Note that it follows normal statement word order, not question word order.)
2. The staff wanted *someone to answer their questions.* (Infinitive verb with its own subject.)
3. They expected *to stay late.* (Infinitive verb without a subject.)
4. They enjoyed *working on important matters.* (Gerund: a verb form that functions partly as a noun, partly as a verb.)
5. The staff people wanted *the ambassador fired.* (Abbreviated infinitive — the phrase "to be" is implied, but not stated.)
6. They considered *him a fool.* (Abbreviated infinitive)
7. Some anticipated his resignation. (Nominalized verb, derived from "He resigned.")

With the exception of abbreviated infinitive phrases, the complex direct object structures can also occur as complex subjects:

1. *That the situation was serious* was not denied. ("That" clause)
2. *How the president avoided an international incident* is a mystery. (Indirect question)
3. *For diplomats to worry* is normal. (Infinitive)
4. *To have no crisis* is rare. (Infinitive)
5. *Coping with emergencies* brings out the best in some people. (Gerund)
6. *People's behavior* is unpredictable. (Verb nominalization)

The Impersonal Use of "it"

When the subject of a sentence is complex, the sentence can usually be rephrased with the subject following the predicate. Such a sentence requires the word "it" to fill the slot left empty by the shifted subject. The sentences above can be rephrased in this way. (Only the gerund in example 5 and the nominalized verb in example 6 do not sound right, unless the "it" clause is followed by a comma; this is correct but somewhat informal.) The following revised sentences show this use of *impersonal "it."*

1a. It was not denied that the situation was serious.
2a. It is a mystery how the president avoided an international incident.
3a. It is normal for diplomats to worry.
4a. It is rare to have no crisis.
5a. *(permissible)* It brings out the best in some people, coping with emergencies.
5b. *(better)* It brings out the best in some people *to cope* with emergencies.
6a. *(permissible)* It is unpredictable, people's behavior.
6b. *(better)* It is unpredictable *how people will behave.*

Gerunds can sometimes be used in sentences with impersonal "it," as in examples 7 and 7a, but the sentences usually sound better if an infinitive is substituted for the gerund, as in 7b:

7. It is difficult getting a visa.
7a. It is difficult, getting a visa.
7b. It is difficult to get a visa.

EXERCISES

Combine the following pairs of sentences by turning the second one in each pair into a complex subject or object, which replaces the word "something" in the first sentence of each pair. Rephrase each resulting sentence in as many ways as possible, and compare the effectiveness of the various paraphrases.
Example:
A. The lawyer believed something. His client was innocent.

The lawyer believed that his client was innocent.
The lawyer believed his client to be innocent.
The lawyer believed in his client's innocence.
It was believed by the lawyer that his client was innocent.

1. Something was discovered by the lawyer's secretary. The client had been in the hospital at the time of the murder.
2. The lawyer wondered something. Why had all the evidence made his client look guilty?
3. Something was obvious. His client had been framed.

B. In the following passage, discuss the author's use of sentences with relative clauses and other noun modifiers, sentences with adverbial clauses and other verb modifiers, and sentences with complex subjects or direct objects. How do these complex sentences clarify the main idea? Why would the passage be less interesting if they were omitted or simplified?

I have discovered that I am not alone in my listening, that almost everyone is listening for something, that the search for places where the singing may be heard goes on everywhere. It seems to be part of the hunger that all of us have for a time when we were closer to lakes and rivers, to mountains and meadows and forests, than we are today. Because of our almost forgotten past, there is a restlessness within us, an impatience with things as they are, which modern life with its comforts and distractions does not seem to satisfy. We sense intuitively that there must be something more, search for panaceas we hope will give us a sense of reality, fill our days and nights with such activity and our minds with such busyness that there is little time to think. When the pace stops we are often lost, and we plunge once more into the maelstrom, hoping that if we move fast enough, somehow we may fill the void within us. We may not know exactly what it is we are listening for, but we hunt as instinctively for opportunities and places to listen as sick animals look for healing herbs.[5]

[5]Olson, pp. 6–7.

SECTION TWO

THE PARAGRAPH

INTRODUCTION

The immediate purpose of writing may be simply to complete an assignment in a composition class. The ultimate purpose of writing — whether the thing to be written is a letter, an essay exam, a job application, a laboratory report, or even a note to the milkman — is to communicate a message to a person or persons to whom the writer cannot speak directly. To accomplish this, the writer must put into words on paper all the relevant ideas that will enable the reader(s) to understand the message. Professors cannot evaluate the knowledge in a student's mind; they can only evaluate the knowledge that a student transfers from mind to paper. Prospective employers cannot guess about a person's qualifications for a job; they can only draw conclusions from the information on a job application. Far-away friends cannot understand why you like pizza if they have never eaten it and you have not described it to them. A person whom you love will not know that you do unless you say so. And the best story in the world cannot entertain anyone if it remains untold.

Before one starts to write, he or she should ask and answer some questions: Who is my audience? What effect do I want to have on that audience? Do I want to inform them, persuade them, reveal my feelings to them, or entertain them? Do I know enough about my subject to write about it in an interesting and informative way? If not, am I sufficiently interested in it to seek additional information? Once those questions have been considered, the writing process can begin. First, the writer must decide what ideas to include. Then he or she organizes those ideas and writes the first draft. Finally, she or he revises and rewrites the first draft, turning it into a polished piece of writing.

CHAPTER 8

Deciding
What Ideas to
Include

There is no such thing as a poor subject, but there are poorly developed subjects. The major cause of a poorly developed subject is overgeneralization, or lack of detail. A two-page essay entitled "Travel" is sure to be poorly developed, full of broad generalizations, with no specific details to provide reader interest. Short papers require very carefully restricted subjects. A two-page theme entitled "Booking a Seat on the London-Dover Boat Train" would probably be better developed and more interesting and informative than one entitled "Travel."

This section is concerned with paragraphs, rather than essays, but the technique of developing a paragraph is essentially the same as expanding an idea into an essay of several paragraphs: the writer considers one subject from several angles, providing details to show the complexity of that subject. The technique is rather like painting a picture: one begins with a roughly sketched outline and proceeds to add various colors, shades, textures, and fine lines. The topic sentence of a paragraph, which makes a general statement, is the roughly sketched outline. The other sentences in the paragraph provide the details. They add the facts, figures, examples, illustrations, and definitions — the coloring, shading, texture, and fine lines of writing.

A detail is a small portion of a larger whole. For any subject, there are dozens of details that might be mentioned. People often get letters from absent family members and friends that are dull because they lack details. Rather than simply writing "I have a new friend," a writer could help the reader visualize and understand that friend:

STATISTICS

He is five feet, ten inches tall, weighs 175 pounds, is twenty years old, and has an IQ of 130. His eyes are

DESCRIPTION

brown, his hair is black, and his skin is light brown. His

OTHER FACTS, DESCRIPTION, OPINION, ILLUSTRATION appear as margin labels.| OTHER FACTS | |
DESCRIPTION	
OPINION	
ILLUSTRATION	

father is a salesman, his mother is an accountant, and he has three brothers and two sisters. He is a biology major from Colombia. He dresses very conservatively, usually in dark colored slacks and jackets, with a light-colored shirt or sweater. But he is a very interesting person, with a delightful sense of humor. Most important, he is very thoughtful of others. His humor and thoughtfulness cheered me up last Saturday. He and I waited over half an hour on a cold street corner for a bus, so we could go shopping. We both wished for a car of our own, so we would not have to depend on a bus every time we wanted to go somewhere. When we got back home, he handed me a small paper bag. Inside was a little model car, with a note saying, "Now you won't ever have to ride a bus again."

Most writing is done to inform or persuade an audience of one or more readers. To inform or persuade a reader a writer cannot simply make a general statement, an assertion, and expect the reader to accept it. Asserting that beings from outer space visited earth in the distant past does not make it true, and the assertion alone is not going to convince most readers that it is true, nor inform those readers of anything except that the writer may believe the assertion. (There are several books in which that assertion is actually made, but they contain several hundred pages of supporting detail, facts and explanations that may persuade readers to believe the assertion. Even after several hundred pages, many readers remain skeptical.) Students often attempt to argue with composition instructors that papers receiving low grades ought to have higher grades, because the writers are entitled to their opinions. This is only partly true. Writing one's opinions is fine, *if* those opinions are supported by carefully organized facts, examples, illustrations, explanations, descriptions, and/or definitions that help the reader understand why the writer holds these opinions.

FACTS

Facts (which include figures and statistics) are highly informative and persuasive; they are hard to refute. A fact is something proven by ample evidence that no rational person disputes (e.g., the sun rises in the east). The statement "Eating carrots improves eyesight" may or may not be true; it is not a fact. It is a fact that many mothers have made the statement to their children. It is a fact that Ingemar Stenmark won the 1980 Winter Olympics gold medal in the giant slalom. It is not a fact that he is the best slalom skier in the world; he may be, but it cannot be proven. The Austrians accept the fact that he won the Olympic medal, but they believe that Hans Enn is a better slalom skier, and they have persuaded at least some other people that they are right.

A *figure* is a numerical fact (e.g., "There are twenty-five students in this class"). *Statistics* are organized numerical data, often phrased in terms of stated or implied ratios: "Three out of four U.S. homes have radios"; "Five hundred people [out of the total population of the U.S.] were killed in car accidents during the Labor Day weekend."

Misleading figures and statistics are sometimes used to give credibility to an assertion. The figures or statistics may be quite true, but with little direct relevance to the subject of the assertion. For example, if the assertion "The teenage population is being drastically cut by accidental deaths," were followed by the statistic, "Accidents are the leading cause of death among teenagers," readers might become very alarmed. Consider for a moment: what else would be likely to be a leading cause of death for that age group? Disease is the leading cause of death in older people, but not in teenagers. The statistic gives no information about the relative numbers of people involved.

EXERCISES

1. In the following paragraph, pick out the facts, figures and/or statistics. Do they support the assertion in the topic sentence? If not, what sorts of facts would support it?

> Senator Blowhard announced that Congressman Yakkity was a crook. Seven of the 450-plus members of Congress have been accused of accepting bribes in exchange for supporting legislation that would require cocoa machines in all college dormitories. Congressman Yakkity drinks cocoa for breakfast.

2. Write a paragraph supporting one of the following generalizations, using only facts, figures, and statistics.

   a. Students from many countries are enrolled in American colleges and universities. (Find out what countries your classmates are from, figure out what percentage are from each country, and determine what percentage of the total number of students in your college or university are foreign students. Use the information to write your paragraph.)
   b. Some of the most popular subjects among foreign students are _____. (Ask your classmates what their majors are.)

3. Discuss how the author of the paragraph below uses facts to develop the topic idea. Is the paragraph informative and/or persuasive?

> One thing everybody from Governor Milliken to tax-cut advocate Robert Tisch agrees about is tax assessment in Michigan: it's a mess. Witness Chrysler's Trenton engine plant, which the company recently said was worth $1 billion when it wanted to use the property to back up a

state loan. That meant the property should have been assessed at $500 million — 50 per cent of true cash value. It was actually assessed at $27 million. Or consider Dearborn, an entire city that simply ignored assessment laws for forty years. The city is now under court order to reappraise all property, but eighteen months after the order was issued, the average house in Dearborn is still assessed at less than $5,000.[1]

4. Discuss how the statistics in the paragraph below clarify and expand the main idea.

Having smoke detectors on guard in your home can save your life — it's as simple as that. According to the U.S. Consumer Products Safety Commission, over 75 percent of all home fire deaths take place while people are asleep. While smoke alarms will not extinguish fires, the alarm they send out will wake you up, increasing your chances of getting up, getting out and calling the fire department. If you are one of those people who think fires happen only to "other people," consider the more than 6,000 people who die and the over 300,000 people who are injured from fires each year who also thought it happened only to "others" before their fire occurred. Smoke detectors are simple to install and moderately priced. Properly placed, they will help to keep you out of the nation's fire statistics.[2]

5. Include as many of the following facts, figures, and statistics as you can to write a paragraph expanding the following sentence: "A possibility exists that the auto unions of the world might become international, but there are problems to solve before this could happen."

   a. One automobile manufacturer has 494,000 hourly workers in twenty-nine different countries.
   b. Almost half that number, 243,800, work in the U.S. and Canada.
   c. There are 10,000 in Spain.
   d. Wage rates in Spain are less than half the U.S. average.
   e. The average U.S. wage is $10.51 per hour.
   f. Spanish auto workers cannot afford to buy the cars they make.
   g. To get to work, the Spanish workers take a company bus.
   h. Three-fourths of the cars made in Spain are exported.

6. Revise your paragraph, correcting errors, combining short sentences by using coordination or subordination, and adding or changing modifiers to improve unclear or uninteresting phrases.

7. Write a paragraph as a job application, including four or five facts about yourself that would support your assertion that you are qualified for the job.

[1]From the *Detroit Free Press*, April 22, 1980, p. 1A.
[2]From *1001 Decorating Ideas*, May 1980, p. 22.

EXAMPLES AND ILLUSTRATIONS

A good way for a writer to clarify what is being said is to use an example:

1. Some of the states in the U.S.A. took their names from Indian words for rivers. For example, the Mississippi, Missouri, and Colorado rivers provided names for three of the fifty states.

2. Some kinds of food should be cooked slowly at low temperatures; others require fast cooking at very high temperatures. For example, the best soup is simmered for several hours and never allowed to boil. Pasta, however, is dropped into rapidly boiling water, a little at a time, so the water boils continuously; and it is drained and quickly rinsed after a few minutes, so it does not overcook.

An illustration is a long example, often taking the form of a short narrative. Like an example, an illustration clarifies the meaning of the topic sentence. One example usually does not constitute an entire paragraph; one illustration often does:

A mirror can often make a small room seem larger. A friend of mine has a living room that measures about eight feet by ten, but that looks twice that size, because one entire wall is covered with mirror tiles. The furniture and pictures in the rest of the room are reflected in the mirror wall, making it look like a large extension of the entire room. Using mirrors is an effective decorating technique.

In the paragraph below, the main idea is stated in the first sentence and the rest of the paragraph is a three-example illustration, effectively using parallel structure.

The key to the art of listening is concentration, to increase your auditory depth perception. My favorite illustration of this involves three people in a room with music playing. One hears the emotional overtones and nuances that the composer felt when he wrote the music; one imperceptibly taps his foot with the rhythm of the music; and one simply hears something in the background. The difference among these three people and their comprehension of music is chiefly concentration.

The following paragraph has some grammar and punctuation problems, but the most serious problem is that the example is too vague.

A doctor has to try to be very accurate. For example, giving prescriptions and knowing what the patient's real problems are. If you are not sure, you might make their life fatal.

The first problem is the sentence fragment in the middle of the paragraph. It could be combined with either the first sentence of the last:

A doctor has to try to be very accurate when he is giving prescriptions and knowing what the patient's real problems are.

A doctor has to try to be very accurate. If you are not sure about giving prescriptions and knowing what the patient's real problems are, you might make their life fatal.

The second problem concerns the shifts of focus from "a doctor" to "you" and from "the patient" (singular) to "their" (plural). Furthermore, "their life" lacks agreement: it should be either "his/her life" (which would also agree with "the patient") or "their lives,"—in which case "the patient" would have to be pluralized to "the patients." With the shifts of focus corrected, and a comma inserted after the introductory phrase in sentence two, the paragraph would read either

A doctor has to try to be very accurate when he is giving prescriptions and knowing what the patients' real problems are. If he is not sure, he might make their lives fatal.

OR

A doctor has to try to be very accurate. If he is not sure about giving prescriptions and knowing what the patients' real problems are, he might make their lives fatal.

There are still a few problems. A doctor should do more than *try* to be accurate; he should *be* accurate. "Giving prescriptions" is rather vague; a doctor may be uncertain either about which prescription to give a patient or about whether or not to give a prescription. Also, one cannot be unsure about *knowing* something; one either does or does not *know* something. Finally, diagnosing patients' problems is necessary before medication can be prescribed, so it should be mentioned first. If we revise the two variations of the paragraph once more, we produce

A doctor has to be very accurate. If he is not sure about what the patients' real problems are or which prescriptions to give, he might make their lives fatal.

OR

A doctor has to be very accurate about diagnosing patients' problems and prescribing medication. If he is not sure, he might make their lives fatal.

And last of all, it would be better English to say that "he might endanger their lives" or "his uncertainty could kill them," rather than "he might make their lives fatal." The word "fatal" describes objects or actions that kill, so a doctor's uncertainty could be fatal — it could kill a patient.

Now the paragraph is ready for an example or illustration:

> A doctor has to be very accurate about diagnosing patients' problems and prescribing medication. If he is not sure, he might endanger their lives [or "His uncertainty could kill them"]. If a doctor prescribes aspirin for an ulcer patient's pain, the patient's ulcer will become much more serious and painful, because aspirin irritates the stomach lining. A person without ulcers can tolerate that irritation, but it could kill an ulcer patient.

EXERCISES

1. Give two or three examples to clarify one of the following statements:
   a. Many words have both literal and figurative meanings.
   b. Water is more important to life than food.
   c. $E = mc^2$
   d. A molecule may be simple or complex.
   e. When they leave home, people often miss things they once took for granted.

2. Write an illustration to clarify one of the following statements:
   a. An unsuccessful job applicant may have only his or her clothes to blame.
   b. Studying all night can lead to failing an important exam.
   c. An engineer needs a solid background in mathematics.
   d. It is not always possible to translate a word in one language into a precise word in another language.

DEFINITIONS

A definition may be very short (as in a dictionary, where one sentence usually suffices) or very long (as in an encyclopedia, where it may go on for several pages) or in between (a paragraph). A word that is of major importance in a piece of writing deserves a full paragraph definition. To define a word, a writer might explain what it is (an inanimate object, an abstract idea, a plant or animal, a process, an emotion, a physical state, etc.), describe it, explain what it is used for, explain how it works, compare it to something that is similar but more familiar to the average person, and/or explain what various parts of the word mean (e.g., "astronaut" is made up of parts of two Greek words, "astron" ("star," in English) and "nautes" ("sailor" in English), and it means something like "star sailor").

Discuss how the following definitions go beyond surface meaning to help readers understand and remember what the words mean.

SHEPHERDS

Shepherds are herders of sheep, people who guard flocks of sheep from predators and other dangers, who herd them to good grazing land, who watch over the ewes during the lambing season and even assist during birth, and who endanger their own lives to rescue lost members of the flock. Shepherds see no other human beings for months at a time; their dogs and their sheep are their only companions. Many shepherds like it that way, avoiding human contact and preferring an audience of attentive animals when they sing, play the guitar, or discuss politics and philosophy.

AN ATOM

An atom is similar to a biological cell or a microscopic model of a solar system. It is the smallest unit of a chemical element, composed of a central nucleus surrounded by electronically charged particles. The word "atom" derives from a Greek word which, in English, means "indivisible," but one of the scientific breakthroughs of the twentieth century was the successful attempt to split the atom. Splitting atoms produces energy, providing us with an alternate source of power to reduce the demand for expensive and diminishing natural sources of energy such as oil and coal.

GRAVITY

"Whatever goes up must come down" is a well-known proverb. Most people also know why the proverb is true: gravity. Gravity is the attraction between objects in the universe that keeps our moon going around the earth, that keeps the earth and the other planets going around the sun, and that brings down to earth an object tossed into the air. So if a rocket is launched into space, should it eventually come back down to its launching point? No. The distance between two objects, as well as their size, or mass, determines the strength of the gravitation force between them, so once a rocket gets a certain distance away from earth, the gravitational attraction of other planets becomes stronger than that of earth. A sufficiently powered engine can propel a rocket beyond the gravitational pull of all of the planets in our solar system. When the power finally runs out, the rocket will wander in deep space until the gravitational attraction of some distant star or planet pulls it in, to crash.

PHOTOSYNTHESIS

Photosynthesis is the process by which green plants feed themselves and do a service to animals at the same time. The cells of green plants convert light into chemical energy, which enables the plants to convert carbon dioxide and water into carbohydrates to nourish themselves. In the process, they release oxygen, which animals need for their survival.

REGENERATION

A starfish has a talent that human beings do not share: it can grow a new arm if one is damaged or destroyed. This ability is called regeneration. Many members of lower branches of the animal kindgom have it, but the more complex forms of animal life, including humans, do not. Scientists are doing research with cells of higher animals in an attempt to find a way to provide human beings with the talent of the starfish.

DEBIT

A debit is a debt, something that is owed, which has been recorded in an account. Debits are usually entered on the left-hand side of an account ledger, so they are the first figures noticed by someone looking at the account. Credits, which are acknowledgements of paid debts, appear on the right-hand side of an account ledger, following the debits. If the amount in the debit column is larger than the amount in the credit column, you are in debt — and you are in trouble!

PROFIT

Everyone complains about rising prices, and almost everyone accuses businessmen of getting rich at other people's expense. Many people do not stop to think what part of the price they pay for something actually goes to the businessman for his personal use. That part is the profit, and usually it is a very small percentage of the total price of an item. Profit is what is left after all expenses have been paid. The wholesale price of an apple may be only one cent, while the grocery store charges seven cents for it, but the profit is not six cents. The grocery store owners have to pay for the building in which the business is located; they have to pay for heat, lights, and water; they have to pay wages to their employees; they have to pay for repairs, maintenance, and insurance; and they have to pay taxes. After all these expenses are added up, there may be no profit at all on that apple.

EXERCISES

1. Write a one-paragraph definition of four of the following nouns, beginning with the statement "A _____ is a (person, process, etc.) who/that _____."

<table>
<tr><td>a. hypothesis</td><td>f. essay</td></tr>
<tr><td>b. family</td><td>g. report</td></tr>
<tr><td>c. calculation</td><td>h. concept</td></tr>
<tr><td>d. poem</td><td>i. vertebrate</td></tr>
<tr><td>e. patient</td><td>j. current</td></tr>
</table>

2. Revise your paragraphs, correcting errors, combining sentences, and changing or adding modifiers as needed.

3. Write a one-paragraph definition of four of the following adjectives, using examples to differentiate the words you are defining from some of their synonyms.

<table>
<tr><td>a. skinny</td><td>f. fascinating</td></tr>
<tr><td>b. hungry</td><td>g. significant</td></tr>
<tr><td>c. miserable</td><td>h. chubby</td></tr>
<tr><td>d. lonely</td><td>i. cozy</td></tr>
<tr><td>e. uncomfortable</td><td>j. attractive</td></tr>
</table>

4. Revise your paragraphs, correcting errors, combining sentences, and changing or adding modifiers as needed.

EXPLANATIONS

General statements often raise questions in readers' minds. By explaining more specifically some of the ideas in a general statement, a writer helps the reader understand the general statement better. A person reading the statement, "Anyone can cross-country ski," might wonder if "anyone" is an exaggeration and might not know what cross-country skiing is. An explanation of those two terms would be helpful:

Anyone can cross-country ski. It is not unusual to see an entire family of retired grandparents, parents, and preschool children together on a weekend outing. They do not have to be wealthy; unlike downhill skiing, cross-country skiing does not require expensive equipment, clothing, or facilities. Cross-country skiers use the local fields and golf courses to enjoy themselves and improve their technique, wearing their jeans and old shoes. Cross-country skiing is easy to learn and easy to do: it's a lot like walking, somewhat like skating, and a little bit like polishing a freshly waxed floor by sliding over it in stocking feet. Anyone can do it, and every winter more and more beginners are joining the increasing numbers of people who enjoy it.

TOPIC SENTENCE

ALL AGES

ALL INCOMES

ALL SKILL LEVELS

CONCLUSION

To explain a general statement like "For many students in the U.S., a car is a necessity," a paragraph could be a discussion of all the different types of students who need cars (those on very tight schedules, those who live too far away to take a bus or walk), or it could be a discussion of the many places students have to get to: grocery stores, department stores, book stores, theatres, restaurants, friends' homes.

EXERCISES

1. Discuss in class what details could be included to explain each of the following sentences.

    a. Most doctors recommend some form of regular exercise to their patients.
    b. Gardening is a pleasant and productive summer hobby.
    c. Modern medicine has dramatically increased life expectancy in the past fifty years.
    d. Inflation has been defined as a spiral involving higher prices, higher wages, higher production costs.
    e. Many professions require a college education.

2. Write a paragraph on one of the five topics above.

One of the differences between a poorly-written paragraph and a well-written one is that the latter contains facts, examples, illustrations, definitions, and explanations, which provide informative details to help the reader understand the main idea. Another difference between a poorly-written paragraph and a well-written one is that the main and supporting ideas of the well-written paragraph are carefully organized to lead the reader from one idea to the next without any abrupt shifts. Organizing the details is the subject of the next chapter.

CHAPTER 9

Organizing
the Details

When you have decided on a topic to write about (or when your laboratory instructor has told you what your report is to include, or when your history professor has handed out the examination questions) you may find it helpful to write a quick outline. Write a word, phrase, or sentence that states the general topic, and then quickly make a list of details that will explain the topic. The list is an outline of your ideas, a summary of what you are going to say. The next step is to organize those ideas. If your list contains details that are subclasses of a general category expressed in the topic word or phrase, your paragraph can be developed by classification. If your list contains details that show the similarities and differences between two things emphasized in the topic, your paragraph can be developed by comparison and contrast. Many topics could be expanded by following any one of several models of paragraph organization. For example, you might use a chronological model to develop a paragraph on the general topic, "Pizza," by telling a reader about the first time you ate pizza (and perhaps did not like it), another time (when you liked it better), and a recent time (after you had developed a liking for it). Or your paragraph might be developed according to a classification model, in which you described several different kinds of pizza. Or you might compare and contrast two different kinds of pizza. Or you might compare and contrast two different brands of pizza. The various models of paragraph organization help the writer to include the most important details about his or her topic without forgetting some and unnecessarily repeating others, and they help the reader to understand clearly what the writer is saying.

TRANSITIONS

Each successive sentence in a paragraph should contain a transition, a link with the preceding sentence. Most of the models of paragraph organization discussed in this chapter are associated with particular transition words and phrases, which are discussed in the individual sections dealing with each of the organizational models. The most common transitional words and phrases are useful, but they should be used only for emphasis, or when more subtle transitions are not possible. One of the most effective transitional devices involves letting each successive sentence in the paragraph repeat a word, phrase, or idea in the preceding sentence. For example, if a writer's topic sentence is, "Many people have installed wood-burning stoves in their homes this year," the idea might be expanded as follows:

Many people have installed *wood* burning stoves in their homes this year. *Wood* is considerably cheaper to burn than *oil*, because home heating *oil* has doubled in *price* in the past twelve months, but the *price* of wood has remained about the same. People who are concerned that rising *oil prices* may force them to choose between eating properly and keeping warm are shopping for attractive, safe, and efficient *wood burning stoves*. Because of the growing interest in these *stoves*, there are dozens of new models, in a wide variety of styles and sizes to choose from. Manufacturers have sold thousands of *these old-time heaters* to homeowners this year.

WORD REPEATED
WORD REPEATED
WORD REPEATED

PHRASE REPEATED

WORD REPEATED

IDEA REPEATED

Another kind of transition uses parallel structure, so the link is between repeated phrase and clause patterns rather than repeated words and ideas.

Farmers raise the grain, fruit, vegetables, and milk- and meat-producing animals that feed a nation. Teachers explain the mathematics, history, science, and literature that educate a nation. Police enforce the rules, regulations, and laws that protect a nation. These three groups of people and thousands of others form a nation.

When Mr. Lee saw the campus of Astral University, he was impressed. When he saw the astronomy building, he was excited. When he saw the telescope, he was ecstatic. Mr. Lee, an astronomy major, was examining the facilities at many universities before deciding which graduate school would best suit his needs. After seeing what Astral University had to offer, he cancelled his visits to other universities.

A robin came and found a juicy worm.
The crocus bloomed and cheered the dusty grass.
Our neighbor's mare produced an early foal.
It's only March, but winter's gone away.

Yet another transitional device is the rhetorical question, a question that does not expect a reader's answer because the questioner is going to answer it

THE PARAGRAPH

him- or herself. The definition of gravity on page 89 relies on a rhetorical question to link the two parts of the paragraph. Rhetorical questions must be used sparingly. More than one or two in a two- or three-page essay can become offensive to a reader. But if they are used sparingly, to emphasize an important idea, they can be effective.

EXERCISES

1. Working in groups of three or four, decide on four or five sentences which develop the general idea, "Education can improve a person's understanding of other cultures." Then write a paragraph containing the sentences, linking the ideas of each successive pair through repetition, parallel structure, or a rhetorical question. Try to vary the transitions. Compare the paragraphs written by your group and the others, and discuss the transitions.

2. Write a paragraph on one of the following topics, linking successive sentences by repetition.

    a. Finding a part-time job in a college town is not easy.

    b. A _____ major is necessary for a career in _____.

    c. One of the things that makes learning English difficult is _____.

    d. For most college students, a roommate is an economic necessity.

    e. One of the first things to do after moving to a new city is to find a good doctor.

3. Rewrite your paragraph linking the sentences by parallel structure.

CHRONOLOGICAL ORDER

With a subject that is linked to a block of time, as short as a minute or as long as a century, it is almost impossible not to use the chronology of events or ideas as a device to organize the subject matter. Explaining to a reader either how pancakes are made or what led to the U.S. boycott of the 1980 Summer Olympics would require step-by-step statements implying "First, ... then ... then ... finally," the most common transitional words in a chronologically organized paragraph. In the following paragraph, the transitional words are italicized.

To build a wood fire that requires minimum tending, you need paper, cardboard, kindling, a few small logs, and two or three large logs. *First,* you should wad up the paper into a tight ball or roll it into a cylinder and tie it into a loose knot. *Next,* fold some of the cardboard over the paper. *Then* lay the kindling over it, forming a pyramid. Use three or four of the small logs around the bottom edge to hold the cardboard in place. *Then* pile the remaining small logs and all the large ones onto the pyramid. *Finally*, light the paper. Once the fire is started, it will need only the occasional addition of another log to keep burning for hours.

The transitional words in the preceding example paragraph are not very subtle. In fact, with the possible exception of "finally," they are not really necessary, because the sentences explaining the steps required to build a fire are in a straightforward chronological sequence, from first to last. Transitions are used to help a reader understand what a writer is saying. If the writer has clearly implied a sequence of actions, transitions as specific as "first, next, then, finally" are not necessary. There are more subtle transitions than these. Prepositional phrases referring to time are one variety (before breakfast, after work, in the morning, on Friday, etc). Another variety involves combining two sentences by subordinating one of them into a "before" or "after" clause. The third and fourth sentences of the preceding example paragraph could be combined this way:

After you have folded some of the cardboard over the paper, lay the kindling over it, forming a pyramid.

OR

Fold some of the cardboard over the paper *before* you lay the kindling over it, forming a pyramid.

In the next example paragraph, the sequence of actions moves from first to last, so few transitions are needed, but there are two of them, "at daybreak" and "after the bath," that reinforce the chronological sequence.

In the life of the Indian there was only one inevitable duty — the duty of prayer — the daily recognition of the Unseen and Eternal. His daily devotions were more necessary to him than daily food. He wakes at daybreak, puts on his moccasins and steps down to the water's edge. Here he throws handfuls of clear, cold water into his face, or plunges in bodily. After the bath, he stands erect before the advancing dawn, facing the sun as it dances upon the horizon, and offers his unspoken orison. His mate may precede or follow him in his devotions, but never accompanies him. Each soul must meet the morning sun, the new sweet earth and the Great Silence alone.[1]

A chronologically organized paragraph need not begin with the first event in the sequence. Sometimes the most interesting, important, or exciting idea

[1]Ohiyesa, quoted in *Touch the Earth: A Self-Portrait of Indian Existence*, compiled by T. C. McLuhan (New York: Outerbridge and Dienstfrey, 1971), p. 36.

enjoy," "some people like," "other people prefer," "those who enjoy," "students who prefer," "those who like."

EXERCISES

1. In which of your other courses is classification used to organize the data? Write a paragraph about some of the subject matter of that course.
2. There are numerous ways one could subcategorize people. Choose one, and write a paragraph about the interesting differences among people.
3. Write a paragraph developing one of the following topics chronologically.

   a. Getting a student visa is a complicated process.
   b. Freeway driving can be a nerve-wracking experience.
   c. A lecture I went to last week was interesting.
   d. Decorating a dormitory room is a challenge.

4. Reread your paragraph and carefully rewrite it, providing transitions, combining sentences that seem choppy, adding modifiers where they would add interest and clarification, and rewriting awkward or unclear sentences.
5. Could the paragraph you wrote for exercise 3 have been developed by subcategorization? If so, how? If not, why not?

COMPARISON AND CONTRAST

Students usually recognize the words "comparison" and "contrast" — often with dismay. These familiar words are very popular in essay exams. Still, many students miss points on comparison and contrast questions, because they do not realize that the question requires discussion of two or more concepts in terms of two sets of features: the similarities and the differences between them. The most common transition words and phrases for comparing — talking about similarities — are "similarly," "similar to," "like," (as in "Like X, Y is . . ."), "also," and "resembling." For contrasting (showing differences), the most common words and phrases are "in contrast to," "unlike," (as in "Unlike X, Y is . . ."), "however," "on the other hand," and "differ from."

There are two models for a comparison-and-contrast paragraph. An item-by-item comparison focuses on the things being compared and contrasted; a point-by-point comparison focuses on the features of each of the two things. If a writer wished to compare and contrast two kinds of mushrooms, his or her paragraphs might look like either of the following:

ITEM BY ITEM COMPARISON
In the button state, when it first appears, the meadow mushroom looks like an elongated white lollipop. When it opens up, it resembles

an open, ivory-colored umbrella. As it matures, the dome flattens somewhat, and the gills on its underside turn form their original pink to tan and then to brown or brownish-purple. The meadow mushroom is a completely safe, delicious addition to any meal. It is sometimes mistaken for another mushroom, the destroying angel.

The destroying angel looks very much like a meadow mushroom. Its appearance also changes from white lollipop to ivory umbrella. However, its gills do not darken as it matures; they are forever white, and deadly poisonous.

POINT-BY-POINT COMPARISON

Both the meadow mushroom and the destroying angel look like elongated white lollipops when they first appear, in the button stage. Both open up and darken slightly to look like open, ivory colored umbrellas. The gills of the meadow mushroom darken as it matures, changing from pink to tan to brownish-purple. The destroying angel's gills remain white. The meadow mushroom is completely safe and thoroughly delicious. The destroying angel is neither; it is deadly poisonous.

A list of the features of both mushrooms would include the following:

1. early shape and color
2. later shape and color
3. color change of dome
4. color of gills
5. edible/poisonous

An outline of the item-by-item comparison would be as follows:

I. Item one: meadow mushroom
  A. early shape and color
  B. later shape and color
  C. color change of dome
  D. color of gills
  E. edible
II. Item two: destroying angel
  A. early shape and color
  B. later shape and color
  C. color change of dome
  D. color of gills
  E. poisonous

Notice the use of repetition and parallel structure in the item-by-item comparison.

An outline of the point-by-point comparison would be as follows:

I. Point one: early shape and color of both
II. Point two: later shape and color of both

III. Point three: color change of domes of both
IV. Point four: color change of gills
    A. meadow mushroom — yes
    B. destroying angel — no
V. Point five
    A. meadow mushroom — safe
    B. destroying angel — poisonous

The following paragraph about apple trees is an item-by-item comparison. One type of tree is discussed first, with references to several features; then the other type is discussed, with reference to those same features, some of which are similar to those of the first type of tree, some of which are different.

Homeowners wanting to grow their own apples can choose from dozens of varieties of apple trees. Once they have decided what kind of apple is best for them, one final choice must be made: should they buy a standard-sized tree or a dwarf? A standard apple tree grows to 25 to 40 feet tall, with a corresponding width. It provides enough shade to protect a small house from direct sun, and it produces enough apples to keep a family crunching raw apples, drinking cider, and eating apple sauce and pie all winter, after giving or selling several bushels to the neighbors. A dwarf stops growing at about six to eight feet, so obviously it will not produce as much shade or as many apples as a standard tree. But it has one great advantage: no one has to climb a 25- to 40-foot ladder to pick the apples; they are all within easy reach. Both the dwarf apple tree and the standard size have advantages; homeowners must choose for themselves.

EXERCISES

1. Make a list of similarities and differences between the two items in one of the following sets:

    a. English sentence structure and the sentence structure of your native language.
    b. Botany and zoology.
    c. Fiction and drama.
    d. Accounting and bookkeeping.
    e. Civil and electrical engineering.
    f. Two other similar fields of study.

2. Write a point by point comparison and contrast of two items.
3. Rewrite the paragraph you wrote for Exercise 1 as an item by item comparison.
4. Decide whether you prefer paragraph 2 or 3 and revise it, including transi-

tions, rewriting awkward and uninteresting sentences, and checking carefully for punctuation and grammar errors.

CAUSE AND EFFECT ORDER

One of the most frequent questions people ask is "Why?" Most people do not believe that things just happen; they believe that there are reasons, or causes, for happenings in their own lives and the lives of others. Causes and their results, or effects, are very important in academic courses. Astronomy answers questions like, "Why do the sun, moon, stars, and planets seem to move?" and "Why does Michigan have hot weather in summer and cold weather in winter?" Zoology answers questions like, "Why do chimpanzees look so much like people?" and "Why do birds and reptiles have similar heads?" Fields of study from biology to philosophy to Victorian prose all raise questions of cause and effect and then try to answer them. In doing so, they often use such transitional words and phrases as "because," "due to," "the reason for," and "since" (preceding statements of cause) and "as a result," "therefore," "thus," "consequently," "so," "this led to," and "followed by" (preceding statements of result).

A paragraph that explains several effects of one cause might follow either of two sequences, one beginning with the cause and continuing with each effect in turn, as in the following example, and the other presenting the effects first and concluding with the cause. The progression of effects might be determined by their chronology or by the relative importance of each one, or, as in the following example, by a loose association of ideas:

> The blizzard last March disrupted many people's lives. Thousands of households were without power for hours and, in some cases, days. Children could not get to their schools, and adults either could not get to their jobs or could not get home from their jobs. Motorists were stranded on snow-blocked roads and highways, and the motels in a three-state area were filled to capacity. It took road crews and power company crews three weeks to undo what the three-day blizzard had done.

Sometimes, a single effect may result from numerous causes. Here again, the paragraph might either begin or conclude with the effect, depending on the author's decision about which would be more effective. If the readers are likely to be familiar with the effect, the author might state it last, to lead the reader from one unfamiliar idea to the next and conclude with what the reader knows. On the other hand, the author might begin with the familiar and then continue with the unfamiliar (or at least not previously considered) causes of that familiar effect.

One cause may produce an effect that becomes the cause of another effect, and so on, as in the following example:

As the price of everything from toothpaste to tuition increases, workers demand higher wages to keep up with rising costs. This can produce further increases in prices or a decreased demand for manufactured goods, or both. Since production tries to keep pace with demand, decreased demand is followed by decreased production. This, in turn, can lead to layoffs and unemployment, which further decrease the demand for goods.

Some subjects are extremely complex, and numerous causes and effects are interrelated, as in the following paragraph:

The U.S. birthrate began to decline in the middle 1950's, resulting in a smaller college-age population starting in the middle 1970's. Something else happened in the 1970's: the price of oil increased tremendously, driving up the price of almost everything and making Americans aware that their large automobiles used a lot of gasoline. At the same time, foreign car manufacturers had begun to produce small fuel-efficient cars in large quantities for the export market. Suddenly, the large, gas-guzzling American cars were no longer attractive to American buyers, who began buying foreign cars by the thousands. The American automobile industry went into a recession. Thousands of automotive workers were laid off, as were thousands of people in industries indirectly connected with the auto industry. People who are laid off tend to keep what money they have for necessities, like food and housing. They do not have the extra money needed to send their children to college. Their children cannot pay their own college costs, because during a recession they cannot find jobs. High unemployment means that more state funds must be used for social services — unemployment benefits and aid to dependent children, for example — than during more prosperous times. It also means that the states have fewer funds than usual, because people are paying fewer taxes. Institutions of higher education depend on two major sources of income to keep them functioning: tuition from students and funds from the states. At the present time, there are fewer students than in the past and fewer state funds available for higher education. The colleges and universities are in trouble.

Note: one of the most common types of faulty argument is deliberate or accidental confusion of chronology and cause/effect: it is raining today because I washed the car yesterday.

EXERCISES

1. Reread the preceding paragraph and discuss the causes of unemployment, of the recession in the American automobile industry, and of declining college enrollments.

2. Write a cause and effect paragraph on one of the following topics:

    a. Businesses fail for many reasons.

    b. Children often resemble grandparents or aunts and uncles more than their parents.

    c. Metal left in humid places will rust.

    d. Doctors and nurses worry more about the effects of shock than of disease or injury.

    e. When a bridge collapses, it is sometimes impossible to know who is responsible.

    f. Misunderstanding American idioms can be embarrassing.

3. Revise your paragraph, including transitions, rewrite awkward and uninteresting sentences, and checking carefully for punctuation and grammar errors.

MIXED ORDER

In many paragraphs, the details are organized by combining two or three models. The paragraphs about Micah's failure to graduate (page 97) use examples as the details in a paragraph that combines chronology with cause and effect. Comparison and contrast can be combined with cause and effect whenever a writer is considering alternate possibilities. An alternate possibility implies a condition, an "if." For example, a writer might want to have readers consider what today's world would be like if World War I had not happened. The writer would compare and contrast examples of the world as it is with examples of the world as it might have been and trace the causes of the differences.

In the following example, the author has organized definitions and examples in a paragraph that combines categorization, chronology, and cause and effect.

Starve

    Americans use the verb "to starve" in the literal sense of "to die of hunger" and in a hyperbolic (exaggerated) sense meaning simply "to be very hungry." Most Britishers also use the word this way. In Yorkshire, however, people use the verb "to starve" to mean "to die of cold" (or hyperbolically, "to be very cold"). A Yorkshireman is thus very puzzled when someone asking directions to a restaurant says "I'm starving." For several centuries after the Germanic language split into Icelandic, Norwegian, Swedish, Danish, English, Dutch, Frisian, and German, the Germanic word which had carried a general meaning "to die" (by unspecified means) kept that meaning in each of the derived languages. In modern German, "sterben" still means simply "to die." In Southern England, however, the meaning of the word became more specific. Perhaps death from hunger was so common that a specific word was needed to talk about it. The meaning of the word also became more specific in the northern part of England, in Yorkshire, a farming area where death from cold may have been more common than death from hunger. Whatever the reasons for the changes of meaning, the verb "to starve" has a curious history.

The following paragraph combines chronology with cause and effect for an effective definition of pollution.

When gasoline and oxygen combine, the result is an explosion. When that explosion occurs in a car's engine, two things happen. First, the car moves. Second, the explosion leaves a chemical residue that dissolves in the air, creating a filthy substance that can kill the creatures that breathe it. The chemical residue is pollution, one of the greatest dangers to modern man. But because the fatal effects occur slowly, the danger goes virtually unnoticed.

EXERCISES

1. Write a paragraph on the following topic, combining chronology, comparison and contrast, and cause and effect:

If I had not decided to enroll in an American college/university, my life would be rather different.

2. Write a paragraph on the following topic, using illustration and statistical details organized by combining categorization and chronological order.

To graduate, I will have to take courses in several different areas of study.

3. Trade paragraphs with a classmate, and carefully correct his or her errors. Then briefly suggest how the paragraphs could be further improved (more details, transitions, rephrased sentences, more careful organization).
4. Rewrite your own paragraphs, incorporating the ideas of your critic, if you think they are helpful.

SUMMARY

A paragraph is a set of sentences, all dealing with the same general idea and linked together in a smooth sequence. The sentences that support and expand the topic may include facts, examples, illustrations, definitions, and explanations. The progression from one sentence to the next is clearer to readers if the writer carefully includes transitions. A transition may be a specific word or phrase associated with a particular model of organization; it may be a word, phrase, or idea from one sentence repeated in the next; it may be the structure of a phrase or clause from one sentence paralleled in the next; or it may be a rhetorical question that links two parts of a paragraph.

The general organization of a paragraph may follow any one of several models, although the subject matter often restricts, and sometimes even dictates, the author's choice of model. For example, any narration of a sequence of events, whether it is a short story or a laboratory report, cannot avoid following a chronological model, alone or with other models.

Thoughtful contemplation of the most effective way to develop an idea, before starting to write about it, can make the difference between a paragraph that will interest, inform, persuade, and please even the fussiest reader and a random collection of sentences that are punctuated like a paragraph but have no collective unity. But no paragraph is finished when a writer writes the last sentence for the first time. At that point, the writer becomes an editor and critic who considers the paragraph from the reader's perspective and realizes that some revision is necessary. Revision is explained in the next chapter.

CHAPTER 10

Revising Rough Drafts of Paragraphs

INTRODUCTION

With few exceptions (essay exams, for example), a piece of writing is not finished when the writer has stated the topic of a paragraph, selected and organized the details to support the topic, and written it all on a piece of paper. The writer has only finished a rough draft. The next step is to revise that rough draft and turn it into an elegant paragraph. The difference between a rough draft and a polished draft is like the difference between a rough, uncut diamond (which looks like any other dull rock) and a skillfully cut and polished stone.

Let's look at a pair of examples. The first example is a rough draft of a paragraph; the second example is a polished, final version of that same paragraph.

Grades are realy important thing for the most of college students. This competition is always hard to be a winner and easy to be a loser. I have been participated this co -mpetition, since I was five years old. However I have never satisfied with past grades. Since I came study in the United States. I have lost relationship with good grades. For example : last year was first expearence of taking regular corse in this University. I had no confidence to succeed with corses.Professors speaks first, writes like cursive letters like a hi-erographycs and I couldn't answer well at the class.I feel li-ke a dumm elementary school kid in the lecture. I studied alot, more than they did. However I dropped one corse and faild English composition class. Finally I got a 2.5 list of corses. I believe

that grading system is good for school
, but they are not everything for the persons ability.

Grades are really important for most college students, because admission to good graduate schools and successful applications for good jobs depend on good grades. In the competition for grades, it is hard to be a winner and easy to be a loser. I have been participating in this competition since I was five years old, and although I achieved good grades, I was never satisfied with less than the highest. Since I came to study in the United States, my grades have been quite low. Last semester, which was my first experience of taking regular courses in this university, I had no expectation that I would succeed. The problem was that I couldn't understand the material nor the questions asked about it, because the professors talked too fast and their handwriting looked like hieroglyphics. I felt like a dumb elementary school kid in the lectures. Although I studied a lot, more than other students did, I could not completely solve the problems. I had to drop one course, to give me more time to study the assignments for the others, and even so, I failed English composition. I finished the semester with a 2.5 grade point average (C+), which is not high enough for admission to most graduate schools nor for employment by most successful businesses. I know that a grading system is necessary for a school, because grades are used by graduate schools and potential employers to assess students' abilities, but grades are not the only measure of a person's ability. Some allowance should be made for students who have to study, to listen to lectures, and to take exams in a language that is not their native one.[1]
Several kinds of revisions caused the dramatic change.

CORRECTIONS

To revise a piece of writing, a writer begins by correcting errors of mechanics, spelling, punctuation, grammar, vocabulary, and sentence structure.

Mechanics M

The following is a check list to help you, as a writer, to ensure that the mechanics of a paragraph are correct.

1. *Margins.* There should be a margin of about one-and-one-half inches (4 cm) on the left side of the paper and about an inch (2.5 cm) on the right.
2. *Indentation.* The first line of the paragraph should begin about an inch to the right of the left margin.

[1]A theme by a student who prefers to remain anonymous.

3. *Hyphens.* If a hyphen is necessary because there is not enough space for an entire word at the end of a line, the hyphen should *end* the line. It should *never* begin the next line. Furthermore, a hyphen can be used only between syllables. One-syllable words cannot be broken by a hyphen.

4. *Abbreviations.* Most words in a piece of writing must be spelled out, not abbreviated. The exceptions are discussed in Chapter 1.

ℓ ⊆ 5. *Capital letters.* The first letter of the first word of each sentence (including quoted sentences which occur in the middle of a longer sentence) is capitalized. Otherwise, only names are capitalized, usually. See Chapter 1 for specific details about capitalization.

Spelling Sp

Using a dictionary to check spelling is recommended. Poor spellers should not be timid about asking for help from those who are good at it. The most effective help is to point out misspelled words to the writer, who then looks them up in a dictionary. Having someone else correct your spelling errors does not improve your spelling.

Punctuation P

Puntuation use and misuse are discussed in detail in Chapter 2. The following list merely enumerates the possible errors.

There is a punctuation error if

1. a sentence ends with no punctuation
   (see Fused Sentences, page 60); Fs
2. a sentence ends with a comma
   (see Comma Splices, page 60); Cs
3. a structure which is not a sentence ends with a period (see Sentence Fragments, page 65); Frag
4. a punctuation mark appears where none belongs; P
5. no punctuation mark appears where one is needed; P
6. the wrong punctuation mark has been used. P

In paragraph (1) below, the mechanical, spelling, and punctuation errors in the example paragraph on page 111 are marked. In paragraph (2), they have been corrected.

⟶   Sp
1. Grades are <u>realy</u> important thing for the most of college

students. This competition is always hard to be a winner and easy

to be a loser. I have been participated this <u>co</u>

M <u>-mpetition,</u> since I was five years old. However I have never satisfied with past grades. Since I came study in the United

States. I have lost relationship with good grades. For example

M : last year was first expearence of taking regular corse in this

University. I had no confidence to succeed with corses. Professors

speaks first, writes like cursive letters like a hi-

Sp, M erograpycs and I couldn't answer well at the class. I feel li-

M ke a dumm elementary school kid in the lecture. I studied alot,

more than they did. However I dropped one corse and faild English

composition class. Finally I got a 2.5 list of corses. I believe

that grading system is good for school

M but they are not everything for the persons ability.

2. Grades are really important thing for the most of college students. This competition is always hard to be a winner and easy to be a loser. I have been participated this competition since I was five years old. However, I have never satisfied with past grades. Since I came study in the United States, I have lost relationship with good grades. For example, last year was first experience of taking regular course in this university. I had no confidence to succeed with courses. Professors speaks first, writes like cursive letters like a hieroglyphics, and I couldn't answer well at the class. I feel like a dumb elementary school kid in the lecture. I studied a lot, more than they did. However, I dropped one course and failed English composition class. Finally, I got a 2.5 list of courses. I believe that grading system is good for school, but they are not everything for the person's ability.

Grammar *Gr*

Our example paragraph contains many grammatical errors, which can be classified into five types: determiners, agreement, word form, reference and omission/inclusion.

Determiners *Det*

Determiners were discussed in detail in Chapter 3. There are three kinds of determiner errors:

1. A determiner has been used where none belongs.
2. No determiner has been used where one is needed.
3. The wrong determiner has been used.

Agreement *Agr*

Agreement refers to the grammatical relationship between the elements of a sentence:

1. Determiners and nouns.
2. Two or more nouns.
3. Subjects and verbs.
4. Two or more verbs.
5. Pronouns and their antecedents.

1. Agreement between determiners and their nouns was discussed in Chapter 3.
2. Agreement is often necessary between nouns in a sentence.

    Errors:
      a. Those kind of people are unusual.
      b. Students have to take a philosophy course.
      c. Bob and George have a sister. (This sentence is correct if Bob and George are brothers.)
      d. Students in New England need a warm coat.

    Corrections:
      a. That kind of person is unusual.
          or
         Those kinds of people are unusual.
      b. Students have to take philosophy courses.
          or
         Each student has to take a philosophy course.
      c. Bob and George have sisters.
          or
         Bob and George each have a sister.
      d. Students in New England need warm coats.
          or
         A student in New England needs a warm coat.

3. Agreement between subjects and their verbs was discussed in Chapter 4, pages 44–49.
4. Verbs in a sentence containing more than one clause must agree in tense, as must verbs in a narrative, however long the narrative is.
    a. My roommate was late for class this morning. She got up, looked at the clock, screamed, and started rushing to get ready.
    b. 1) John said that he was sick.
       2) John says that he is sick.
    c. 1) When Tom was a child he wanted to be a policeman.
       2) Since Tom was a child, he has wanted to be a policeman.
    d. 1) When Sassan finished working, he was ready to have fun.
       2) When Sassan had finished working, he was ready to have fun.
       3) When Sassan finishes working each day, he is ready to have fun.
       4) When Sassan has finished working each day, he is ready to have fun.

5) When Sassan has finished working today, he will be ready to have fun.

6) When Sassan finishes working today, he will be ready to have fun.

e. When/While Simon was driving to class, he $\begin{Bmatrix} \text{listened} \\ \text{was listening} \end{Bmatrix}$ to the radio.

f. 1) I wondered if Khadiga would go to the concert.
   2) I wonder if Khadiga will go to the concert.

g. 1) If Hamad goes to New York, he will tell us.
   2) If Hamad went to New York, he would tell us.
   3) If Hamad had gone to New York, he would have told us.

5. Agreement is also necessary between a pronoun and its antecedent, the noun it replaces.

   a. *Error:* Each student brought their registration card.
      Correction: Each student brought his or her registration card.

   b. *Error:* One of the boys said they were sick.
      Correction: One of the boys said he was sick.
      (Unless the writer meant that all the boys were sick.)

   c. *Error:* Vincent wants to take a science fiction course, but they aren't being offered this term.
      Correction: Vincent wants to take a science fiction course, but $\begin{Bmatrix} \text{one isn't} \\ \text{none is} \end{Bmatrix}$ being offered this term.

Word Form   WF

Errors of word form occur when a singular noun is used in a phrase or clause that requires a plural, or when a plural is used in a phrase or clause that requires a singular; when an incorrect verb form is used ("goed," rather than "went"); when an incorrect verb suffix is used (see Chapter 4, pages 46–50); or when an incorrect part of speech is used, as in the following examples.

                                   WF
1. *Error:* Ski is fun.

   Correction: Skiing is fun.
                             WF   WF
2. *Error:* I was really *depress; depress* is common among students during exam week.

   Correction: I was really depressed; depression is common among students during exam week.

Reference   Ref.

An error of reference occurs when a pronoun has no antecedent or is too far from its antecedent for clarity; the reader is not sure what the pronoun refers to.

1. *Error:* Sam is a gardener. He enjoys watching <u>them</u> grow. [Ref]
   Correction: Sam is a gardener. He enjoys watching plants grow.
2. *Error:* Amir has one daughter and two sons. Mohammed is a carpenter and Ari is a businessman, while she is an economist.
   Correction: Amir has one daughter and two sons. Mohammed is a carpenter and Ari is a businessman, while Suzanne (OR his daughter) is an economist.

Omission/Inclusion Om

Omission means leaving out a word or words which are necessary to a sentence (prepositions are frequently forgotten); inclusion means including a word which does not belong in the sentence.

1. *Error:* My mother was annoyed [OM] my brother.

   Correction: My mother was annoyed at my brother.
2. *Error:* I attended [OM] the class most [OM] days.

   Correction: I attended class most days.

Corrections of Your Papers

The grammatical errors in our example paragraph are marked below, and they are discussed in detail in the following pages.

(Grades) are really important thing [Agr] for the [det] most [OM] college   1

students. (This) competition is always hard to be a winner and   2

easy to be a loser. I have been <u>participated</u> [wf] this competition [OM]   3

since I was five years old. However, I have never [OM] satisfied   4

with past grades. Since I came [OM] study in the United States, I have   5

lost [det] relationship with good grades. For example, last year was [det]   6

first experience of taking regular <u>course</u> [wf] in this university. I   7

had no confidence to succeed with [det] courses. Professors <u>speaks</u> [agr]   8

first, <u>writes</u> [agr] li[OM]e cursive letters like a hieroglyphics, [agr] and   9

I couldn't answer well at the <u>class.</u> I <u>feel</u> [wf] like a dumb elementary [agr tense]   10

school kid in the lecture. I studied a lot, more than <u>they</u> did. [ref]   11

However, I dropped one course and failed [det] English composition   12

class. Finally, I got a 2.5 list of courses. I believe that [det] grading   13

Revising Rough Drafts of Paragraphs

system is good for^det school, but (they)^ref are not everything for (the)^det   14

person's ability.   15

Determiner Errors *det*

a. *Line 1.* "The" and "most" are both determiners, so normally they do not occur together. There are two apparent exceptions. When the word "most" is used with adjectives to express superlative degree ("The most intelligent person I know"), it is not a determiner. The word is also sometimes used with nouns to express the idea "the greatest number of something" (compared with something else), as in the sentence, "In 1971, this university had the most graduate students in its history." When "most" is used as a determiner, it means "the majority of something."

b. *Line 2.* "This" is incorrect, because the word is supposed to specify a previously identified noun, but the noun "competition" has not been mentioned previously. In this line, no determiner should be used, because "competition" is a non-count noun (we are not talking about one athletic or intellectual competition out of many), which is not specific. The meaning of the sentence is still unclear after "this" is omitted; further revision will be discussed later.

c. *Line 6.* A determiner is needed, since we have the singular form of a count noun, "relationship." To specify whose relationship was lost, a possessive pronoun would be the best choice: "my relationship."

d. *Line 7.* A determiner is needed with the ordinal number "first." Again, to specify whose first experience is involved, a possessive pronoun would be the best choice: "my first experience."

e. *Line 8.* "Courses" cannot refer to all courses in the university, so the reference should be specified: "my courses."

f. *Lines 12-13.* The word "class" is the singular form of a count noun, and it is specific, so the definite article "the" is needed. If the writer preferred, he could omit the word "class" and say simply, "I failed English composition."

g. *Line 14.* The words "system" and "school" are singular forms of count nouns, so they require determiners. If the author is referring to his own school's grading system, then the definite article is called for: "I believe that the grading system is good for the school." If the writer just means that any school's grading system is a good idea, then the indefinite article should be used: "I believe that a grading system is good for a school."

h. *Line 15.* In this sentence, "person" is not specific. The implication is "any person," so either the word "any" or the indefinite article "a" should be used.

Agreement Errors *Agr*

a. Line 1. "Grades" is plural, so "thing" must also be plural.

b. Lines 8-9. "Professors" is plural, so the verbs must also be plural: "speak" and "write."

c. Line 9. The indefinite article is singular; "hieroglyphics" is plural, so it cannot be preceded by a singular determiner. Since "letters" is plural, "a hieroglyphic" would be incorrect. The phrase should read, "letters like hieroglyphics."

d. Line 10. All of the verbs in the personal narrative part of the paragraph are in the past tense; "feel" should also be in the past tense.

Errors of Word Form   *wf*

a. Line 3. The verb "participate" is intransitive, so it cannot occur in a passive sentence, which this is. (The active version would be "This competition has participated me," which makes no sense.) With the auxiliaries "have been," the only possible verb form is "participat*ing*."

b. Line 7. "Course" is a count noun, so it needs either a determiner or a plural ending. If one assumes that the writer took more than one course, the plural would be the correct form.

c. Line 10. Unless the writer had more than one professor for a particular class, the plural, "classes," is needed.

d. Line 11. The implication of the entire paragraph is that the writer "felt like a dumb kid" in more than one lecture, so it should be "lectures."

Errors of Reference   *ref*

a. Line 11. The reader will search in vain for the noun to which "they" refers. A noun or noun phrase, perhaps "other students," should replace the pronoun.

b. Line 14. "They" apparently refers to a word not in the sentence: "grades." "They" could refer to "grading system," but it does not agree in number. Since "system" is singular, the pronoun should be "it," not "they." This error might also be marked as an agreement error.

Errors of Omission *oM* *λ* or Inclusion *oM* *χ*

a. Line 1. The preposition "of" is used with "most" only if the definite article or a demonstrative pronoun follows: "most of the college students." In this sentence, the writer is not talking about a specific group of college students, but college students in general.

b. Line 3. One participates "in" something.

c. Line 4. The passive sentence is missing the word "been."

d. Line 5. The word "study" explains the purpose for which the writer came, so the word "to" or the phrase "in order to" is needed. The only verbs that can be followed immediately by another verb are the auxiliaries and "make," "hear," "saw," "watched"; all others require a word or phrase between them:

> I came to study.
> I came and studied.

I came in order to study.
I came so that I could study.
I want/intend/plan/expect/hope to study.
I want you to study.
You made me study.
I heard you sing.
I saw you run.
I watched you play tennis.

e. Line 9. Professors may write like small children who have not yet learned how to form their letters very well, but they do not write like cursive letters, because cursive letters cannot write. The phrase "cursive letters" is the direct object of "write," and the word "like" in front of the phrase should be omitted. The word "like" before "hieroglyphics" is correct; it means "similar to."

Vocabulary: Wrong Words   *WW*

After making the grammatical corrections discussed above, our paragraph is clearer, but there are still problems. Some of the vocabulary items are confusing; the meaning is not clear. Problem words are marked below.

Grades are really important things for most college	1
students. Competition is always hard to be a winner	2
and easy to be a loser. I have been participating in this com-	3
petition since I was five years old. However, I have never	4
been satisfied with past grades. Since I came to study in the United	5
States, I have lost my relationship with good grades. For example,	6
last year was my first experience of taking regular courses in	7
this university. I had no confidence to succeed with my courses.	8
Professors speak first, write cursive letters like hierogly-	9
phics, and I couldn't answer well at the classes. I felt like	10
a dumb elementary school kid in the lectures. I studied	11
a lot, more than other students did. However, I dropped one course	12
and failed English composition. Finally, I got a 2.5 list	13
of courses. I believe that a grading system is good for a school,	14
but it is not everything for a person's ability.	15

Corrections

a. *Line 6.* One does not lose relationships, and one has relationships with other people (or animals), not with inanimate things like grades. (In humorous essay, a writer might discuss his/her relationship with an inanimate object like a car, but it would require attributing human characteristics to the car.) Vocabulary errors can be corrected in many different ways, because there are many different ways to express a given idea. If a writer begins by stating the idea as simply as possible, he or she can consider other ways of expressing it. Often, the simplest way is the clearest. Presumably, the author of our example wanted to express the idea that he stopped getting good grades after he came to study in the United States. The idea could be stated just that way: "Since I came to study in the United States, I have stopped getting good grades." If the writer does not care for that simple statement, it can be rephrased:

> I have been unable to get good grades.
> I have received poor grades.
> My grades have been unsatisfactory.
> My grades have not been very good.
> My grades have been very bad.
> My grades have been quite low.

b. *Line 8.* "Confidence" is usually followed by the preposition "in" and a noun phrase or a "that" clause. "Succeed" is usually followed by "at" or "in." This sentence could be rephrased as:

> I had no confidence in my ability to succeed in my courses.
> I had no confidence that I would succeed in my courses.

The word "confidence" implies certainty, so the sentence suggests that the writer was merely unsure of success. If the intended meaning is that he knew that success was impossible, "confidence" is the wrong word. "Hope" or "expectation" would be better:

> I had no hope that I would succeed.
> I had no expectation that I would succeed.
> I had no hope of success.
> I had no hope of succeeding.
> I had no expectation of success.

c. *Line 9.* "Fast," not "first," is evidently what the author meant to write.

d. *Line 10.* People are "in" classes, not "at" them.

e. *Line 13.* The original sentence implies that the writer got a list of courses in which he was guaranteed grades averaging C+ (4.0 for A, 3.0 for B, 2.0 for C). What is obviously meant is that he averaged C+ in the courses he took. A student's average grades on a numbered scale are referred to as the grade point average (GPA). So the sentence should be revised to read:

> Finally, I got a 2.5 grade point average.

f. *Line 15.* The meaning which the writer wants to convey in this sentence seems to be that grades are not the only means of evaluating a student's ability. But it does not say that. The words "everything for" create confusion. Writers frequently use the word "everything" when they mean "the only thing," especially in negative sentences, but it does not always express the same meaning. The word "for" does not make sense in this sentence. Replacing those two words will clarify the meaning:

$$\ldots \text{ it is not the only thing to } \left\{ \begin{array}{l} \text{indicate} \\ \text{show} \\ \text{prove} \end{array} \right\} \text{ a person's ability.}$$

$$\ldots \text{ it is not the only } \left\{ \begin{array}{l} \text{measure of} \\ \text{way to measure} \\ \text{means of evaluating} \end{array} \right\} \text{ a person's ability.}$$

Replacing inaccurate words with accurate ones changes our example paragraph into this:

Grades are really important things for most college students. Competition is always hard to be a winner and easy to be a loser. I have been participating in this competition since I was five years old. However, I have never been satisfied with past grades. Since I came to study in the United States, my grades have been quite low. For example, last year was my first experience of taking regular courses in this university. I had no expectation that I would succeed in my courses. Professors speak fast, write cursive letters like hieroglyphics, and I couldn't answer well in the classes. I felt like a dumb elementary school kid in the lectures. I studied a lot, more than other students did. However, I dropped one course and failed English composition. Finally, I got a 2.5 grade point average. I believe that a grading system is good for a school, but it is not the only measure of a person's ability.

Sentence Sense   SS

After errors have been corrected, a sentence may still fail to make sense to a reader. The problem may be faulty sentence structure, which was reviewed in Chapters 4 through 7.

Sometimes a sentence is unclear because it contains too many unnecessary words. This may happen because the writer cannot think of the right word. More often, it happens because the writer mistakenly believes that long words, phrases, and clauses are better than short ones. This is not necessarily — or even usually — true. The following examples illustrate the effectiveness of careful cutting.

1. *Original:* Giving the ball a really solid kick, a player on the soccer team that was losing the game succeeded in getting the ball through the opposing team's goal post.

Revision: Kicking the ball solidly, a soccer player on the losing team scored.

2. Original: Some people are unduly concerned about the way in which other people will perceive their physical appearance.

Revision: Some people worry too much about their appearance.

3. Original: The cause of the cessation of John's continuance in the physical science field was his inability to successfully complete the examination at the conclusion of the term.

Revision: John dropped out of physics because he failed the final exam.

4. Original: All of my courses which I am taking in this university will prove to be extremely valuable in my plan for the future, when I hope to become an engineer.

Revision: All my courses will be valuable in the future, when I become an engineer.

Original

Fear is merely a result of one's mind and thought reaction to the unknown that generates ambiguity. For example, one might fear to fail to achieve a goal, by not anticipating the goal, but rather thinking about the failure first. Another example would be a person's fear of beasts and objects. Examples of the former are lions, snakes, and other frightening and fearful animals, and the latter, objects, are like power-generating machines, electrical devices, or knives. Books might result in creating fear, like horror books. One unconsciously unnoticed fear, which comes up to reality at different stages and the last stage of life, would be the fear of death, which may be the worst experience in the life of a person. Not knowing what could be accomplished by understanding may be another way that fear can dominate a person's mind, since he has a fear of the unknown.[2]

Cutting the Original

Fear is ~~merely~~ a ~~result of one's mind and thought~~ reaction to the unknown ~~that generates ambiguity. For example,~~ One [person] might fear ~~to fail~~ [failure.] ~~to achieve a goal, by not anticipating the goal, but rather thinking about the failure first.~~ Another ~~example would be~~ [might] a person's fear ~~of beasts and~~ [animals such as] objects. ~~Examples of the former are~~ [or inanimate] lions, [or] snakes, ~~and other frightening and fearful animals, and the latter, objects, are~~ like power-generating

[2]Hamid Dastkar, a student theme.

machines, electrical devices,^or knives.^Books ~~might result in~~ *deliberately* creating fear **.**
~~like~~ (horror) ~~books~~. One ~~unconsciously~~ ~~unnoticed~~ fear, ~~which comes up~~
~~to reality at different states and the last stage of life, would be~~ *is* the fear
of death, ~~which may be the worst experience in the life of a person. Not~~
~~knowing what could be accomplished by understanding may be another~~
~~way that fear can dominate a person's mind, since he has a fear of~~ the
final unknown **.**

Revision

Fear is a reaction to the unknown. One person might fear failure. Another person might fear animals such as lions or snakes, or inanimate objects like power-generating machines, electrical devices, or knives. Horror books deliberately create fear. One widespread fear is the fear of death, the final unknown.

Original

(1) Ecology, the science that deals with man and his environment, is becoming increasingly important. (2) Pollution, the cause of accelerated ecological development, is subject to future discussion. (3) It wasn't until the early 1940's that technology began to undergo some important changes. (4) Before long, nearly all sectors of the New World industrial complex implemented these changes. (5) The auto industry, clothing manufacturers, and the development of new chemicals as food preservatives are a few of the technological changes. (6) Technology created not only comfort, but a new problem as well. (7) This side effect is today commonly known as pollution. (8) Pollution is formed by the residue of the chemical combustion that occurs when gasoline and oxygen combine and produce an explosion, causing the movement of a car. (9) Once the explosion occurs, two effects are manifested. (10) First is the movement of the car and second is the residual remains of the chemical combustion. (11) This residue dissolves in the air, thus creating a filthy substance which can cause death to the creatures that breathe it. (12) Pollution is considered one of the most dangerous risks modern man lives with today. (13) Because the fatal effects occur slowly and over a long period of time, the danger goes virtually unnoticed.

Suggestions for Cutting, Revising, and Combining

1. OK, but use a comma at the end.
2. due to pollution (combine with sentence 1).
3. In the early 1940s, technology produced many changes,

4. which most industries implemented (combined with sentence 3),
5. including manufacturers of automobiles, clothing, and food preservatives (combine with sentences 3 and 4. The original sentence is unclear: "the auto industry" and "clothing manufacturers" are not examples of changes.)
6. OK, but use a dash or colon at the end.
7. pollution (combine with sentence 6),
8. Pollution results when gasoline and oxygen combine in a car's engine to produce an explosion.
9. Once the explosion occurs, two things happen.
10. First, the car moves. Second, the chemical
11. residue of the explosion dissolves in the air, creating a filthy substance which can kill the creatures that breathe it.
12. Pollution is one of the greatest dangers in modern life.
13. Because the fatal effects occur slowly, the danger goes virtually unnoticed.

Revision

Ecology, the science that deals with man and his environment, is becoming increasingly important, due to pollution. In the early 1940's, technology produced many changes, which most industries implemented, including manufacturers of automobiles, clothing, and food preservatives. Technology created not only comfort, but a new problem as well: pollution. Pollution results when gasoline and oxygen combine in a car's engine to produce an explosion. Once the explosion occurs, two things happen. First, the car moves. Second, the chemical residue of the explosion dissolves in the air, creating a filthy substance which can kill the creatures that breathe it. Pollution is one of the greatest dangers of modern life. Because the fatal effects occur slowly, the danger goes virtually unnoticed.

When you begin to cut a rough draft, be ruthless. If any word, phrase, or clause is unclear, uninformative, or unnecessarily repetitive, omit it. This will give more space for necessary details which may be missing from the first draft.

The final version of the preceding paragraph about pollution appears on page 109. The writer decided that the introductory information about ecology and technological changes was unnecessary in a paragraph about pollution.

In our example paragraph about grades, there are a few sentence sense problems. (The most recent revision is on page 122.)

1. The sentence beginning in line 1 and ending in line 2 is not clear. A competition is a contest among two or more individuals to determine which one is the winner and which ones are the losers. But the sentence says "competition is hard to be a winner and easy to be a loser." It does not make

sense. Presumably, the competition the author is thinking about is the competition among college students for grades. If the word "competition" is put into a prepositional phrase clarifying that idea, the sentence will no longer puzzle its readers:

> In the competition for grades, is always hard to be a winner and easy to be a loser.

The sentence is now ungrammatical, but at least the meaning is clear. This is the kind of sentence which requires an expletive "it" to fill the subject position. (The actual subject is "to be a winner and to be a loser.") If "it" is added, the sentence is both correct and meaningful:

> In the competition for grades, it is always hard to be a winner and easy to be a loser.

2. The sixth and seventh sentences, lines 5–7, are rather choppy, and they seem to be closely related, so combining them is recommended. The idea in the first sentence is less important than the idea in the second one, so the first sentence should be subordinated. Keeping the phrase "last year" as an introductory phrase with which to begin the sentence "I had no expectation that I would succeed in my courses" links the time reference to the statement. The information that "last year" was the author's first experience with regular courses can be rephrased as a relative clause modifying "last year":

> For example, last year, which was my first experience of taking regular courses in this university, I had no expectation that I would succeed in my courses.

3. The next sentence (lines 7-9) is a general observation, not closely related to the idea in the previous sentence. If "professors" is preceded by a definite article (specifying those professors who taught the courses the author took) and if the verbs are rephrased in the past tense (to reinforce the time frame of "last year"), this sentence explains the causes of the author's feeling of hopelessness in the preceding sentence:

> The professors spoke too fast and wrote cursive letters like hieroglyphics.

The last half of this sentence is ambiguous: it is not clear whether the professors' handwriting looked like hieroglyphics or the professors wrote like hieroglyphics do. Since the paragraph is not meant to be amusing, the first meaning is the intended one. The next clause in the original sentence shifts the subject from "professors" to "I," so it should be a new sentence, not just an addition to this one.

4. The last half of line 8, the clause we just took out of the sentence which begins "The professors," explains why the author "felt like a dumb elementary school kid in the lectures," so it should be connected to it. Either idea could be subordinated to the other in a cause/effect sentence:

> Because I couldn't answer well in the class, I felt like a dumb elementary school kid in the lecture.
> I couldn't answer well in the classes, so I felt like a dumb elementary school kid in the lectures.

Actually, the reason for the author's inability to answer well is implied in the previous sentence, and could be stated directly:

> Because I couldn't understand the questions, I couldn't answer them, so I felt like a dumb elementary school kid in the lectures.

5. The sentences in lines 9 to 11 seem to contradict one another: dropping one course and failing another do not seem the likely results of studying a lot. What the author wants to say, presumably, is that in spite of studying harder than other students, he was forced to drop one course, and he failed another. Let's revise the sentence so that it conveys the idea that dropping a course was not something he wanted to do, but something he had to do:

> However, I had to drop one course, and I failed English compositon.

After these revisions, our example paragraph looks like this:

> Grades are really important things for most college students. In the competition for grades, it is always hard to be a winner and easy to be a loser. I have been participating in this competition since I was five years old. However, I have never been satisfied with past grades. Since I came to study in the United States, my grades have been quite low. For example, last year, which was my first experience of taking regular courses in this university, I had no expectation that I would succeed in my courses. The professors spoke too fast, and their handwriting looked like hieroglyphics. Because I couldn't understand the questions, I couldn't answer them, so I felt like a dumb elementary school kid in the lectures. I studied a lot, more than other students did. However, I had to drop one course, and I failed English composition. Finally, I got a 2.5 grade point average. I believe that a grading system is good for a school, but it is not the only measure of a person's ability.

SELECTING DETAILS

In our example paragraph, errors are the main cause of the reader's uncertainty about the writer's meaning. Correcting the errors results in a pretty good paragraph, which clearly states the basic ideas. Furthermore, the author has included details to support those ideas; there are both facts and examples. However, two or three of the ideas could be more fully developed and explained.

An idea at the beginning of the paragraph needs to be explained: why grades are important. Readers know the reasons, but it is the writer's job to remind them:

> Grades are really important for most college students, because admission to good graduate schools and successful applications for good jobs depend on good grades. In the competition for grades, it is hard to be a winner and easy to be a loser.

The next three sentences contain an implication that is not stated. They also contain an apparent contradiction. The implication is that the writer had better grades before he came to the U.S. than he has had since. The contradiction is in lines 4 and 5, "I have never been satisfied with past grades." The ideas would be clearer to the reader if the implication were stated and the apparent contradiction were rephrased:

> I have been participating in this competition since I was five years old, and although I achieved good grades, I was never satisfied with less than the highest. Since I came to study in the United States, my grades have been quite low.

The next six sentences are intended to be an expansion of one general idea, so the first one begins with the words "For example." However, there is no example until the sixth sentence, where a specific course is named. Failing a course is, indeed, an example of getting a low grade. But the previous sentences do not include any example. Rather, they are an explanation of the causes of the low grades. This should be made clear:

> Last semester, which was my first experience of taking regular courses in this university, I had no expectation that I would succeed in my courses. The problem was that I couldn't understand the material nor the questions asked about it, because the professors talked too fast and their handwriting looked like hieroglyphics. I felt like a dumb elementary school kid in the lectures.

The next two sentences concern the same idea. The implication of the "however" at the beginning of the second one is that all the author's hard studying was not enough to overcome the problems mentioned earlier. Again, the implications need to be clearly stated, not just implied. Beginning the first sentence with the subordinating conjunction "although," prepares the reader for the statement "I could not completely solve the problems." The next sentence then explains two specific results of the unsolved problems.

> Although I studied a lot, more than other students did, I could not completely solve the problems. I had to drop one course, to give me more time to study the assignments for the others, and even so, I failed English composition.

The next to last sentence does not provide any information about the meaning of a 2.5 grade point average. The word "finally" at the beginning could suggest to some readers that the problems were eventually overcome and the author considers 2.5 a good average. Presumably, this is not at all how the author felt, so the sentence needs to be rephrased and perhaps expanded:

I finished the semester with a 2.5 grade point average (C+), which is not high enough for admission to most graduate schools nor for employment by most successful businesses.

The last sentence is a problem. The entire paragraph up to that sentence is a discussion of the importance of good grades and some of the reasons international students have trouble getting good grades in U.S. colleges and universities. The last sentence abruptly shifts to a different idea, which is not explained or discussed. Again, there is an implication: the author considers himself a better student than a GPA of 2.5 would suggest. The following revision would clarify how this sentence is associated with the rest of the paragraph:

I know that a grading system is necessary for a school, because grades are used by graduate schools and potential employers to assess students' abilities, but grades are not the only measure of a person's ability. Some allowance should be made for students who have to study, to listen to lectures, and to take exams in a language that is not their native one.

Our example paragraph has now been revised to read as follows:

Grades are really important for most college students, because admission to good graduate schools and successful applications for good jobs depend on good grades. In the competition for grades, it is hard to be a winner and easy to be a loser. I have been participating in this competition since I was five years old, and although I achieved good grades, I was never satisfied with less than the highest. Since I came to study in the United States, my grades have been quite low. Last semester, which was my first experience of taking regular courses in this university, I had no expectation that I would succeed. The problem was that I couldn't understand the material nor the questions asked about it, because the professors talked too fast and their handwriting looked like hieroglyphics. I felt like a dumb elementary school kid in the lectures. Although I studied a lot, more than other students did, I could not completely solve the problems. I had to drop one course, to give me more time to study the assignments for the others, and even so, I failed English composition. I finished the semester with a 2.5 grade point average (C+), which is not high enough for admission to most graduate schools nor for employment by most successful businesses. I know that a grading system is necessary for a school, because grades are used by graduate schools and potential employers to assess students' abilities, but grades are not the only measure of a person's ability. Some allowance should be made for students who have to study, to listen to lectures, and to take exams in a language that is not their native one.

ORGANIZING THE DETAILS

The final stage of revision is to check the organization of details and to ensure that each sentence follows naturally from the last. Particularly with an introductory paragraph, a writer should carefully consider whether he or she wants the main idea to introduce the paragraph or to conclude it. A categorization paragraph usually begins with a topic statement that introduces the general category to be discussed, and the rest of the paragraph explains the subcategories or subclasses that make up the general topic. A cause and effect paragraph could go either way: several effects of a single cause might follow the statement of cause, or they might lead up to it. After-dinner speakers often begin with an example, using it to lead up to the statement of the main idea. The decision to begin or end with the topic statements is a matter of personal style, of subject matter, of organizational model, and of audience.

Our example paragraph mixes cause and effect with chronological organization, and it works well. The chronological sequence begins with a reference to the author at the age of five, continues through his coming to the United States, and ends with the immediate past, the preceding year. Within the chronological sequence, the causes of his poor grades are explained. Together, the chronology and the cause and effect statements lead to the general topic statement — that although grades are important, they do not accurately measure the intellectual ability of a foreign student. The first three sentences function as an introduction to the rest of the paragraph. The writer mentions the general subject, grades; he observes that getting good grades is very difficult; and he then prepares the readers for the shift from college students in general to one student in particular, himself.

To ensure that each sentence follows naturally from the preceding one, a writer should look for transitional words or phrases; for repetition of key words, phrases, or ideas; for parallel structure; or for a carefully placed rhetorical question. If there is no link between one sentence and the next, the writer should try out various possibilities, including the addition of a transitional sentence.

In our example paragraph, the major transitional device is repetition of words or ideas, sometimes using opposites, with connectives like "not only," "although," etc. Some of the transitions were present in the original draft of the paragraph; others were added as the paragraph was revised. Turn back to pages 111 and 112 and compare the first draft with the final one.

There are very few pieces of writing that could not be improved by revision. Revision is a careful step-by-step process that begins with the correction of errors — mechanics, punctuation, and grammar — continues with vocabulary and sentence structure revision, and ends with careful consideration of the organization of ideas and the transitions between one idea and the next.

The following example paragraph seems, at first, to be much better than the first draft of the previous example. There are no obvious errors and the vocabulary seems to be very impressive. Actually, this paragraph is worse, in some ways, than the previous one.

(1) Both botany and zoology are the study of living organisms. (2) Autotrophs are the organisms that manufacture their own foods either by photosynthesis or chemosynthesis. (3) The concepts of zoology emphasize the human, his structure and functions, and key issues and problems confronting human beings. (4) Heterotrophs are those organisms that must obtain their food by ingesting other organisms. (5) Botany is the study of the structure and function of seed plants and representative lower plants, together with the fundamentals of plant heredity, ecology, and evolution. (6) Both botany and zoology are scientific studies. (7) Botany is in the group of producers, while zoology is the consumers. (8) Organisms can be distinguished on the basis of nutrition into two categories.

The primary problem with the paragraph is the lack of organization. The similarities and differences between botany and zoology are stated, but the comparison does not follow either an item-by-item nor point-by-point order. If the sentence order is changed so that the ideas are presented point by point, the result is as follows:

(1) Both botany and zoology are the study of living organisms. (6) Both botany and zoology are scientific studies. (8) Organisms can be distinguished on the basis of nutrition into two categories. (7) Botany is in the group of producers, while zoology is the consumers. (5) Botany is the study of the structure and function of seed plants and representative lower plants, together with the fundamentals of plant heredity, ecology, and evolution. (2) Autotrophs are the organisms that manufacture their own foods, either by photosynthesis or chemosynthesis. (3) The concepts of zoology emphasize the human, his structure and functions, and key issues and problems confronting human beings. (4) Heterotrophs are those organisms that must obtain their food by ingesting other organisms.

Sentences 1 and 6 could be combined. Sentences 3 and 5 seem to deal with differences between botany and zoology, but they actually deal with similarities more than differences. (Although 3 does not say so, zoology deals not only with human beings' structure and functions, but with the structures, functions, heredity, ecology, and evolution of all animals, including human beings. Furthermore, the key issues and problems confronting human beings are not just physical ones, which would be part of the subject matter of zoology, but also psychological, social, political, economic, historical, and artistic ones.)

Some of the ideas of sentences 3 and 5 could be combined with those of sentences 1 and 2 to produce the following sentence:

Botany and zoology are scientific studies of the structures, functions, heredity, ecology, and evolution of living organisms.

This leaves sentences 8, 7, 2, and 4, as well as some ideas from sentences 3 and 5. The average reader may never have seen or heard the word "autotrophs" before, but sentence 5 contains a synonym, "plants." Combining sentence 2 with a simplified version of the first part of sentence 5 and one word from sentence 7 produces this sentence:

Botany is the study of plants, or "autotrophs," organisms which produce their own food, either by photosynthesis or chemosynthesis.

This leaves sentences 8 and 4, and parts of sentences 3 and 7. Combining them so that the resulting sentence parallels the sentence about botany produces the following:

Zoology is the study of animals, or "heterotrophs," organisms which obtain their food by consuming other organisms.

A reader who is not a biologist would probably appreciate one further revision: the addition of definitions of "photosynthesis" or "chemosynthesis," or the substitution of less technical terms. A final version of the paragraph might look like this:

Botany and zoology are scientific studies of the structures, functions, heredity, ecology, and evolution of living organisms. Botany is the study of plants, or "autotrophs," organisms which produce their own food from inorganic substances. Zoology is the study of animals, or "heterotrophs," organisms which obtain their food by consuming other organisms.[3]

Revising the paragraph by reorganizing the ideas and combining sentences has incidentally provided the paragraph with transitions, which are absent from the original draft. The second sentence of the revised version repeats two words from the first sentence. The third sentence parallels the structure of the second and also repeats the word "organisms."

[3]Joseph Ekpo, a student theme.

1. Correct the errors in the following paragraph:

Naval Engineering is type of Engineering that studies the design and buildings of ships. Naval Engineering also teaches how those ships are moved, therefore I find it very interesting due to its different ways of designing and building ships. It requires the study of Mathematics and Physics which are main subjects used in calculations. Naval Engineering have a lot opportunity for people who want get a good job.

2. The following paragraph is not well organized. The ideas are jumbled, and there are few transitions between the sentences. Change the order of the sentences so that the classification of the properties of various gasses is clearer, and add transitions to emphasize the relationships between ideas:

We need to drink liquids, so we must have a fresh supply of air every few minutes to go on living. Some of the gasses can be distinguished by their smell or color. Gasses have their own properties. The exceptions to the rule of colorless gasses are fluorine and chlorine, which are pale yellow-green; bromine, and nitrogen dioxide, which are reddish brown; and iodine, which is violet. All gasses are transparent, and most of them are colorless. Every gas will disperse to fill space, unless a force prevents it from doing so, but their mobility differs. Gasses have wide variations in density under various conditions. The physical characteristics of gasses can be altered. Gas laws and the properties of gasses help us to determine whether an element will be a liquid, a solid, or a gas in various conditions. There are four gas laws.

3. Rewrite the following paragraph to clarify the similarities and differences between the two subjects, using either a point-by-point or an item-by-item comparison and contrast model of organization. You may wish to combine some sentences and add or change some transitions.

Civil engineering and architectural engineering are very similar, but there are many differences between them. A good building is produced by a civil engineer and an architectural engineer working together. It takes a person four years to be a civil engineer, while it takes about six years to be a architectural engineer. Architectural engineering is closer to art than engineering. Most universities teach civil engineering, while very few teach architectural engineering. An architectural engineer uses colors in his work. Civil engineering and architectural engineering have many things in common.

4. Reorganize the sentences in the following paragraph to emphasize the cause and effect relationship between the ideas.

A student is a person who doesn't sleep very much, a person who doesen't eat very well, and a person who doesn't have much free time. We must realize that students spend most of their time working and trying not to get behind, so they don't notice that there is not enough time for rest. Some teachers notice that there is not enough time for rest. Some teachers give too much work to their students; they don't realize that students may have other things to do. That is why we say that a student is a person who needs to sleep a bit more. A student may not be eating properly because of the pressures that he or she has: homework, papers, and all the things that always come to make a student's life really hard. In conclusion, we can say that a student is someone who may be unhealthy.

5. Discuss the following paragraph. What is the main idea? What are the major supporting ideas? What details could be added to improve the paragraph? Which sentences repeat ideas of other sentences? Do the repetitions serve as transitions? If not, could the repetitions be omitted? Are transitions needed?

The meaning that education has is very important for us, because education is a mixture of ideas and developed beliefs, and learning these ideas is very important for us. Education is a tool for a good future. Education is not just knowing the alphabet, but also helping other people. It is important to me because it shows me the bad and good meanings of life. The importance that education has is very great. It was used in schools hundreds of years ago. The idea of it was very important because it was a way for a better future. Education is a tool to help other people, because the best way that we can use education is to help mankind. People are interested to gain education, because they can face problems with an educated, clear mind. The ways that we get education are different. One of them is experience, which is a kind of education that we acquire gradually.

6. a. Write a cause and effect paragraph on the topic "Education can help mankind."
   b. Read each sentence carefully, correcting mechanical, punctuation, grammatical, spelling, and sentence sense errors.
   c. Reread your revised paragraph. Is the organization clear? Does each sentence follow naturally from the previous one? Are enough details provided? Rewrite the paragraph.
   d. Reread your revised paragraph. Is it concise and clear, or could some of it be omitted? Rewrite a final draft.

SUMMARY

A well-written paragraph is a joy to the reader and a source of satisfaction to the writer. Writing a good paragraph is not difficult, but it does require both careful thought and careful revision. Revising what someone else has written is easier than revising your own work, because you know your own thoughts, whether or not you included them in your first draft.

But you can be sure of the thoughts of another writer only if they appear on paper. When you begin to revise your own work, try to consider it from the viewpoint of someone else. Assume that there are errors; you will probably find some. Consider different synonyms for some of the words you have used. Try rephrasing sentences: some might sound better as passives; some modifiers might be shifted; some words might be omitted; some sentences might be combined. If a reader might be unfamiliar with your topic, consider adding an example, illustration, or definition to clarify your idea. Look at the sequence of ideas: are the transitions smooth? are the ideas clearly organized?

Whenever you write something, remember your purpose: to communicate your ideas to a reader.

SECTION THREE

THE THEME

INTRODUCTION

The word "theme" often carries a restricted meaning, especially in introductory composition courses. In this restricted sense, a theme is a short writing assignment (two to four pages) with approximately five paragraphs — an introductory paragraph, three paragraphs which develop the main idea set forth in the introduction, and a conclusion.

In this book, the word "theme" is used in a broader sense to designate any piece of writing which consists of several paragraphs about one main idea. The word is thus used to refer to a wide variety of writing, including literary essays, extended definitions, explanations, discussions, reports, letters, and even stories. Most of the writing exercises in this section ask for short themes, but these need not be 500-word, five-paragraph writing exercises. A theme should be as long as it has to be to present the main idea clearly and to discuss it thoroughly.

Writing a theme is like writing a paragraph, except that in a theme, the ideas of the individual sentences in an introductory paragraph are expanded into full paragraphs. The paragraphs in a theme have the same relationship to each other as do the sentences in a paragraph.

In the previous section we used facts, figures, statistics, examples, illustrations, descriptions, definitions, and explanations to support and explain the main ideas of single paragraphs. Facts, figures, statistics, examples, illustrations, descriptions, definitions, and explanations are also used to support the main ideas of individual paragraphs in a theme. Each paragraph in a theme develops one aspect of a broader subject, or thesis, which is usually introduced in the first paragraph.

The following chapters are concerned with the selection of details for a theme, the organization of those details, and the revision of first drafts. The examples, exercises, and reading selections cover a broad range of subject matter, most of which will be familiar to college or university students since it reflects the content of general college courses in several fields of study.

CHAPTER 11

Selecting
the Details for
a Theme

Selecting the details to include in a theme is easier than selecting the details for a single paragraph, because a theme allows the writer more space for details. Many writers assume that they will not have enough to say if they choose narrow topics to write about, but the most common problem with student themes is that the topics are too general, allowing no room for details. No reader is going to be very enthusiastic about reading a theme that begins with the statement, "I am going to write about economics" (or cats, cars, trees, poetry, sodium chloride, the solar system, asteroids, starfish, or dishwashers). Books of several hundred pages have been written on most of those topics, none of them claiming to be complete. If it takes an entire term to complete an introductory course in economics or poetry, neither subject can be discussed adequately in a short theme. Once a writer has chosen a general subject, what is needed next is a statement about one carefully limited aspect of that general subject:

(Economics)	I need a part-time job to help pay my expenses.
(Cats)	Cats are great high jumpers.
(Cars)	The car has shaped modern society.
(Trees)	If the fuel crisis continues, we will run out of trees.
(Poetry)	Poetry expresses sensory impressions in verbal images.
(Sodium Chloride)	Sodium chloride—common table salt—can kill.
(The Solar System)	A big bang may have created our solar system.

(Asteroids)	An asteroid may have killed the dinosaurs.
(Starfish)	Starfish can grow extra arms.
(Dishwashers)	If a dishwasher is going to go haywire, it will do so when you have guests.

This *thesis statement* both limits the subject and tells the reader what the theme is really about. Usually, the thesis statement appears in the first, or introductory paragraph of a theme. The other sentences in the introduction briefly expand the thesis statement, by comparing the subject with something else, giving an illustration or a few examples, explaining background information, presenting some facts, or defining an important word.

Once a writer has decided what he or she wants to say and has written it in a single sentence at the top of a piece of paper, she or he is ready to begin selecting details to explain prove, define, and illustrate the idea. One way to begin to decide what details might be included in a theme is to consider the models of paragraph organization and figure out the details that would be needed to write one paragraph following each model. If a writer began with the idea "Many American prefer imported cars to American-made ones," a rough outline of the paragraphs might look like this:

I. Thesis statement and supporting sentences
II. The causes of interest in imported cars
III. Categories of imported cars
IV. Chronology of increasing sales of imported cars
V. Similarities and differences between domestic and imported cars
VI. Conclusion

This is not intended as a model of a final draft, but it can be useful as an outline of types of details to be included in a rough draft.

If a writer begins with this sort of rough outline of the entire theme, with each heading in the outline representing the topic idea of one paragraph, the next step is to select the details needed to develop each idea, each paragraph. For the second heading above, the writer would need facts, examples, an illustration, a description, an explanation, and/or a definition of one or two causes of interest in imported cars. Facts could include actual prices of two or three cars and statistics about their fuel economy. The two or three cars discussed would be examples.

One could write a three- or four-page theme on just one of the main ideas in the outline. If all the ideas were to be included in one short theme, the details would need to be selected very carefully. Some of the ideas could be combined. For example, prices and fuel economy are the major causes of interest in imported cars because they compare favorably with the prices and fuel economy of American-made cars. Separate paragraphs about the causes of interest and about the similarities and differences between domestic and imported cars are not necessary: the details can be combined in one paragraph.

The major problem with this example topic is that many writers would find they had too many details, rather than too few. Their rough drafts would be too long, so during the revision, many details would be omitted. This is good. Writing a rough draft that contains too many details forces a writer to differentiate between essential details and less important ones. Often, it also makes the writer aware that the original topic is too broad.

The following example illustrates what often happens when students begin a writing assignment:

How to Build a Bookcase

Put some bricks on the floor where you want your bookcase and then put a board on top of the bricks. Continue alternating bricks and boards until the bookcase is the desired height.

These instructions are not particularly informative. They do not suggest how many bricks are necessary, nor what kinds of bricks work best. They do not mention how long or how wide the boards should be, nor what kind of wood should be used. They do not tell the reader where to get the materials. They do not warn the unwary bookcase-maker that this kind of bookcase is unstable if it gets too high, nor that some floors will not support a very large bookcase of this type. (Books are extremely heavy, but bricks are heavier yet.) The paragraph does not contain enough details. There are few facts, no definitions (what is a "desirable" height?), no examples or illustrations, no descriptions, and no explanations.

The kinds of details that could be used in a theme about bookcases include facts about different kinds of bookcases, the materials and tools needed for each kind, techniques for assembling each kind, descriptions of the appearance of each kind, etc.

These details seem to fit into a several paragraph theme following this outline:

I. Introduction — The Convenience of a Bookcase
II. Type 1: Brick and Board
  A. materials
  B. tools
  C. techniques
  D. appearance
III. Type 2: Wall Brackets with Wood Shelves
  A.
  B.
  C.
  D.

and so on.

The introductory paragraph has three main responsibilities: to tell the reader the general subject of the theme, to interest the reader, and to suggest the basic ideas that will explain the general subject. The need for a bookcase frequently confronts students, so an introductory paragraph for a theme entitled "How to Build a Bookcase" might be written as follows:

There you stand in your new home, a dorm room or an apartment. Your clothes are all carefully hung up or put away in dresser drawers; your dishes, pots, pans, and tableware are neatly stacked in cupboards and drawers. The furniture is arranged to your satisfaction; the bed is made; and the curtains are hung. But your new home is not yet totally tidy: that pile of books in the middle of the floor must be put somewhere. You need a bookcase. Buying one is impossible: the lovely inlaid mahogany one you saw in a furniture store last week costs over five hundred dollars. Your budget will barely allow one hundred, with which the only thing you can buy is an ugly metal contraption. Making a bookcase seems to be your only option. It is not difficult, but it requires some careful thought and planning before you rush out to the lumber yard or hardware store. A bookcase should complement the style of the room it is in. If you have colonial, traditional, or elegant modern furniture, you may not want a brick-and-board bookcase, which is better suited to casual surroundings. If you are renting an apartment or a dorm room, you probably are not allowed to drill holes in the walls, so a built-in bookcase or a wall-bracket one would be a poor choice. An all-wood bookcase may suit your needs best. Before you buy the materials to make any type of bookcase, decide whether you will paint it, stain it, or leave the boards natural.

This introductory paragraph appeals to readers by addressing them directly and suggesting imaginary circumstances that many readers would have actually experienced. It states the general thesis (making a bookcase is not difficult) and suggests what ideas will follow in subsequent paragraphs (information about building different types of bookcases).

In the next paragraph, one type of homemade bookcase is described:

If you decide that a brick-and-board bookcase would suit you, make sure that the floor is strong enough to hold it and that the bookcase will be no more than four shelves high. Then start measuring. You need to know how long a bookcase you want and how tall and how wide your books are, so the bookshelves will be wide enough and far enough apart to hold them. If you have a few very large books, you might decide to have the bottom shelf of the bookcase wider than the others, to hold the large books and perhaps your phonograph records as well. The height of the books and the length of the bookcase determine how many bricks you will need. Before you go to the lumberyard, draw a diagram of your planned bookcase, including accurate measurements. A standard brick is two inches thick, four inches wide, and eight inches long. There are larger bricks, but they are not easy to locate and they are heavier than regular bricks. (Remember, you are going to have to carry the materials.) You will need a brick support at each end of each shelf and at three or four foot intervals along its length. If the first shelf is to be six feet long and twelve inches high, you will need eighteen bricks to support it: six piled on top of each other at each end and six more in the middle. If the next shelf is to be six feet long and eight inches high, you will need twelve more bricks for it: four at each end and four in the middle. . . .

Let's stop there for a moment. This theme already contains over four hundred words and the instructions for building the first type of bookcase are not finished yet. If instructions for building four or five different types are included, this theme is going to be over two thousand words. If the assignment calls for a five-hundred-word theme, this is going to be far too long. As was the case with the draft outline for a theme about imported cars, this draft outline requires too many details. In a short theme, it would be possible to describe four or five different types of bookcases, but explaining how to build each type requires a much longer theme. The best revision in this case would be to limit the topic. Instead of "How to Build a Bookcase," it would be limited to "How to Build a Brick-and-Board Bookcase."

When students are asked to write an examination or a laboratory report, they rarely fear that they will not have enough to say. When they write letters to family or friends, they often apologize for the lack of anything interesting to say. When they are asked to write a composition, they panic. The letters and the compositions both need details — not to meet an arbitrary requirement of a certain number of words, but to provide enough information about the general subject matter to interest, persuade, and/or inform the readers.

The subject matter of examinations and laboratory reports is limited by the questions asked by the instructor. The subject matter of letters and compositions is usually quite general. Knowing the approximate amount of time available, the writer must limit the general topic to allow time to develop it by including carefully selected and organized details. If one is writing home for money, one does not write a five-thousand-word essay on the general state of the world's economy; one states the topic, "Please send me some money," and supports the request with details about the high cost of toothpaste, the unexpectedly cold weather that demands a warm new coat, the unexpectedly warm weather that demands a new wardrobe, etc. The topic has been carefully narrowed and the details carefully selected.

A student who wanted to write about home construction realized that the topic was too general for the assignment, a ten page report, so he narrowed the topic to allow thorough discussion of one type of home construction. He began by writing a one-paragraph draft, each sentence of which could become the topic sentence of a separate paragraph in a longer composition. The following paragraph was the first step.

(1) Underground construction is one of the least publicized methods of energy conservation. (2) Underground living has been in man's history almost since the beginning. (3) Most people have the idea that an underground house has to be dark, damp, and dirty. (4) It is true that there are certain disadvantages to building underground. (5) However, there are numerous advantages to an underground home. (6) Some popular myths about the underground house need to be dispelled. (7) The American Solartron Corporation accepted the challenge to disprove those myths by building a prefabricated underground house. (8) At present, underground homes are not energy self-sufficient; that is the next step. (9) Even now, however, the popular view of underground houses seems to be changing; they are gaining acceptance every year. (10) As to the future, who knows what it will bring?

To complete the final report, "Underground Houses and Construction," which is the next reading selection, the writer carefully expanded ideas, corrected errors, rephrased sentences, changed the order of sentences, and omitted unnecessary or repetitive phrases and clauses. (Topic sentences have been numbered to correspond with the numbered sentences in the draft paragraph.)

READING SELECTION

UNDERGROUND HOUSES AND CONSTRUCTION
by Philip Brose

In these times of energy shortages and rising energy prices, we find most of our attention being focused on alternate energy sources. However, these alternate sources (for example, wind power, solar power, geothermal power, and nuclear fusion) only become plausible when technology increases enough to support them. Currently there are several offshoots from energy research that may be utilized, such as better insulation, solar collectors, heat pumps, more gas-efficient cars, passive solar design (if you are building a house), and underground construction. I would like to concentrate on (1) *underground construction, because it is one of the least publicized methods of energy conservation* and, possibly, the one with the most interesting potential.

(2) *Underground living has been in man's history almost since the beginning.* Prehistoric man lived in caves for many years until he settled into an agrarian economy, which did not allow living near cave sites. There are areas in the Middle East where, in Biblical times, caves served as monasteries for certain religious sects. At the American Mesa Verde site, Indians lived in cave dwellings for several centuries, and in modern day Spain there are people who are still living in a cave city that is centuries old. The American pioneers used sod houses to protect themselves on the plains, and in cases of emergency they dug holes in the ground to survive severe storms. I must point out, however,

A student theme, reprinted by permission.

THE THEME

that in the case of the pioneers, earth dwellings were the last choice, as is still the case today.

There are many people who think of caves, basements, and root cellars when you mention underground houses. As a matter of fact, it is often difficult to find a financial institution that will finance the construction or sale of an underground home, because they consider it a fad. (3) *Most people have the idea that an underground house has to be dark, damp, and dirty.* They have not seen what can be done with modern methods, as I will explain later.

I must admit that (4) *there are certain disadvantages to building underground,* but how much of a hindrance are they in reality? The primary difficulty lies in expanding an existing house. It can be done, but it is much more time-consuming and costly than with a conventional frame house. And you do have to be careful where and how you build an underground home. It is not desirable to build one in the water table (because of water leaks) or in solid rock (because of the expense). There is definite need to have a forced air ventilation system in order to prevent the buildup of carbon dioxide or carbon monoxide gases, as well as to increase the oxygen supply. The last problem that I am familiar with is community building codes, which tend to prevent or entangle the building of "exotic" structures. These disadvantages should be carefully weighed against the advantages before a conclusion is made.

(5) *The advantages of an underground home are numerous.* The most appealing is the reduction in heating and cooling costs. This is a result of the moderating effect the earth has on temperature changes. Generally speaking, the changes in ground temperature lag the air temperature by three months, so that when you need heating the earth is warmer, and when you need cooling, the earth is cooler. The peak-to-peak variation in the ground temperature is smaller as you go deeper into the earth: therefore it is more controllable. Although it varies somewhat from area to area, the temperature of the earth at 10 feet below the surface is between 50 and 58 degrees Fahrenheit.

Two proven examples of the energy efficiency of underground homes are the Andy Davis family home in Armington, Illinois, and The American Solartron Corporation's model home in Centralia, Illinois. The Andy Davis family used 2½ cords of wood to heat their underground home during the worst winter in Illinois history (1977–78), compared to their $165 per month heating bill in their previous above-ground house. The Davis house is 1200 square feet and has approximately three feet of earth over it. The American Solartron Corporation's model home, in spite of having an exposed central courtyard and a parade of sightseers, had a $15.75 heating bill during December of that same winter, with a projected yearly bill of $128. Underground houses also integrate well with other energy savings systems, such as solar heating and heat pumps.

Another advantage of underground houses is the lack of exterior maintenance that is required. Most of the designs for the houses have at least one side of the house exposed (usually the south side for solar heating effect), but even if you use stone or brick, little maintenance is required. Being underground reduces the chance of storm damage almost to the point of nonexistence, provided you have good drainage. Since the exterior shell of an underground house is virtually fire-proof and is not subject to the elements, some insurance companies are offering a 20 to 30 per cent discount in insurance rates to the owners because of the lower risk.

A third advantage could be the ability of the underground house to blend with the environment. With underground construction it is not necessary to clear an entire lot of trees and plants. As a matter of fact, the most desirable location for a building site is a hillside, where drainage is good. The Andy Davis family literally has a garden growing on their roof. The only problem that they have with it is that the cows from neighboring pastures sometimes get into it, and they can't bear them in the house! One man even specified to his architects that he wanted full-grown trees over his house (which did add some additional expense because of the increased weight).

Another man who lives on the seashore has a house that looks like a sand dune and affords a beautiful view of the ocean. These are just a few examples of harmonizing with the environment, and there are undoubtedly many more.

(6) *There are a few popular myths about the underground house which need to be dispelled.* Probably the most prominent belief is that there would be a problem with dampness and leaks, which come with the automatic association with caves and old basements. If there is a layer of porous material placed around the unit and a good sealant is used, there should be no problem of this nature at all. (The latest sealants are much better than the ones of a few years ago.) Most basements leak or seep due to a build-up of water next to an improperly sealed cement or block wall (block has the most problems because of the number of connections in a wall, compared to one continuously poured cement wall). This is avoided with proper usage of materials. If humidity is still a problem, a small dehumidifier should alleviate it. At this point, it should be reinforced that care must be taken in locating the house above the water table; otherwise there would be no drainage. The ideal location for drainage is on a hillside so that the water may not accumulate.

The next point to dispel is the association of the underground house with darkness. Designers have incorporated light and passive solar heating in the same concept to provide well-lighted rooms which have the ability to catch winter sunlight directly (for heat), but the strong summer sun only indirectly (to help cooling). Perhaps one of the best designs for sun-catching is the courtyard design, where the house is a square or rectangle surrounding an open central court. The house is earth-covered on all sides except for the side facing the open court. The court itself may be covered with a transparent dome during the winter to maintain heating efficiency and to provide a solarium of sorts. An easier method to achieve the proper effects is to build the house into a hill with a southern exposure and cover the windows so that they can't receive sunlight from directly overhead. This way only the winter sun will shine in during the warmest part of the day. Both of the methods described will allow plenty of light in at any time of the year.

There is also a misconception about the cost of building a house underground. It is usually not more expensive and is sometimes less expensive than building its counterpart on the surface. A definite example of this is the Davis family's home, which cost them $15,000 to build and furnish. They spent $7000 on materials and the rest on the land and furnishings, including all new appliances.

(7) *The American Solartron Corporation accepted the challenge to build a prefabricated underground house* and to lower the price as much as they could. They first tried using precast cement slabs, but they were too heavy to handle efficiently and tended to

make the cost higher instead of lower. Then the idea of using Fiberglassed material occurred to them, bringing the weight down to a manageable 300 pounds. Using Fiberglassed material had other benefits (besides the reduction in weight): it was strong enough, it was relatively rot-free, and it was waterproof. Cement, when exposed constantly to water, will seep slightly because it is porous. This seepage will eventually cause crumbling. Fiberglas has essentially no pores and, except on seams, needs no sealing compound. This prefab concept allows a house to be constructed in eight hours, and it brought the price down to the cost of a comparable surface home. It is necessary to point out, though, that even at par value with a surface home, considering reduced energy bills, reduced exterior maintenance costs, and probably reduced insurance costs, it does not take long for the cost scales to tip in favor of the underground home.

(8) *The next step in the evolution of the underground home is energy self-sufficiency.* The current problems involved in this are watt-consuming appliances such as refrigerators, freezers, stoves, and heating systems. These problems are being attacked, with partial success, on several fronts.

Heating and cooling have been pretty well covered except for the few extra steps needed for self-sufficiency. One method can be combined with others to increase its efficiency, and that is the use of the heat pump. The heat pump can actually pull heat from air that is anywhere above 14 degrees Fahrenheit in temperature, and when the exchanger is placed in a well, in a basin of gravel below the frost line, or in a solar-heated heat storage area (such as a loose gravel basin or water storage tank), it can provide enough additional heat (in most cases) to keep you comfortable with a minimum expenditure of electricity. A heat pump can also be reversed to become an air conditioner.

A second method is to supplement your passive heating with solar collectors and use hot water heating. In northern areas, though, this probably would not be enough by itself.

The third method uses wind power to generate electricity. This method would probably only be used by those houses built into hillsides. The present plans call for using the convection air flow generated by heat rising up through the house to drive the wind propeller at the top. The propellers would also be angled slightly to pick up surface winds.

Solar cells may some day generate enough electricity for household use, but presently it requires too many of them to be an effective energy source.

The successful method will most probably be a combination of these technologies, and the combination will probably vary with the climate and terrain. It might also be said that all of these principles can be utilized on surface homes as well, but not with anywhere near the efficiency of the underground home. The underground home is computed to be capable of being 60 per cent more efficient than the equivalently sized surface home. The surface home is not anywhere close to being energy self-sufficient, while for the underground home it appears to be right around the corner.

Some research foundations have set up totally self-sufficient homes. These homes, usually constructed in-ground, have incorporated waste recycling systems as well as energy generating and saving systems. Everything that is needed to support life with little or no waste is contained in these units, but it will be several years before this type of approach is usable by the man on the street. The constant attention that is necessary and the cost make such an operation almost impossible for the average man.

(9) *The popular view of underground houses does seem to be changing, however.* In October of 1977, an Oklahoma firm won the contract for a 237,400 square foot state office building in California. It was to be an underground, passively solar heated complex with computer controlled heat distribution. Also, in 1977, the University of Minnesota contracted an underground book store and office complex. This effort incorporated energy consumption monitoring, which the university used for data collecting and research. The university not only benefitted from the 35 to 40% energy savings, but also received the honor of establishing the federal heat dissipation standards for underground construction. Due to the increasing public recognition and federal project funding, the University of Arizona and the University of Minnesota now offer courses on underground construction. The staffs of these universities are also writing papers on the subject. This acceptance at the academic level definitely indicates a change in status for underground construction.

Today there are a few large scale usages of underground sites. One of the sites is the limestone quarries under Kansas City. Since limestone is mined in layers, a relatively flat floor and ceiling is left behind. This left-over cavern has a constant temperature and humidity (approximately 50%) and is ideal for long term storage of perishable items. Lately, businessmen have been leasing space for their offices to take advantage of the low heating and cooling bills. Now there are established rail heads and shipping docks in this great underground maze that are part of a rapidly expanding business district.

(10) *As to the future, who knows what it will bring?* Science writers have been predicting for years that man will move underground in the future. Their reasons differ (population explosion, conservation of energy, war, pollution), but their net prediction is the same. They describe everything from thousands of small cubicles, miles beneath the surface, to vast cities honeycombing the entire crust of the Earth. The people they envision are everything from semi-intelligent moles to superbeings. These examples may seem to be rather extreme exaggerations of the basic concept of the underground home, but they must be viewed as possibilities. When we look back through history and see that man has come from underground only to return underground once more, perhaps it isn't so farfetched after all.

As the population increases year after year and the amount of arable land decreases, something will have to be done to allow us to grow more food. Underground construction would allow the topsoil to be used for agriculture and possibly for parks and recreation areas. Our fossil fuel resources are running out, and nuclear fission is too contaminating for long-term usage. This only leaves our alternate energy sources, which are far from sufficient by themselves at this point in time. I believe that we need conserving measures like the underground home, and to me this alternative is not all that unattractive.

References

Calvert, Terri. "The Solartron Prefabricated Earth-Sheltered Home." *The Mother Earth News,* **57** (May/June 1979), 157–159.

Gettings, T. L. "Digging in: How a Family Lives Underground." *Organic Gardening and Farming,* **25** (June 1978), 98–100.

Martindale, David. "New Homes Revive the Ancient Art of Living Underground." *Smithsonian,* **9** (Feb. 1979), 96–100.

Smay, V. Elaine. "Underground Houses." *Popular Science,* **210** (April 1977), 84–89.

"Subterranean Design Wins California Office Competition." *Engineering News Record,* **199,** 13 Oct. 1977, 14.

Questions about the Reading Selection

1. Why did the author expand some of his ideas (e.g., the discussion of the advantage of underground homes) into more than one paragraph?
2. What facts does the author include? Are they informative? Persuasive?
3. What figures or statistics are used? Are they informative? Persuasive?
4. How many examples are used? Are they informative? Persuasive?
5. Are difficult or unfamiliar terms defined?
6. Is the theme sufficiently detailed? Too detailed? What, if anything, should have been added or left out?
7. Do the sentences in the general paragraph on page 144 follow a logical order, or do some seem out of place? Do the paragraphs in the theme follow a logical order, or do some seem to belong elsewhere?

EXERCISES

1. Write a general paragraph on one of the following subjects:

   a. Good leadership requires certain qualifications.
   b. Children model their behavior on the behavior of their parents, either positively or negatively.
   c. Careful accounting can help people learn to save money.
   d. Modern biological research is solving some of medicine's ancient problems.
   e. A bridge is a work of art supported by careful mathematics.

2. Using your general paragraph as an outline, write a two to four page theme on the subject you chose, using examples, definitions, facts, figures, etc., to develop your main idea.

3. Discuss ways of limiting the following topics for assignments of various lengths.

Example: The English language (several books would be needed)

    A. The problems international students have with the English language (several hundred pages)

    B. The problems international students have with English verb forms (at least fifty pages)

       C.   The problems international students have with English
           auxiliary verbs (at least ten pages)
       D.   The problems international students have with
           English modal verbs "will" and "would" (with care,
           two to four pages)

    a. Inflation
    b. Ecology
    c. Mental Illness
    d. Transportation
    e. Leisure Activities
    f. Weather
    g. Nutrition
    h. Heredity
    i. Electricity

4. Select details which would be included in a two- to four-page theme about one of the topics in Exercise 3. (Several of the topics could be considered if the class splits up into small groups.)
5. Write a theme about one of the topics in Exercise 3.

CHAPTER 12

Organizing the Details of a Theme

The paragraphs in a theme need to be as carefully organized as the sentences in a paragraph, using the same models which are used for organizing sentences: chronology, space, categorization, comparison and contrast, cause and effect, and mixed order.

CHRONOLOGICAL ORDER

Chronological order, as we noted in Chapter 9, means "order of occurrence in time." A chronologically organized theme moves, paragraph by paragraph, through a sequence of events. A report of an automobile accident, a science lab report, a diagnostic report on a patient, a fictional murder mystery, a description of a graduation ceremony, a set of instructions for putting a child's swing set together—all would present the topic ideas of the paragraphs in a chronological sequence, although the sentences within each individual paragraph might follow some other organizational model. For example, a report of an automobile accident might include a paragraph describing the weather and road conditions, a paragraph explaining the relative locations of the cars involved in the accident (a spatially organized paragraph), and a paragraph explaining the cause(s) of the accident and the effects on the vehicles and people involved. All these paragraphs would be linked together by the time frame of events and circumstances immediately before, during, and after the accident.

The most common transitional words and phrases linking chronologically ordered paragraphs are "first," "second," "next," "then," "before," "after," "while," "when," "finally." As is true of all transitions, the more varied and subtle they are, the better. The most common ones should be used only for emphasis or to provide a link between two paragraphs when a more subtle transition is either impossible or insufficient for clarity.

In the following illustration, the author carefully informs the reader that the story ends fifteen years after it started, and he uses chronological transitions to mark the passing of time between the events described in one paragraph and those of the next paragraph.

READING SELECTION

THE BET
by Anton Chekhov

It was a dark autumn night. The old banker was pacing from corner to corner of his study, recalling to his mind the party he gave in the autumn fifteen years before. There were many clever people at the party and much interesting conversation. They talked among other things of capital punishment. The guests, among them not a few scholars and journalists, for the most part disapproved of capital punishment, found it obsolete as a means of punishment, unfitted to a Christian State, and immoral. Some of them thought that capital punishment should be replaced universally by life-imprisonment.

"I don't agree with you," said the host. "I myself have experienced neither capital punishment nor life-imprisonment, but if one may judge *a priori,* then in my opinion capital punishment is more moral and more humane than imprisonment. Execution kills instantly, life-imprisonment kills by degrees. Who is the more humane executioner, one who kills you in a few seconds or one who draws the life out of you incessantly, for years?"

"They're both equally immoral," remarked one of the guests, "because their purpose is the same, to take away life. The State is not God. It has no right to take away that which it cannot give back, if it should so desire."

Among the company was a lawyer, a young man about twenty-five. On being asked his opinion, he said:

"Capital punishment and life-imprisonment are equally immoral; but if I were offered the choice between them, I would certainly choose the second. It's better to live somehow than not to live at all."

There ensued a lively discussion. The banker who was then younger and more nervous suddenly lost his temper, banged his fist on the table, and turning to the young lawyer, cried out:

"It's a lie. I bet you two millions you wouldn't stick in a cell even for five years."

"If you mean it seriously," replied the lawyer, "then I bet I'll stay not five but fifteen."

"Fifteen! Done!" cried the banker. "Gentlemen, I stake two millions."

"Agreed. You stake two millions, I my freedom," said the lawyer.

So this wild, ridiculous bet came to pass. The banker, who at that time had too many

THE THEME

millions to count, spoiled and capricious, was beside himself with rapture. During supper he said to the lawyer jokingly:

"Come to your senses, young man, before it's too late. Two millions are nothing to me, but you stand to lose three or four of the best years of your life. I say three or four, because you'll never stick it out any longer. Don't forget either, you unhappy man, that voluntary is much heavier than enforced imprisonment. The idea that you have the right to free yourself at any moment will poison the whole of your life in the cell. I pity you."

And now the banker, pacing from corner to corner, recalled all this and asked himself:

"Why did I make this bet? What's the good? The lawyer loses fifteen years of his life and I throw away two millions. Will it convince people that capital punishment is worse or better than imprisonment for life? No, no! all stuff and rubbish. On my part, it was the caprice of a well-fed man; on the lawyer's, pure greed of gold."

He recollected further what happened after the evening party. It was decided that the lawyer must undergo his imprisonment under the strictest observation, in a garden wing of the banker's house. It was agreed that during the period he would be deprived of the right to cross the threshold, to see living people, to hear human voices, and to receive letters and newspapers. He was permitted to have a musical instrument, to read books, to write letters, to drink wine and smoke tobacco. By the agreement he could communicate, but only in silence, with the outside world through a little window specially constructed for this purpose. Everything necessary, books, music, wine, he could receive in any quantity by sending a note through the window. The agreement provided for all the minutest details, which made the confinement strictly solitary, and it obliged the lawyer to remain exactly fifteen years from twelve o'clock of November 14th, 1870, to twelve o'clock of November 14th, 1885. The least attempt on his part to violate the conditions, to escape if only for two minutes before the time, freed the banker from the obligation to pay him the two millions.

During the first year of imprisonment, the lawyer, as far as it was possible to judge from his short notes, suffered terribly from loneliness and boredom. From his wing day and night came the sound of the piano. He rejected wine and tobacco. "Wine," he wrote, "excites desires, and desires are the chief foes of a prisoner; besides, nothing is more boring than to drink good wine alone," and tobacco spoiled the air in his room. During the first year the lawyer was sent books of a light character; novels with a complicated love interest, stories of crime and fantasy, comedies, and so on.

In the second year the piano was heard no longer and the lawyer asked only for classics. In the fifth year, music was heard again, and the prisoner asked for wine. Those who watched him said that during the whole of that year he was only eating, drinking, and lying on his bed. He yawned often and talked angrily to himself. Books he did not read. Sometimes at night he would sit down to write. He would write for a long time and tear it all up in the morning. More than once he was heard to weep.

In the second half of the sixth year, the prisoner began zealously to study languages, philosophy, and history. He fell on these subjects so hungrily that the banker hardly had time to get books enough for him. In the space of four years about six hundred volumes were bought at his request. It was while that passion lasted that the banker received the following letter from the prisoner: "My dear jailer, I am writing these lines in six languages. Show them to experts. Let them read them. If they do not find one single mistake, I beg you to give orders to have a gun fired off in the garden. By the noise I shall know that my efforts have not been in vain. The geniuses of all ages and countries speak in different languages; but in them all burns the same flame. Oh, if you knew my heavenly happiness now that I can understand them!" The prisoner's desire was fulfilled. Two shots were fired in the garden by the banker's order.

Later on, after the tenth year, the lawyer sat immovable before his table and read only the New Testament. The banker found it strange that a man who in four years had mastered six hundred erudite volumes, should have spent nearly a year in reading one book, easy to understand and by no means thick. The New Testament was then replaced by the history of religions and theology.

During the last two years of his confinement the prisoner read an extraordinary amount, quite haphazard. Now he would apply himself to the natural sciences, then he would read Byron or Shakespeare. Notes used to come from him in which he asked to be sent at the same time a book on chemistry, a text-book of medicine, a novel, and some treatise on philosophy or theology. He read as though he were swimming in the sea among broken pieces of wreckage, and in his desire to save his life was eagerly grasping one piece after another.

The banker recalled all this, and thought:
"To-morrow at twelve o'clock he receives his freedom. Under the agreement, I shall have to pay him two millions. If I pay, it's all over with me. I am ruined forever . . ."

Fifteen years before he had too many millions to count, but now he was afraid to ask himself which he had more of, money or debts. Gambling on the Stock-Exchange, risky speculation, and the recklessness of which he could not rid himself even in old age, had gradually brought his business to decay; and the fearless, self-confident, proud man of business had become an ordinary banker, trembling at every rise and fall in the market.

"That cursed bet," murmured the old man clutching his head in despair. . . . "Why didn't the man die? He's only forty years old. He will take away my last farthing, marry, enjoy life, gamble on the Exchange, and I will look on like an envious beggar and hear the same words from him every day: 'I'm obliged to you for the happiness of my life. Let me help you.' No, it's too much! The only escape from bankruptcy and disgrace— is that the man should die."

The clock had just struck three. The banker was listening. In the house every one was asleep, and one could hear only the frozen trees whining outside the windows. Trying to make no sound, he took out of his safe the key of the door which had not been opened for fifteen years, put on his overcoat, and went out of the house. The garden was dark and cold. It was raining. A damp, penetrating wind howled in the garden and gave the trees no rest. Though he strained his eyes, the banker could see neither the ground, nor the white statues, nor the garden wing, nor the trees. Approaching the garden wing, he called the watchman twice. There was no answer. Evidently the watchman had taken shelter from the bad weather and was now asleep somewhere in the kitchen or the greenhouse.

"If I have the courage to fulfil my intention," thought the old man, "the suspicion will fall on the watchman first of all."

In the darkness he groped for the steps and the door and entered the hall of the garden-wing, then poked his way into a narrow passage and struck a match. Not a soul was there. Some one's bed, with no bedclothes on it, stood there, and an iron stove loomed dark in the corner. The seals on the door that led into the prisoner's room were unbroken.

When the match went out, the old man, trembling from agitation peeped into the little window.

In the prisoner's room a candle was burning dimly. The prisoner himself sat by the table. Only his back, the hair on his head and his hand were visible. Open books were strewn about on the table, the two chairs and on the carpet near the table.

Five minutes passed and the prisoner never once stirred. Fifteen years' confinement had taught him to sit motionless. The banker tapped on the window with his finger, but the prisoner made no movement in reply. Then the banker cautiously tore the seals from the door and put the key into the lock. The rusty lock gave a hoarse groan and the door creaked. The banker expected instantly to hear a cry of surprise and the sound of steps. Three minutes passed and it was as quiet inside as it had been before. He made up his mind to enter.

Before the table sat a man, unlike an ordinary human being. It was a skeleton, with tight-drawn skin, with long curly hair like a woman's, and a shaggy beard. The color of his face was yellow, of an earthy shade; the cheeks were sunken, the back long and narrow, and the hand upon which he leaned his hairy head was so lean and skinny that it was painful to look upon. His hair was already silvering with gray, and no one who glanced at the senile emaciation of the face would have believed that he was only forty years old. On the table, before his bended head, lay a sheet of paper on which something was written in a tiny hand.

"Poor devil," thought the banker, "he's asleep and probably seeing millions in his dreams. I have only to take and throw this half-dead thing on the bed, smother him a moment with the pillow, and the most careful examination will find no trace of unnatural death. But, first, let us read what he has written here."

The banker took the sheet from the table and read:

"Tomorrow at twelve o'clock midnight, I shall obtain my freedom and the right to mix with people. But before I leave this room and see the sun I think it necessary to say a few words to you. On my own clear conscience and before God who sees me I declare to you that I despise freedom, life, health, and all that your books call the blessings of the world.

"For fifteen years I have diligently studied earthly life. True, I saw neither the earth nor the people, but in your books I drank fragrant wine, sang songs, hunted deer and wild boar in the forests, loved women. . . . And beautiful women, like clouds ethereal, created by the magic of your poets' genius, visited me by night and whispered to me wonderful tales, which made my head drunken. In your books I climbed the summits of Elbruz and Mont Blanc and saw from there how the sun rose in the morning, and in the evening suffused the sky, the ocean and the mountain ridges with a purple gold. I saw from there how above the lightnings glimmered, cleaving the clouds; I saw green forests, fields, rivers, lakes, cities; I heard sirens singing, and the playing of the pipes of Pan; I touched the wings of beautiful devils who came flying to me to speak of God. . . . In your books I cast myself into bottomless abysses, worked miracles, burned cities to the ground, preached new religions, conquered whole countries. . . .

"Your books gave me wisdom. All that unwearying human thought created in the centuries is compressed to a little lump in my skull. I know that I am cleverer than you all.

"And I despise your books, despise all worldly blessings and wisdom. Everything is void, frail, visionary and delusive as a mirage. Though you be proud and wise and beautiful, yet will death wipe you from the face of the earth like the mice underground; and your posterity, your history, and the immortality of your men of genius will be as frozen slag, burnt down together with the terrestrial globe.

"You are mad, and gone the wrong way. You take falsehood for truth and ugliness for beauty. You would marvel if suddenly apple and orange trees should bear frogs and lizards instead of fruit, and if roses should begin to breathe the odor of a sweating horse. So do I marvel at you, who have bartered heaven for earth. I do not want to understand you.

That I may show you in deed my contempt for that by which you live, I waive the two millions of which I once dreamed as of paradise, and which I now despise. That I may deprive myself of my right to them, I shall come out from here five minutes before the stipulated term, and thus shall violate the agreement."

When he had read, the banker put the sheet on the table, kissed the head of the strange man, and began to weep. He went out of the wing. Never at any other time, not even after his terrible losses on the Exchange, had he felt such contempt for himself as now. Coming home, he lay down on his bed, but agitation and tears kept him a long time from sleeping. . . .

The next morning the poor watchman came running to him and told him that they had seen the man who lived in the wing climb through the window into the garden. He had gone to the gate and disappeared. The banker instantly went with his servants to the wing and established the escape of his prisoner. To avoid unnecessary rumors he took the paper with the renunciation from the table and, on his return, locked it in his safe.

In the first paragraph of "The Bet," people at a party are discussing the effect of imprisonment on a human being. The next eight paragraphs are dialogue, statements made by one person after another, in chronological order. The next two paragraphs continue the chronology, informing the reader that the previous dialogue occurred before supper and adding a further bit of dialogue that occurred during supper. The next three paragraphs explain what took place after the party. About one-third of Chekhov's story deals with the events of one evening in the lives of the characters. The reader knows that the entire sequence of events lasted fifteen years, and that if the events following the party are presented in as much detail as those during the party, this will have to be a novel, not a short story.

However, after the account of the events at the party, the chronology of events becomes less detailed. One paragraph begins "During the first year"; the next paragraph beings "In the second year" and skips to "the fifth year."

The next paragraph moves to "the second half of the sixth year" and includes the next four years. The next paragraph refers to events "after the tenth year," and the following one summarizes events "During the last two years." Then Chekhov summarizes in one paragraph the events of the previous fifteen years in the banker's life, to explain the cause of his decision. The fifteen-year time frame of the story is almost finished, but not quite. The author has telescoped the events of the middle of the story, because the most dramatic events occur at the beginning and the end.

Now Chekhov slows down the chronology to provide more details about the dramatic events of the last few hours, as he slowed down the chronology of the first few hours of the story. The events of the last few hours take up nearly half of the story's length. It is three o'clock in the morning of the day the lawyer is to be set free to claim the two million. The next several paragraphs detail the minute-by-minute actions of the banker, including his reading of the letter. In the last two paragraphs of the story, the chronology speeds up again slightly. The action moves from "When he had read," to "The next morning . . . the banker instantly went . . . and, on his return, locked it in his safe."

The next example differs considerably from Chekhov's short story; it is a clinical report of the diagnosis and treatment of a young patient's problems. However, the story and the report have one thing in common: chronological organization of the topic ideas of the paragraphs.

READING SELECTION

A CASE STUDY IN SPEECH THERAPY
by Marjorie Chamberlain

A four-year, ten-month-old male was referred to the University Speech and Hearing Clinic for articulation therapy. Informal assessment of his receptive and expressive language indicated normal language development. However, his spontaneous speech was characterized by multiple articulation errors consisting of substitutions and omissions. According to developmental norms given in the *Weiss,* the majority of the patient's errors were above his age level. However, several consistent errors were noted on phonemes below his age level. Of the phonemes below his age level, most were stimulable on either the syllable or word level. A featural analysis revealed forwarding of place to be his most prominent error. Both fine and gross motor abilities appeared normal.

Examination of the patient's oral mechanism revealed no physical abnormalities. Mobility of the lip, tongue and velum appeared normal. The diadochokinetic rate for repetition of /pʌ/, /tʌ/ and /kʌ/ was normal. A complete audiological examination was performed by a staff audiologist at the University Speech and Hearing Clinic, in December, 1979. The hearing evaluation indicated normal hearing for both pure tones and speech. Impedance measurements revealed normal functioning middle ears.

Observation of the patient's interaction with his mother and sisters indicated a close,

A student theme, reprinted by permission.

friendly relationship. His mother stated that he was a very social child and related well to his peers. Although he exhibited a slight initial shyness in his interactions with the clinicians, this was quickly overcome. The patient occasionally refused to cooperate in therapy, saying, "I don't want to," or, "I'm tired." However, with slight coaxing, he was easily persuaded to participate. During most tasks, he displayed an exceptionally long attention span for a child of his age. He exhibited frustration when articulation errors prevented the clinician or his mother from understanding his speech. Rather than repeating himself, he frequently said, "Never mind."

In accordance with the test results of the evaluation performed on 12/7/79, the following therapy goals were established.

To improve articulation, the patient will:

1. produce the /p/ in all positions of short phrases and sentences with 90% accuracy following a verbal model.
2. produce the /k/ in all positions of short phrases and sentences with 80% accuracy following a verbal model.
3. produce the /d/ in the initial and medial position of two syllable words with 90% accuracy when given a visual cue.
4. produce the /t/ in the final position of words with 100% accuracy following a verbal model.
5. produce the /g/ in the initial position of single syllable words with 75% accuracy following a verbal model.

The patient was enrolled for individual therapy for one-hour sessions, two days per week. He was responsive to both drill accompanied by secondary motivating activities and structured play activities. He especially enjoyed card games, board games, dot-to-dot, and color-and-paste activities. Discrimination tasks utilizing the Voice Mirror and the Voice Lite proved to be effective as well as highly motivating. Flannel board activities and role playing activities were particularly effective in eliciting spontaneous speech. As the boy became restless when seated for long periods of time, activities that required movement helped to alleviate restlessness and maintain his interest.

In response to visual stimuli, the patient is able to:

1. produce the /p/ in the initial, medial and final positions in short sentences with 95%, 100% and 97% accuracy, respectively.
2. produce the /k/ in the initial, medial and final positions in short sentences with 88%, 95%, and 100% accuracy, respectively.
3. produce the /d/ in the initial position in short sentences with 100% accuracy, and the /d/ in the medial position in two and three syllable words with 82% accuracy.

Following a verbal model, the patient is able to produce the /t/ in the final position of one-syllable words with 100% accuracy. Administration of the *Weiss* toward the end of the therapy period also revealed spontaneous improvement in articulation of the /s/ in the initial position, and the /r/ and /t/ in the medial position of the words. Substantial improvement in the patient's articulation of the /p/ and /k/ in all positions, and /d/

in the initial and medial positions and the /t/ in the final position has considerably increased patient's overall intelligibility.

The patient is extremely cooperative and attentive in therapy. He appears proud of his improvement in articulation and is clearly concerned with his performance in therapy. He proudly displays any small prizes received for substantial improvement to his mother, explaining to her, "I got this for doing so well." He is generally more communicative in the therapy room now than he was at the beginning of therapy. Substantial improvement in intelligibility resulting from improved articulation appears to have lessened his frustration with and improved his attitude toward speech.

The patient's mother is extremely supportive of her son's attempts to improve articulation. She frequently observes him during therapy and warmly praises his effort and progress. She has also reinforced the therapeutic effort outside of clinic by working with the boy on informal home assignments. She reports that he frequently self-corrects when he is outside of the therapy setting. She also states that both she and his preschool teachers have noticed a substantial improvement in his overall intelligibility.

It is recommended that the patient continue to receive individual articulation therapy at the University Speech and Hearing Clinic during the Spring semester for one hour sessions twice a week, to focus on improving production of the /k/ in the initial position, the /g/ in the initial position, the /n/ in the medial and final positions, and the /t/ and /d/ in the final position.

It is further recommended that the patient's mother continue to work with the boy on carefully structured home assignments to reinforce the therapeutic effort outside of clinic and facilitate carry-over.

An outline of the report using key verbs indicates the chronological sequence of events:

1. First, the boy was *referred* to the clinic.
2. Then, he was *assessed.*
3. Next, he was *examined.*
4. Then his interaction with other people was *observed.*
5. After therapy goals were *established* (based on the previous assessment, examination, and observation),
6. he was *enrolled* for therapy sessions.
7. After initial therapy, the boy *is able to produce* sounds that previously were difficult or impossible. (Notice the tense shift.)
8. Further therapy *is continuing.*
9. Recommendations *are made* for further treatment.

There are other chronological references. For example, in the third sentence of the third paragraph, the reader is told, "Although he exhibited *initial* shyness, . . . this was *quickly overcome.*"

The next example of chronological organization differs from the other two, both in subject matter and style. It is neither a story nor a report; it is an expository essay, an explanation.

READING SELECTION

You, The Multi-Purpose Pronoun
by Judith Johnson

English makes some distinctions among pronouns which other languages do not make, and it fails to make some distinctions that other languages do. For its first person pronouns, English has an eight-form set, four singular ones and four plural ones: *I, my/mine,* and *me* refer to a single speaker; *we, our/ours,* and *us* refer to more than one. For third person (neither speaker nor listener), there are further distinctions in the singular to differentiate masculine, feminine, and neuter. However, the second person set of pronouns, used to address a listener or listeners, does not have eight forms. There are only three: *you* and the possessive forms *your* and *yours.*

This was not always the case. A thousand years ago, the second person pronoun set had the same number of forms as the first person set. There were pronouns for addressing a single listener and different ones for addressing a group. If English still had all those forms, the singular ones would be *thou,* the subject form; *thy* and *thine,* the possessive forms; and *thee,* the object form. The plurals would be *ye, your/yours,* and *you.*

All eight forms can still be found in texts dating from the sixteenth century. However, a close look at those texts indicates that the distinction between the two sets of pronouns is not simply a distinction between singular and plural. Frequently, the plural forms are used when a speaker is addressing a single listener. The singular set is never used to address more than one listener, so the explanation is not simply that people mixed up the two sets.

What had happened began to occur in the twelfth and thirteenth centuries. A social distinction as well as a grammatical one affected one's choice of second person pronouns. It was correct to use *thou, thy/thine,* and *thee* to address one listener only if that listener was younger than the speaker, socially inferior to the speaker, or socially equal to the speaker and very familiar with him or her: a friend or sweetheart. However, if the listener was older, socially superior, or not familiar, the speaker used the "respectful" pronouns: *ye, your/yours,* and *you.*

By the seventeenth and eighteenth centuries, the social barriers between classes were crumbling, and the middle class was acquiring political power. Using the "familiar" pronouns could give offense to a listener, even though no offense was intended. A person might wish to show friendly feelings toward another, so he or she would address the other person as *thou.* The other person might mistakenly assume that the speaker used *thou* because she or he felt that the listener was a social inferior. To avoid giving offense, speakers of English gradually stopped using the familiar pronouns altogether, preferring *ye, your/yours,* and *you* to address all listeners: a single person or a group; a younger person, one the same age, or one older; social inferiors, social equals, or social superiors; close friends and perfect strangers.

Before the eighteenth century was over, the eight pronoun forms of the second person set had been reduced to four. The formal plural forms now served a dual function

An unpublished lecture, reprinted by permission.

as both singulars and plurals. One of those four forms soon joined the singular ones in oblivion. The old subject form *ye* no longer exists in English.

Sixteenth- and seventeenth-century texts include both *ye* and *you*, but the subject-object distinction is not always maintained. *Ye* does not appear as an object, but *you* frequently appears as a subject. No one can be sure of the reasons for the incorrect use of *you* as a subject, but one can make an intelligent guess. Perhaps repeated grammatical errors led to the loss of *ye*. Many speakers of modern English use object forms when the grammar calls for subject forms, especially in compound phrases like "Bob and me went to class." Repeated use of *you* in the sixteenth-century sentences which should have had *ye*, as in "Arthur and you should go to France next week," could have led to the use of *you* alone as a subject, as in "You should go to France next week." That sentence is grammatically correct now, but it was not correct four hundred years ago.

If a speaker of modern English said to a friend, "Will Tom and thou meet me at noon, and will ye have lunch with me?" the friend would think the question sounded peculiar. Yet the question would have sounded quite ordinary—and would have been grammatically correct—to speakers of English living before the latter part of the seventeenth century. English has lost all of its second person singular pronouns and one of its plural ones. All that remain are the plural possessives and *you*, the multi-purpose pronoun.

In the essay, the chronology covers centuries, not weeks or years. It begins and ends with the present; the middle paragraphs begin with the tenth century, move to the sixteenth, backtrack to the twelfth and thirteenth centuries, go forward to the seventeenth and eighteenth centuries, and go back briefly to the sixteenth and seventeenth centuries before concluding with the present. A chronologically organized theme does not have to begin, in the first paragraph, with the earliest events being discussed and progress in sequence from next to next to last, as long as there are specific time references to help the reader understand the temporal relationships among the ideas.

EXERCISES

1. The following set of paragraphs is disorganized. It contains transitions, but they are not effectively linking one paragraph to the next. Change the sequence of the paragraphs so the essay is chronologically organized.

At 1:45 a.m., December 14, a car driven by Julius Cato was hit from the rear by a pickup truck. The driver of the truck was killed. His name is being withheld until his family can be located and notified. Two passengers in the car are in serious condition in a local hospital.

By midnight, the sideroads and highways were like ice-skating rinks.

They were covered with a hazardous half-inch glaze of smooth ice on which no vehicle could move safely at a speed of more than 20 miles per hour. Most motorists slowed their cars and trucks to a crawl. The few who tried to maintain high speeds quickly began to create accidents.

Freezing rain had begun to fall about ten o'clock the night of December 13. At first the rainfall was slight, and there was no buildup of ice on the highways.

2. Write a chronologically organized two- to four-page theme on one of the following subjects, remembering to limit your topic to provide adequate space for interesting, informative details.

    a. The way I use my native language is different from the way my grandmother uses it.

    b. One hundred years ago, my country was different from the way it is today.

3. Revise each paragraph in your theme, correcting errors, omitting unnecessary words and details, organizing the sentences, and adding or changing transitions as necessary.

4. Rewrite your theme, providing transitions between your revised paragraphs.

SPACE ORDER

Some subjects almost demand that the writer organize the ideas according to the physical position of one thing with reference to another. Descriptions of buildings, parts of cities or towns, or the biological structure of plants or animals progress from a starting point to a point nearby, to a point closer to the second one than the first, and so on. In the following essay, the discussion of body language uses space order as an organizing technique.

READING SELECTION

SOUNDLESS COMMUNICATION
by Ge Zhixing

Paragraph 1. Can you communicate with others when you live in a foreign country with no or little knowledge of its language? Of course, it is possible. You can convey your moods and intentions to one another without words, because all human beings share a large repertoire of common visual signals. These signals are as effective as words are during communication. However, in daily life when people talk with others in their native

A student theme, reprinted by permission.

                            THE THEME

language, they are not aware that they are using these signals to express their ideas at the same time. These signals are called body language. Paying a little attention to one's gestures when that person is talking, we can understand more than by only hearing one's words. Wordless communication acts to qualify the words.

Paragraph 2. The gestures of the head play a key role in body language. The vertical head movements, called nods, signify "yes" almost everywhere in the world. People use such a head gesture to express their agreement. It is very interesting that this gesture has been used by people born deaf and blind. No doubt, it strongly suggests that affirmative nodding may be an inborn action for the human species—a pattern of body language designed by our genes. Similarly, the horizontal head movements are also virtually global in range and are always a negative sign. This pattern of body language may be traced from our early infancy when we were nursed at the breast or the bottle. When a baby is not hungry, he rejects the breast by turning the head sharply to the side. It may be argued that one is born with this instinct.

Paragraph 3. The movements of eyes and eyebrows are as important as head movements in body language, but there are many differences among nations in using this pattern of body language. Americans are very subtle about eye movements. During their conversation, eye movements may have several meanings. For instance, people avoid looking into another's eyes for more than a few seconds because it may be thought of as a sign of disrespect. In England, however, staring at the speaker attentively may be considered as nothing more than a sign of interest. English people also like to blink their eyes occasionally during the conversation as a signal of agreement. That eye-blinking means nothing to Americans, who expect the listener to nod or to murmur something. Rage is another emotion eyes and eyebrows may reveal. Contracting one's eyebrows closely is regarded as a strong facial symbol of disagreement or anger that is used not only by Americans and Englishmen, but also by people everywhere.

Paragraph 4. Besides the gestures of the head or the movements of the eyes and eyebrows, the action of arms, hands and legs also are a large part of body language. Extending one's arm and shaking hands with others is a greeting in both formal and informal cases. This part of body language might be traced back to primeval tribes. Early human beings established a major division of labor, with the male hunter leaving the group for some time, then returning home with the kill. Before the male left and after he came back, there were great ceremonies. The main part of the ceremony was when actual body contact was made; at full intensity this consisted of a total embrace with much hugging, patting, squeezing, and even weeping. After many thousands of years, this kind of greeting has developed into the present customs, such as handshaking—one of the important elements in the modern body language dictionary.

Paragraph 5. Like handshaking, there are still many other forms of body language presented by hands. Raising one's hand and making a circle with his thumb and forefinger signals that something is OK. Clasped hands raised above the head, a traditional picture adopted by sportsmen after winning a fight, is a display of triumph that grows out of a surge of feeling following a victory. Waving one's hands, a speaker can make his words more powerful and vigorous.

Paragraph 6. In addition to hand gestures, there are times when a person says something with his legs as well as with his head and eyes. The leg gestures often reflect one's attitude towards something or someone that person is with. For example, if you pay a little attention, you will notice that when one is impatient listening to someone, his foot might beat the floor constantly and restlessly, as if it had its own life. In such a case, although he says not a word, in fact his body gesture reveals nearly everything. The same thing will happen when a person sits with someone whom that person dislikes. In this situation, not only will his legs jiggle, but also he will change the way his legs are crossed frequently. These postures reflect one's uncomfortable feeling.

Paragraph 7. According to the above facts, body language has offered a more reliable way to understand one's mind by means of gestures. It is just like Sigmund Freud once wrote: "No mortal can keep a secret. If his lips are silent, he chatters with his finger tips; betrayal oozes out of him at every pore." Body language is a communication tool. Like English, French, Spanish, and other languages in the world, though body language is soundless and wordless, once you understand it, you will feel the world is bigger than you realized.

The organization of the preceding essay can be outlined as follows:

I. Introduction: People convey moods and intuitions through body language.
II. Gestures of the Head
   A. General
   B. Specific: movements of eyes and eyebrows
III. Actions of Arms
   A. Specific example: handshaking
   B. Other examples
IV. Leg Gestures
V. Conclusion

In the second paragraph, the author begins to develop the idea introduced in the first paragraph. The specific topic of paragraph two is the wordless communication of the head gestures. Gestures involving two specific parts of the head, the eyes and eyebrows are then discussed. Next, following a spatial line from the top of the human body to the bottom, the author discusses arm movements and then leg movements. The conclusion functions as a general summary of the main ideas.

The organization of the separate paragraphs is independent of the overall organization of the theme. The first paragraph introduces the general idea and briefly explains it, using a cause-and-effect organization. The second paragraph uses cause and effect, also, to suggest how head gestures evolved. In the third paragraph, comparison and contrast is used to discuss eye and eyebrow movements. In the fourth paragraph, cause and effect organization is again used; this time, it serves to suggest why a particular hand gesture developed. Categorization of various other hand gestures serves to organize the information in paragraph five. Cause and effect links the examples of the sixth paragraph. In the final paragraph, the author uses cause and effect to summarize the specific ideas and to restate the thesis: awareness of body language can help a person to understand other people.

The author has effectively used transitions to link each paragraph to the preceding one. In the first paragraph, three synonymous phrases are defined: "soundless communication," "body language," and "wordless communication." One of these phrases, "body language," is repeated in the first sentence of paragraph two, thus linking the paragraphs. Paragraph two is a discussion of head movements; the phrase "head movements" is repeated in the first sentence of paragraph three. Paragraph four begins with the words "Besides the gestures of the head or the movements of the eyes and eyebrows," referring back to the topics of the preceding two paragraphs and signalling that another related topic will be discussed in this paragraph; the topic is handshaking. Paragraph five begins with the transition words, "Like handshaking." Paragraph six uses as a transition the words, "In addition to hand gestures," referring back to the topics of the previous two paragraphs. The conclusion begins with the phrase, "According to the above facts," and preceeds to summarize those facts in a general definition of body language.

Explanations of charts, diagrams, or figures are usually spatially organized, to help the reader relate the discussion to specific parts of a larger whole. In its original form, the following essay describing the human skeletal system was illustrated by two figures showing the axial skeleton and the skull, respectively. The figures have been omitted here, because the description has been so carefully organized by spatial relations between one part of the human skeleton and the next that pictorial figures are not necessary.

READING SELECTION

THE HUMAN SKELETAL SYSTEM

The human skeleton consists of two main parts: (1) the axial skeleton, composed of the bones that form the upright portion of axis of the body (skull, ear bones, hyoid bone, vertebral column, sternum, and ribs), and (2) the appendicular skeleton, made up of the bones attached to the axial skeleton as appendages (shoulder, hips, arms, and legs).

The skull, which is formed from twenty-eight irregularly shaped bones, including those of the inner ear, is composed of the bones of the cranium (brain case) and the face. Of the eleven paired and six single bones of the skull, only one, the mandible (lower jaw bone) is movable. The bones of the skull, excepting the articulation of the mandible, are joined together by jagged-edged immovable articulations, the sutures.

At birth, several cranium bones are not completely sutured (fused) so that six spaces are left without any bony covering. These spaces, called fontanels, allow alteration of the shape of the child's head in passing through the birth canal (vagina) during birth and allow for brain growth. The fontanels are almost completely fused by the second year of life.

The hyoid bone is a single bone in the neck—a part of the axial skeleton. Its U shape may be felt just above the larynx and below the mandible where it is suspended. The

From *Life Science*, 2nd ed., pp. 304–307. Eds. Gerard J. Tortora and Joseph F. Becker. Copyright 1978. Reprinted by permission of Macmillan Publishing Co., Inc.

hyoid is the only bone in the body which does not articulate (join) directly with any other bone.

The vertebral column constitutes the longitudinal axis of the skeleton on which the head is balanced. It consists of twenty-four separate bones called vertebrae, so joined to each other to permit forward, backward, and sideways movement of the column. The seven cervical vertebrae comprise the skeletal framework of the neck; the next twelve, the thoracic vertebrae, lie behind the thoracic (chest) cavity; the next five spinal bones, the lumbar vertebrae, form the small of the back; and below the lumbar vertebrae lie the sacrum and the coccyx. In the adult, the sacrum is a single bone which has resulted from the fusion of five separate vertebrae, whereas the coccyx is a single (or double) bone formed by the fusion of four or five separate vertebrae.

Although the vertebrae exhibit characteristic specializations in different regions of the column, all are constructed on the same basic plan. The body, or centrum, of a vertebra is the thick, disc-shaped anterior portion. The upper and lower surfaces of the body are roughened for attachment of intervertebral discs of fibrocartilage, whereas the anterior surface is perforated with numerous openings for blood vessels. The neural arch forms the dorsal portion of the vertebra. The arch bears three processes for attachment to muscles: two transverse processes, one on either side, which serve as points of attachment for the ribs, and a spinous process which projects dorsally and serves as a point of attachment for muscles and ligaments. The arch also bears four articular processes (two superior and two inferior) for articulation with the vertebrae above and below. The opening formed by the arch, called the vertebral foramen, serves as a passageway for the spinal cord. Pairs of small openings, the intervertebral foramina, occur between the vertebrae and permit the passage of nerves to and from the spinal cord. The laminae form the remainder of the arch and constitute the posterior wall of the vertebral column. Individual vertebrae are held together by ligaments, connective tissue masses that attach bone to bone. Between each of the vertebrae are cartilaginous pads, the intervertebral discs.

The bony chest cage, or thorax, is formed by the twelve thoracic vertebrae, twelve pairs of ribs, and the sternum (breast bone). Each rib articulates with one or more adjacent thoracic vertebrae and curves outward, forward, and downward. Anteriorly, each of the first seven ribs is directly attached to the sternum. Because the cartilage of the eleventh and twelfth ribs does not attach them even indirectly to the sternum, they are referred to as floating ribs.

The human appendicular skeleton consists of 126 bones and includes the bones of the arms and legs and the bones comprising the girdles which attach the appendages to the axial skeleton. The pectoral girdle (clavicle and scapula) attaches the arm to the axial skeleton. Each clavicle (collarbone) forms a joint with the breastbone at the inner end and a joint with the scapula (shoulder blade) at the outer end. The scapula is attached to the axial skeleton by muscles and tendons, an anatomical feature which accounts for the flexibility and freedom of movement of the shoulders and arms. A socket on the scapula serves as the point of attachment for the arm. Each arm consists of three long bones: (1) the humerus, or upper arm bone which articulates with the shoulder socket. (2) the ulna, or lower arm bone on the little finger side, and (3) the radius, or lower arm bone on the thumb side. The eight short bones of the wrist, collectively called the carpals, are held together in two rows of four by a series of ligaments. The hand consists of five bones of the palm called the metacarpals and fourteen finger bones, or phalanges. Each finger has three phalanges, the thumb has only two. A thumb is a digit, but not a finger.

The pelvic girdle is composed of the two osso coxae or hip bones and with the sacrum constitutes a stable, circular base that supports the trunk and to which the legs attach. Each hip bone is composed of three fused bones. The fused vertebrae of the sacrum complete the circle at the back, leaving a large opening through which offspring pass in the birth process in the female. The dimensions of this opening are one of the clues used in determining the sex of a skeleton since the pelvic girdle of the female is broader than that of the male, a feature that facilitates the child-bearing function.

The upper leg bone, or femur, is the longest and heaviest bone of the body. Its proximal end (end nearer the trunk) fits into a deep socket in one of the hip bones and, although this joint is much more secure than the arrangement in the shoulder region, it does not have equivalent freedom of movement. This movement is limited by muscles. At the distal end (end farther from the trunk) the femur forms the knee joint with one of the two lower leg bones, the tibia (shin bone). The other lower leg bone, the fibula, is smaller and lies on the outside of the leg. The knee joint is protected anteriorly by the kneecap, or patella. The structure of the foot is similar to that of the hand, with certain differences which adapt it for supporting weight. Each foot has twenty-six bones, seven ankle bones, or tarsals; five matatarsals, which correspond to the metacarpals of the palm; and fourteen phalanges, three in each toe except the large one, which has only two.

Some of the most common (although not necessarily the most effective) transitions associated with spatial organization are identical to those associated with chronological organization: "first, second, next, before, after, finally," etc. Other common transitions are "over, under, above, below, beneath, across from, on top of, next to," etc. In the preceding essay describing the human skeletal system, these common transitions are not used between paragraphs, although some of them are used within paragraphs. In the fifth paragraph, for example, the description of the vertebrum column contains these transitions: "the *next* twelve," "*behind* the thoracic (chest) cavity," "the *next* five," and "*below* the lumbar vertebrae."

Exercises

1. Outline the paragraph topics of the essay, "The Human Skeletal System."
2. Describe the organization of each of the paragraphs.
3. List the transitions between paragraphs and discuss how each works.
4. Pick out those words that are apt to be unfamiliar to a student who has not taken a course in human biology. In one column, list those which are clearly defined in the essay. In a separate column, list those that are not clearly

defined. As a class exercise, formulate definitions of the words in both columns. (If any students in class have taken a human biology course, they will be your resource people. Otherwise, a dictionary may be needed.)

The spatial organization of the following essay involves references to astronomical charts.

READING SELECTION

THE UNICORN OF CETUS
by Carl Sagan

In the night sky, when the air is clear, there is a cosmic Rorschach test awaiting us. Thousands of stars, bright and faint, near and far, in a glittering variety of colors, are peppered across the canopy of night. The eye, irritated by randomness, seeking order, tends to organize into patterns these separate and distinct points of light. Our ancestors of thousands of years ago, who spent almost all their time out of doors in a pollution-free atmosphere, studied these patterns carefully. A rich mythological lore evolved.

Much of the original substance of this stellar mythology has not come down to us. It is so ancient, has been retold so many times, and especially in the past few thousand years by individuals unfamiliar with the appearance of the sky, that much has been lost. Here and there, in odd places, there remain some echoes of cosmic stories about patterns in the sky.

In the Book of Judges there is an account of a slain lion discovered to be infested by a hive of bees, a strange and apparently pointless incident. But the constellation of Leo in the night sky is adjacent to a cluster of stars visible on a clear night as a fuzzy patch of light, called Praesepe. From its telescopic appearance, modern astronomers call it "The Beehive." I wonder if an image of Praesepe, obtained by one man of exceptional eyesight, in days before the telescope, has been preserved for us in the Book of Judges.

When I look out into the night sky, I cannot discern the outline of a lion in the constellation Leo. I can make out the Big Dipper, and if the night is clear, the Little Dipper. I am at a loss to make out much of a hunter in Orion or a fish in the constellation of Pisces, to say nothing of a charioteer in Auriga. The mythical beasts, personages, and instruments placed by men in the sky are arbitrary, not obvious. There are agreements about which constellation is which—sanctioned in recent years by the International Astronomical Union, which draws boundaries separating one constellation from another. But there are few clear pictures in the sky.

These constellations, while drawn in two dimensions, are fundamentally in three dimensions. A constellation, such as Orion, is composed of bright stars at considerable distances from Earth and dim stars much closer. Were we to change our perspective, move our point of view—with, for example, an interstellar space vehicle—the appearance of the sky would change. The constellations would slowly distort.

THE THEME

Largely through the efforts of David Wallace at the Laboratory for Planetary Studies at Cornell University, an electronic computer has been programmed with the information on the three-dimensional positions from the Earth to each of the brightest and nearest stars—down to about fifth magnitude, the limiting brightness visible to the naked eye on a clear night. When we ask the computer to show us the appearance of the sky from Earth, we see . . . the northern circumpolar constellations, including the Big Dipper, the Little Dipper, and Cassiopeia; . . . the southern circumpolar constellations, including the Southern Cross; and . . . the broad range of stars at middle celestial latitudes, including Orion and the constellations of the zodiac. If you are not a student of the conventional constellations, you will, I believe, have some difficulty making out scorpions or virgins. . . .

We now ask the computer to draw us the sky from the nearest star to our own, Alpha Centauri, a triple-star system, about 4.3 light-years from Earth. In terms of the scale of our Milky Way Galaxy, this is such a short distance that our perspectives remain almost exactly the same. From α Cen the Big Dipper appears just as it does from Earth. Almost all the other constellations are similarly unchanged. There is one striking exception, however, and that is the constellation Cassiopeia. Cassiopeia, the queen of an ancient kingdom, mother of Andromeda and mother-in-law of Perseus, is mainly a set of five stars arranged as a W or an M, depending on which way the sky has turned. From Alpha Centauri, however, there is one extra jog in the M; a sixth star appears in Cassiopeia, one significantly brighter than the other five. That star is the Sun. From the vantage point of the nearest star, our Sun is a relatively bright but unprepossessing point in the night sky. There is no way to tell by looking at Cassiopeia from the sky of a hypothetical planet of Alpha Centauri that there are planets going around the Sun, that on the third of these planets there are life forms, and that one of these life forms considers itself to be of quite considerable intelligence. If this is the case for the sixth star in Cassiopeia, might it not also be the case for innumerable millions of other stars in the night sky?

One of the two stars that Project Ozma examined a decade ago for possible extraterrestrial intelligent signals was Tau Ceti, in the constellation (as seen from Earth) of Cetus, the whale. . . . The computer has drawn the sky as seen from a hypothetical planet of τ Cet. We are now a little more than eleven light-years away from the Sun. The perspective has changed somewhat more. The relative orientation of the stars has varied, and we are free to invent new constellations—a psychological projective test for the Cetians.

I asked my wife, Linda, who is an artist, to draw a constellation of a unicorn in the Cetian sky. There is already a unicorn in our sky, called Monoceros, but I wanted this to be a larger and more elegant unicorn—and also one slightly different from common terrestrial unicorns—with six legs, say, rather than four. She invented quite a handsome beast. Contrary to my expectation that he would have three pairs of legs, he is quite proudly galloping on two clusters of three legs each, one fore and one aft. It seems quite a believable gallop. There is a tiny star that is just barely seen at the point where the unicorn's tail joins the rest of his body. That faint and uninspiringly positioned star is the Sun. The Cetians may consider it an amusing speculation that a race of intelligent beings lives on a planet circling the star that joins the unicorn to his tail.

When we move to greater distances from the Sun than Tau Ceti—to forty or fifty light-years—the sun dwindles still further in brightness until it is invisible to an unaided human eye. Long interstellar voyages—if they are ever undertaken—will not use dead-reckoning on the Sun. Our mighty star, on which all life on Earth depends, our Sun, which is so bright that we risk blindness by prolonged direct viewing, cannot be seen at all at a distance of a few dozen light-years—a thousandth of the distance to the center of our Galaxy.

| **EXERCISES** |

1. Describe a constellation that you have seen, using spatial organization to draw a word picture of that constellation for a reader who has never seen it.
2. Using spatial organization, explain the relative positions of the sun, Mercury, Venus, Earth, and Mars by describing an imaginary journey of a space-traveller.
3. Make a list of the transitions used in "The Unicorn of Cetus," and discuss how the author has added to the interest of the essay by careful selection of subtle transitions.

Travel is another general topic that lends itself well to spatial organization. In the following excerpt from the book *Hunter,* space references provide the general organization; they are also used within some of the paragraphs.

READING SELECTION

LION HUNTING IN MASAILAND
by J. A. Hunter

One spring about the middle of the twenties, I was called into the office of Captain A. T. A. Ritchie, O.B.E., M.C., head of the Kenya Game Department. Captain Ritchie laid before me one of the most remarkable offers ever made to a professional hunter.

To understand the reasons behind his offer, you must first know the unusual conditions prevailing in part of the colony at that time.

In the center of Kenya lies a great tableland—the home of a warlike tribe of herdsmen named the Masai. The Masai are a nation of spearmen. They scorn the bow and arrows as the tools of cowards who are afraid to close with their enemies. The young warriors of the tribe, called the moran, subsist mainly on a diet of fresh blood and milk. This they consider the only proper food for fighting men. The neighboring tribes lived in terror of the Masai for none of them could stand against a Masai war party. For sport, the moran amuse themselves by killing lions with their spears—a feat I would have considered well-nigh impossible. In the old days, the Masai had lived almost completely on other tribes, much as any predatory animal lives on its weaker neighbors.

Now it is a strange fact that although the true hunting animals that insist on killing their own prey, such as hawks and wild dogs, have no natural enemies they seldom increase in numbers. They live at such a high pitch that they use themselves up very quickly. Also, in spite of their strength and ferocity, they are strangely delicate while their prey is apt to be much more hardy. This is also true of humans. When the British government stopped the raiding, the tribes near the Masai increased so in population that they became a major problem. But the Masai, with their whole way of life changed, were threatened with extinction. They were forced to raise more cattle as a means of livelihood. Partly as a result of the overcrowding caused by the increased herds, a terrible epidemic of rinderpest swept the district. The cattle died by the thousands until only a minor number of breeding stock remained.

Lions readily became scavengers, and with the plains littered by the carcasses of cattle, these big cats increased greatly in numbers. Weakling cubs that would soon have died under normal conditions grew to maturity and thus in a surprisingly short space of time the Masai country was overrun with lions. When the epidemic had run its course and there were no more dead cows lying about, the lions turned on the live cattle. The Masai sallied out with spear and shield to defend the precious remnants of their breeding stock but for every lion killed, one or two of the young moran were mauled. A wound made by a lion almost invariably causes blood poisoning, for the claws of the animals are coated with a rotting film from their prey. Thus even a superficial scratch often means death to a native. So many of the warriors were injured fatally in these lion hunts that the elders of the tribe feared the Masai were losing all their best men. In the old days, the Masai would have corrected this state of affairs by raiding other tribes for more women and cattle. But under present conditions they had no solution except to appeal to the government for help.

The District Commissioner of the Masai Reserve was a young chap named R. Pailthorpe. He went out to reduce the number of lions, using a magazine rifle. To my mind, a magazine rifle is not the ideal weapon for close-up work in the thick bush. After a shot, it takes a second or so for the next cartridge to enter the breech. This delay can be fatal. Although I use a magazine rifle for shooting from a hide or for hunting in the open, I prefer a double-barreled rifle for dense cover. The double barrel gives you two shots and you can fire them almost simultaneously. If your first shot misses, you can fire again instantly. In case of a charge, this is an important consideration.

The majority of lions lie up in thick bush and if you wish to wipe out the lions in a district you must go into the cover after them. Mr. Pailthorpe had previously shot lions only for sport — in the open. Now he went into the bush and fired at a lioness. The lioness charged before he could get another cartridge in the breech, and knocked him down and started mauling him. He would surely have been killed had not one of his native policemen fired and killed the animal on top of him. As it was, Pailthorpe was badly injured and taken to the hospital.

"After Pailthorpe's experience, I don't think it wise to allow this work to be handled by ordinary sportsmen," Captain Ritchie told me. "This is a task for an experienced hunter. After considerable discussion, the game department decided that you are the man best qualified for the task. We want the trouble-giving lions killed in the next three months to bring the lion population within control. You will be allowed to keep the hides as your pay."

The skins of first-class, black-maned lions were then bringing twenty pounds each and even lioness hides were worth three pounds. Although the risks were great, this would mean a large sum of money for Hilda and me. We had four children by this time and it is surprising how much children cost to raise, even in Kenya.

That evening I talked the matter over with Hilda. To kill ten or even twenty lions in brush country could be done by an experienced hunter without too great risk. But to kill a hundred in the short space of time mentioned would almost certainly mean a serious mauling sooner or later. Hilda, who is a very shrewd person, came up with an excellent idea.

"Do you remember Captain Hurst's pack of hounds that you used to hunt lions in Ngorongoro? They were a great help to you. Why don't you use dogs in this work?"

Here was an inspiration, but Captain Hurst's kangaroo hounds had long ago been sold by his brother and I had no idea where to get a similar pack. After trying vainly to purchase some suitable hounds, I finally went in despair to the dog pound at Nairobi. There was a motley collection of twenty-two dogs, all awaiting their doom as worthless strays. They were all sizes, shapes and breeds. At least with me they would have a chance for their lives, so I purchased the whole collection at ten shillings apiece and took them home. Hilda's face fell when she saw my pack of lion dogs and it fell far worse in the next few days, for none of the creatures was housebroken. They barked by day and howled by night. They fought with each other and with our houseboys. When things grew dull, they went out and attacked the sedate dogs of my neighbors. But in a week, I had the collection—I can hardly call it a pack—under some sort of discipline and was ready to set out for the Masai Reserve.

The government had provided me with six oxen, for dragging bait to different spots in the reserve. With these valuable but slow-moving creatures, a few native porters and my dogs, I set out for Masai land.

We followed the main highway to Konza about eighty miles southeast of Nairobi and then turned almost due west. After a day's trek, we began to leave behind the forested country and come into the open plains. The thatched huts of the Kikuyu, an agricultural people who were long the favorite prey of the Masai, grew fewer. The cultivated shambas disappeared and ahead of us lay the open grassland, dotted with game. Here was perfect grazing country and here, for untold ages, the Masai had lived, pasturing their cattle beside the herds of zebra, and wildebeest. The air was clear and cool, a pleasant thing to breathe, and not a house or a road to mar the sweep of the great rolling country. We went on and on farther and farther into the wilds of the reserve. Except for Hilda, I would have little cared if I never returned to Nairobi, for here was Africa as God made it before the white man arrived and began to deface the country with villages and farms. At night we camped wherever we happened to stop and when the sun rose over the hills, we went on again following no guide but our own wills.

One evening after we had penetrated deep into the reserve, I heard lions grunting around the camp. From the deep-drawn quality of the sounds, I knew them to be males. At dawn the next morning, I saw my first Masai, two young moran who were out lion hunting and had seen my camp. Completely self-possessed, they came strolling up to my tent and stood leaning on their long spears as they studied me. They were different from any natives I had yet met—tall, slender men with very delicate features more finely cut than those of a white man. There is even a theory that the Masai are the

THE THEME

descendants of the ancient Egyptians who traveled south on some great migration in the distant past. These young warriors had their faces painted red with ocher and outlined with white chalk made from powdered bones. Each man wore only one piece of clothing, a blanket thrown carelessly around his body and fastened at the shoulder.

I told the moran that I had come to kill the lions. The warriors seemed rather amused at this idea and said I would have trouble killing lions with nothing but a gun. A spear was the proper weapon to use on a lion. The Masai have a great contempt for firearms, dating back to the old days when a Masai war party had little trouble defeating Arab slave traders armed only with muzzle-loading muskets.

Apparently to call my bluff, one of the young men told me that he knew of two lions not far from camp. His friend chimed in, saying these animals were particularly fine specimens and he would be delighted to see me have a go at them. Now I had not intended making my first hunt before such a critical audience. The dogs were completely untrained and I had no idea in what kind of country these lions might be. But as the two young men were regarding me with amused contempt, I felt duty bound to do my best. I told them to lead on, calling to one of my porters to uncouple the dogs.

The Masai led me to a drift, the dry bottom of a ravine that in the rainy season turns to a roaring torrent. The floor of the drift was covered with sand and the Masai easily picked up the lions' spoor and began tracking. The dogs trotted along, examining the strange scent doubtfully. We rounded a bend in the winding course of the drift and saw before us two lions lying stretched out on the sand like big cats. They both rose and stood glowering at us. When the dogs saw what they had been trailing, they took one horrified look and most of the pack fled, yelping in panic. None of them had ever seen a lion before or even imagined that such a creature existed. But four dogs of Airedale strain bravely stood their ground.

Neither the Masai nor I could spare any thought for the dogs. The two moran stood with their spears upraised waiting for the charge. A noble sight. I took quick aim for the chest of the largest cat and fired. He reared at the impact of the bullet, grunted and fell heavily on his side. His companion promptly bolted into some heavy bush on the left bank of the drift. Instantly my four Airedales charged in and began to worry the dead lion. I let them pull at the mane to their hearts' content, and when the rest of the pack gingerly returned, I encouraged them to do the same. There were two other dogs of remote collie ancestry that also seemed to show pluck and I hoped with these six animals to build up a true pack of lion dogs.

When the dogs had wearied of worrying the dead lion, I went on with them toward the bush where the second cat had taken refuge. As we approached, I heard the lion give a low, harsh growl of warning. The Airedales and collies promptly charged the bush, barking in fury, while the rest circled the cover, giving tongue but not caring to approach. One of the Masai tossed a stone into the cover. The lion charged out a few feet, making a feint at one of the furious Airedales, and then dodged back before I could get in a shot.

The dogs were now growing bolder. I could tell where the lion was from the movements of the upper twigs in the cover. The braver dogs were crawling through the bush to drive him out, keeping up a furious yelling. I knew it would not be long now before the lion charged and steadied myself to meet the attack.

Suddenly the bushes swayed violently and the lion burst out and came for me at uncanny speed. He was bunched up almost in a ball, his ears flattened back and his back arched. He seemed to fly through the air across the sandy bottom. One of my gallant Airedales met the charge full on and tried to seize the monster by the throat. The lion knocked him over as a child might knock over a toy. Without even pausing in his charge he rushed toward me, ignoring the rest of the pack that were snapping at his flanks.

When he was within ten yards, I fired. The bullet hit him fairly between the eyes. He dropped without a quiver. In the cool morning air, a tiny curl of smoke rose from the bullet hole.

EXERCISE

Some paragraphs in the excerpt "Lion Hunting in Masailand" have nothing to do with the space references of the hunter's journey to the area where the lions were or of the hunt itself. What models or organization are used in those paragraphs? How has the author made sure that those paragraphs fit naturally into the narrative?

Theme Revision Using Spatial References

The following essay is confusing, because there is no progression from one paragraph to the next. As you read it, pay particular attention to the first sentence of each paragraph and try to determine whether the sentence contains a clue to the paragraph's proper place in the sequence of paragraphs.

Paragraph 1. The spinning line of light on the screen had begun to paint the first dim echoes at the limits of its range. Land lay ahead, ten miles below and two hundred miles away—the land that Dirk had never seen though it was sometimes more real to him than the country of his birth. From those hidden shores, over the last four centuries, his ancestors had set out for the New World in search of freedom or fortune. Now he was returning, crossing in less than three hours the wastes over which they had labored for as many weary weeks. And he was coming on a mission of which they, in their wildest imaginings, could never have dreamed.

Paragraph 2. Now the liner was dropping toward a cloudscape so white and dazzling that it hurt the eyes. At first it seemed broken only by a few slight undulations but, presently, as it rose towards him, Dirk realized that the mountains of cloud below him were built on a Himalayan scale. A moment later, the peaks were above him and the machine was driving through a great pass flanked on either side by overhanging walls of snow. He flinched involuntarily as the white cliffs came racing towards him, then relaxed as the driving mist was all around and he could see no more.

Paragraph 3. Dirk Alexson threw down his book and climbed up the short flight of stairs to the observation deck. It was still much too soon to see land, but the journey's approaching end had made him restless and unable to concentrate. He walked over to the narrow, curving windows set in the leading edge of the great wing and stared down at the featureless ocean below.

Paragraph 4. The luminous image of Land's End had moved halfway across the radar screen before Dirk first glimpsed the advancing coastline, a dark stain almost lost in the horizon mists. Though he had sensed no change of direction, he knew that the liner must now be falling down the long slope that led to London Airport, four hundred miles away. In a few minutes he would hear again, faint but infinitely reassuring, the rumbling whisper of the great jets as the air thickened around him and brought their music once more to his ears.

Paragraph 5. The cloud layer must have been very thick, for he caught only the briefest glimpse of London and was taken almost unawares by the gentle shock of landing. Then the sound of the outer world came rushing in upon his mind.

Paragraph 6. Cornwall was a gray blur, sinking astern too swiftly for any details to be seen. For all that one could tell, King Mark might still be waiting above the cruel rocks for the ship that brought Iseult, while on the hills Merlin might yet be talking with the winds and thinking of his doom. From this height the land would have looked the same when the masons laid the last stone on Tintagel's walls.

Paragraph 7. There was absolutely nothing to be seen: from this height the Atlantic's mightiest storms would have been invisible. He gazed for a while at the blank grayness beneath and then moved across to the passengers' radar display.

For a reader familiar with the general geography of the southern part of England, the place references provide clues for reorganization. Flying east across the Atlantic Ocean, one first sees Land's End, the southwestern tip of Cornwall. Crossing Cornwall and other shires of southern England, one finally approaches London, in the southeast.

Even without a knowledge of English geography, however, a reader can find space references that are not in sequence. Paragraph 7 refers to "nothing to be seen" and "the blank grayness" of the Atlantic Ocean and to Dirk's moving to a radar screen so he can see something. Paragraph 1 describes what he sees on that radar screen and repeats the information that the plane is not yet over land. Paragraph 4 mentions "the advancing coastline," the first sight of land. That land is specifically named, as is Cornwall in paragraph 6, over which the plane is still flying very high and very fast: it has just begun to descend for the landing in London. Paragraph 5 must be the last one: the plane has landed in London at the end of the journey.

Only paragraphs 2 and 3 remain to be considered. Paragraph 3 should introduce the others: the character's full name is given nowhere else, and this paragraph provides the explanation for his looking out the window and at the radar screen. It also mentions the "featureless ocean below," which becomes the transition idea between this paragraph and paragraph 7. The space references in paragraph 2 are "the liner was dropping," "the peaks were above him," etc., referring to the gradual descent of the plane toward London, through the clouds. The clouds are the transition between this paragraph and paragraph 5.

The spatial relationships between the ideas of these seven paragraphs should be used as the organizing principle. If the paragraphs are rearranged in the sequence 3 7 1 4 6 2 5, the essay becomes easier to read:

READING SELECTION

COMING HOME
by Arthur C. Clarke

Dirk Alexson threw down his book and climbed up the short flight of stairs to the observation deck. It was still much too soon to see land, but the journey's approaching end had made him restless and unable to concentrate. He walked over to the narrow, curving windows set in the leading-edge of the great wing and stared down at the featureless ocean below.

There was absolutely nothing to be seen: from this height the Atlantic's mightiest storms would have been invisible. He gazed for a while at the blank grayness beneath and then moved across to the passengers' radar display.

The spinning line of light on the screen had begun to paint the first dim echoes at the limits of its range. Land lay ahead, ten miles below and two hundred miles away — the land that Dirk had never seen though it was sometimes more real to him than the country of his birth. From those hidden shores, over the last four centuries, his ancestors had set out for the New World in search of freedom or fortune. Now he was returning, crossing in less than three hours the wastes over which they had labored for as many weary weeks. And he was coming on a mission of which they, in their wildest imaginings, could never have dreamed.

The luminous image of Land's End had moved halfway across the radar screen before Dirk first glimpsed the advancing coastline, a dark stain almost lost in the horizon mists. Though he had sensed no change of direction, he knew that the liner must now be falling down the long slope that led to London Airport, four hundred miles away. In a few minutes he would hear again, faint but infinitely reassuring, the rumbling whisper of the great jets as the air thickened around him and brought their music once more to his ears.

Cornwall was a gray blur, sinking astern too swiftly for any details to be seen. For all that one could tell, King Mark might still be waiting above the cruel rocks for the ship that brought Iseult, while on the hills Merlin might yet be talking with the winds and thinking of his doom. From this height the land would have looked the same when the masons laid the last stone on Tintagel's walls.

Now the liner was dropping toward a cloudscape so white and dazzling that it hurt the eyes. At first it seemed broken only by a few slight undulations, but presently, as it rose towards him. Dirk realized that the mountains of cloud below him were built on a

Himalayan scale. A moment later, the peaks were above him and the machine was driving through a great pass flanked on either side by overhanging walls of snow. He flinched involuntarily as the white cliffs came racing towards him, then relaxed as the driving mist was all around and he could see no more.

The cloud layer must have been very thick, for he caught only the briefest glimpse of London and was taken almost unawares by the gentle shock of landing. Then the sound of the outer world came rushing in upon his mind.

Sometimes an essay can be improved by revising the order of paragraphs to emphasize the organizing principle of spatial relationships among ideas. Sometimes all that is needed is the addition of spatially related transitions between paragraphs. To understand clearly what a writer is saying, a reader needs to be able to follow that writer's thought processes. The careful organization of ideas allows that.

COMPOSITION EXERCISES

1. Write six paragraphs about your campus or public library, each one describing or explaining the purpose of one of the following. (Use a separate piece of paper for each paragraph.)

   a. the card catalogue.
   b. the reference desk.
   c. the circulation desk.
   d. the stacks.
   e. the microfilm room.
   f. the audio-visual center.

Draw a diagram showing the location of each. Then pick a natural starting point and draw a line from that point to the next closest one, going from one point to the next until your line connects all of them. Arrange your paragraphs in the same sequence as the points on the line. Then add transitions between successive pairs of paragraphs, and rewrite the separate paragraphs as a unified composition. Your introductory paragraph should contain a thesis statement that is developed in general terms (e.g., "The college/university library is a valuable resource center for detailed information not found in general textbooks," *not* "I am going to describe the library").

2. Write four or five paragraphs (using a separate piece of paper for each), each describing a different place you have visited in a particular city. Draw a rough map showing the location of each place. Then pick a natural starting point and draw a line connecting the four or five places. Arrange your paragraphs in the same sequence as the points on your map. Write an introductory paragraph with a carefully considered thesis statement (for example, a statement like "Rome is full of reminders that Christianity was once a persecuted religion"

is less likely to produce a dull list of the names of buildings and the objects within them than a statement like "I really enjoyed my visit to Rome"), and add transitions that will both link successive pairs of paragraphs and reinforce the thesis statement.

3. Using spatial organization, write a theme explaining a chart from one of your textbooks.

CATEGORIZATION

Any subject that can be divided into a relatively limited number of major classes or component parts can be organized so that each major class is discussed in a separate paragraph. Poetry can be divided into epic, narrative, lyric, and ballad, to name a few classes. Plants can be subcategorized into a hierarchy of classes, as can animals. In the field of chemistry, the elements can be categorized in terms of their valences, their atomic numbers, or their uses. Generally, there should be no less than three categories and no more than five or six. A theme about cars in which each of thirty different cars is discussed in a separate paragraph should be revised, and a smaller number of categories should be established: eight-, six-, and four-cylinder cars; or Japanese, German, and American cars; or regular, compact, and subcompact cars. In a long theme about cars, there might be an introductory paragraph for each of the three categories, followed by three or four paragraphs giving more detailed information about specific cars in that category. In such a theme, category order would be used twice, once for the general classes, and once for the subclasses within each general one. An outline might look like this:

  I. Introduction: general thesis introduced in one paragraph
 II. First major category
     A. Topic paragraph to introduce one set of paragraphs
     B. A paragraph for each subcategory
III. Second major category
     A. Topic paragraph to introduce the second set of paragraphs
     B. A paragraph for each subcategory
 IV. Third major category
     A. Topic paragraph to introduce the third set of paragraphs
     B. A paragraph for each subcategory
  V. Conclusion

In a shorter theme of two to four pages, an introductory paragraph followed by one paragraph for each major category or class is sufficient.

In the following theme, different types of letters are discussed, and the discussion is organized categorically.

READING SELECTION

LETTER WRITING
by Victor Ezeibe

Generally speaking, letter writing can be classified into three categories: formal, semi-formal, and informal. In each of these three types of letters, language and tone differ. While slang and unnecessary abbreviations are not allowed in formal or semi-formal letters, they can be used to a greater or lesser extent in an informal letter, depending on the person to whom you are writing.

A formal letter is normally written to a person in an official capacity. It requires two addresses: the address of the writer and the date appear in the top right hand corner; the name, title, and address of the recipient appear in the left hand corner. The correct salutation is "Dear Sir/Madam" (if the recipient's name is unknown) or "Dear Mr./Ms./Dr. _____." Examples of formal letters are a letter of application for employment, a letter of protest, a letter of apology, or a letter of application for admission to a college. When writing an application for college admission, I would follow the general model of the following example:

> 1234 Main Street
> Anywhere, Any State
> April 1, 1983

Dr. John Doe, Director of Admissions
General College
Somewhere, Somestate

Dear Dr. Doe:
    I am a freshperson at Specific College, enrolled in a pre-pharmacy curriculum. Since Specific College does not offer a pharmacy major, I hope to transfer to General College at the end of my sophomore year. Would you please send me a copy of your admission forms and information regarding the procedures for transfer students' admission?
    Thank you for your prompt attention to this request.

> Yours faithfully,
>
> (signature)
> Victor Ezeibe

Note that the closing salutation is very formal and that the writer's name is given in full.

Like a formal letter, a semi-formal letter is written in polite language and a humble tone; no slang is allowed. However, unlike a formal letter, a semi-formal one does not require two addresses. Examples of semi-formal letters include a letter to a family friend who is not my friend directly, a letter to an instructor concerning my academic work, or

A student theme, reprinted by permission.

Organizing the Details of a Theme

a letter to my resident advisor concerning my absence from a floor meeting. The last example might look like this:

April 1, 1983

Dear Julie:
    As one of the rules of the floor is that any member absent from a scheduled floor meeting which is not an emergency should inform the resident advisor of the cause in writing, I hereby regretfully inform you of my inability to attend tonight's meeting, scheduled for nine o'clock. Due to a botany exam coming up tomorrow, the instructor decided to give the class a review tonight at nine o'clock. Unfortunately, the time coincides with that of the floor meeting, making it impossible for me to attend the meeting. Nevertheless, I will call in at eleven o'clock to find out how the meeting went. I hope that it will go smoothly.
    Thank you.

Yours sincerely,

(signature)
Victor Ezeibe

As the example indicates, "thank you" is correct; the slang version, "thanks," would be incorrect. Also, "nine o'clock" and "eleven o'clock" are spelled out: the abbreviations "9:00" and "11:00" would be incorrect.

Slang and abbreviations are allowed in informal letters, because they are substitutes for informal conversation, providing a way of communicating with close relatives or friends who are far away. Casual, chatty language and tone are allowed in informal letters, although they should be suited to the recipient. The tone and language I use in a letter to my parents is different from those I use for my brothers or my friends. A letter to my father might look like this:

April 1, 1983

My dear papa,
    How are you and the rest of the family doing? I hope everybody is all right. How is your job going. Hopefully, good. Papa, before I comment further, may I apologize for delaying my reply to your last letter. It was due to the series of exams I have had the past two weeks. However, they are all over now. . . .

In the next paragraph I might tell him how my academic work is going, the grades I am making in my courses, and what I expect from each subject at the end of the semester. In another paragraph I might describe the weather, and how I am adapting myself to the new environment. In yet another paragraph, I might tell him about the residence hall, how I eat here compared with how we ate at home, and how I like the food being served here. In the last paragraph, I might describe my problems, such as homesickness, and might request a plane ticket for a visit home at Christmas. Finally, I would send my greetings to the rest of the family and to family friends, and close with an informal salutation such as "Affectionately, Vic."

From the examples above it is quite obvious that there are different types of letters.

The language, tone, and content of each type depend on the type of letter and my relationship with the recipient.

The author of the preceding essay has organized the discussion of letter writing by classifying letters into three types, which are named in the introductory paragraph. Each type is then discussed in a separate paragraph, and the final paragraph summarizes the ideas.

Within each of the separate paragraphs of discussion, the author uses spatial order and comparison and contrast to organize the examples. Starting at the top of each type of letter and moving step by step to the end, he describes the inside addresses and opening salutations, the specific contents of the letters, and the closing salutations.

The transition between the introductory paragraph and the second one uses phrase repetition: "The person you are writing to" is echoed in "to a person in an official capacity." The link between paragraphs two and three is the phrase "Like a formal letter," referring to the previous topic. Paragraph two ends with examples of slang and abbreviation which are not permitted in semi-formal letters; paragraph three begins with the words "Slang and abbreviations are allowed in informal letters." The conclusion is introduced, not with the overly obvious phrase "In conclusion," but with a reference to what has already been said: "From the examples above."

The author of this essay has done a good job of organizing and linking his ideas so a reader can easily follow them.

The following discussion of management is organized in terms of categories.

READING SELECTION

MANAGEMENT LEVELS
by Dalton E. McFarland

Managers are the agents of activity and change in organizations. They require a high capacity for analyzing problems and isolating their causes, marshaling resources, and initiating the action of colleagues and subordinates. As decision makers, they are responsible for identifying and achieving the purposes of the organization.

The term *top management* includes the corporate officers and the echelons of presidents, executive vice presidents, vice presidents, and assistant vice presidents, who may also be referred to as executives or administrators. Corporate officers are elected from the group at the top, as shown in Figure 3.1. They usually include the chairman of the board of directors, board members, the president, executive or group vice presidents, and frequently, several vice presidents. Corporate officers are concerned primarily with the major direction of the enterprise, overall policies, large-scale and long-

From *Management: Foundations and Perspectives,* 5th ed. pp. 41–46. Copyright 1979. Reprinted by permission of Macmillan Publishing Co. Inc.

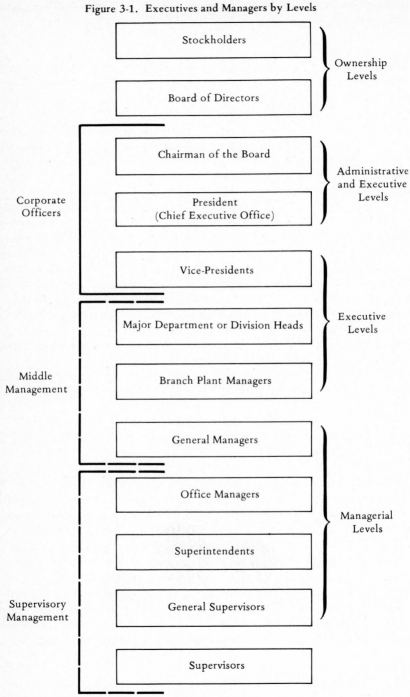

Figure 3-1. Executives and Managers by Levels

FIGURE 3-1. Executives and Managers by Levels

THE THEME

run strategies and commitments, legal matters, the security of the company and its assets, the choice of major goals, and the profitability that ensues from all these elements. The roles and responsibilities of corporate officers are specified in corporate bylaws, and are governed by the laws of the state in which the organization is incorporated.

At executive levels, vice presidents, major department or division heads, or the manager of a plant formulate and carry out policies, decisions, and plans. They are also concerned with the implementation and communication of basic administrative decisions pertaining to goals, strategies, and policies. These managers perform the top-level day-to-day management work of the company, with the responsibility for major actions affecting the company's success. The term executive aptly pertains to the members of this group.

Figure 3.1 also identifies, approximately, a group known as *middle management.* This term, popularized by Niles in the early 1940's, identifies a group that tends to overlap the executive and lower management groups. The concept of middle management does not refer to exact boundaries, but it provides a useful focus for examining certain critical management problems, such as promotions, training, career aspirations, organization design, human relations, communications, and leadership.

At intermediate levels of an organization, the term *manager* comes to supplant *executive,* but the term also applies to those at the lower levels of the management hierarchy, such as first-line supervisors; *middle management* usually includes below the vice-presidential level, such as the heads of functional departments, and the managers of technical and staff units such as purchasing, engineering, and research and development.

At the supervisory level, typically, are general foremen, group supervisors, and first-line supervisors. Essentially these positions relate closely to operating units such as maintenance, manufacturing, or office-clerical supervision. General foremen or departmental superintendents supervise first-line supervisors, who in turn are in direct contact with rank-and-file blue-collar, office-clerical, or technical workers.

The supervisory levels are considered to be managerial in character (although supervision is also a function that administrators and executives perform). Managers usually have less discretion in the manner of carrying out their responsibilities and less scope for policy decisions than executives. Their function is to carry out operating plans, policies, and procedures within frameworks developed by higher levels. The term *manager* is most frequently applied to persons who direct relatively small and well-defined units or who operate at close to a day-to-day level of responsibility.

The managerial relationships just described pertain to what is technically known as the *hierarchy.* An organization consists of levels, each having an appropriate status and degree of authority for position holders. This hierarchy is of central importance to organization theory and practice, which will be examined in later chapters. It is also a key factor in understanding managerial behavior. The hierarchy poses difficulties for managers: its very existence has an impact on their judgments, actions, thinking, and decisions. Moreover, the way the hierarchy operates has much to do with career advancement within an organization.

The hierarchy consists not only of levels but also of horizontally differentiated units at each level, thus permitting the scope of the various positions to be defined in terms of tasks and responsibilities so that managers can specialize in a major function within a limited sphere of action.

| **EXERCISES** |

1. Using the essay on management careers as a model, do an outline for a theme about careers in your field of study.
2. Decide which of the models of paragraph organization would be most effective for developing the main idea in each of your proposed paragraphs.
3. Following your outline and your chosen models of paragraph organization, write an essay about careers in your field of study, paying particular attention to transitions.

Each of the following five themes is organized in terms of categories. As you read each theme, outline the categories, determine the organizational model used for each paragraph, and underline or list the transitions between paragraphs.

READING SELECTION

BIOMES

Biomes are large areas with a uniformity of climate and vegetation and its associated fauna. The vegetative types are determined mainly by climatic conditions. Even though seeds and spores show many adaptations for wide dispersal (many are readily carried by wind and water even over such geographic barriers as wide expanses of oceans, deserts, or mountains), plants and fungi are not evenly distributed over the earth. They are limited to distribution to specific areas by such factors as temperature, soil conditions, precipitation, and specific adaptations of the particular species. The tundra, taiga, deciduous forest, grassland, desert, and tropical rain forest are the six major types of biomes.

TUNDRA

Within the polar climate group is found the tundra biome. It is the most geographically continuous of the biomes and includes the northernmost land areas of North America, Europe, and Asia. The climate is cold and the subsoil is permanently frozen. The surface area is characterized by gently rolling plains with many lakes, ponds, and bogs. Trees, when present, are quite small and scrubby. There are numerous, small, perennial herbs, grasses, sedges, and dwarf woody plants. However the dominant flora are low ground mosses such as sphagnum and lichens such as reindeer moss. The plants of this

From *Life Science*, 2nd ed. pp. 640–646. Eds. Gerard J. Tortora and Joseph F. Becker. Copyright 1978. Reprinted by permission of Macmillan Publishing Co. Inc.

THE THEME

region are well adapted to the stresses of the cold climate, the continuous night during the winter season, and the continuous daylight of low intensity during the summer season. During the short growing season great splashes of color cover large areas of the tundra where brilliantly colored flowers bloom simultaneously.

In spite of the extremely severe environment, the tundra teems with life. There are considerable numbers of certain mammals such as the caribou, musk ox, arctic fox, arctic hare, and lemming. In addition, vast numbers of migratory birds are found during the short summer. Conspicuous among animal life are swarms of flies and mosquitoes. Although the number of individuals is large, there are relatively few species, showing that while successful adaptation has occurred in only a few species, once it is achieved, large populations can thrive.

TAIGA

South of the tundra, stretching in broad belts across the northern continents, are vast evergreen forests. These constitute the taiga biome. Here winters are long and severe, and the growing season is limited to a few months during the summer. However, the soil completely thaws for a short period of time, thereby making sufficient water available to support large evergreen forests. The dominant species are spruces, firs, hemlocks, and pines. Some deciduous trees such as the paper birch and aspen are also present. In those land areas where mountains extend down into southern zones as they do in parts of North America, the taiga may be continuous with the evergreen forests of the mountains much farther south. The taiga, like the tundra, has many lakes, ponds, and bogs. The number of species of animals, however, is larger than in the tundra. Moose, black bear, wolf, lynx, squirrel, and small rodents abound. Large numbers of birds are present during the short summer. Like the tundra, the taiga is subject to pronounced seasonal periodicity of populations.

DECIDUOUS FOREST

South of the taiga biome the regions show wide variations in temperature and precipitation that result in great differences from one area to another. In those parts of the middle latitude climatic zones where there are warm summers, cold winters, and abundant rainfall, the deciduous forest biomes are found. These are dominated by broadleaf hardwood trees such as oak, maple, ash, and hickory. The seasonal variations in temperature are great in this biome. The plants are adapted to the low temperatures of winter by ceasing to grow. The number of species is greater than in the taiga, but less than in the more humid biomes. The familiar animals of the deciduous forest biome are deer, bears, raccoons, foxes, squirrels, and many varieties of birds and insects. The major deciduous forest biome is distributed over the eastern United States and Europe.

GRASSLAND

The grassland biomes are found in both the middle latitude and equatorial tropical climatic zones. The major controlling factor is the rather sparse or erratic rainfall of about 10–40 inches annually. The grasses vary from short buffalo grass to tall elephant grass and bamboo.

There are various regional designations for the grassland biomes. The savannas are found in the tropical plains of Africa, India, and South America. The climate is characterized by a long dry winter season alternating with a wet summer season. The temperature remains relatively warm throughout the year. The prairies are widespread in central United States, eastern Europe, and in the South American countries of Argentina and Uruguay. There are great annual variations in temperature because of their middle latitude location, and rainfall tends to be scanty. The grasses vary from tall to short species. The steppe, which is drier than the prairie, contains short grass species and is located in interior plains and plateaus that are semiarid. Within the United States the higher plains extending from the Canadian border to Texas represent this type of biome. Steppe grasslands are found in western North America but are most extensive in central and southwest Asia. Grasslands support a large number of species of animal life. Most notable is the great variety of grazing mammals and rodents.

DESERT

Major desert areas are located on each continent except Europe. The desert shrub and desert waste biomes are found wherever the average annual rainfall is less than the annual evaporation. Rain, when it falls, occurs in a few heavy cloudbursts and evaporates rapidly soon after it reaches the earth. Both plant and animal forms are uniquely adapted to this biome. Some plants flower and produce seeds during a brief period of time after a rainfall. Other plants, such as the cacti of the Western Hemisphere and the euphorbia of Africa, have thick stems that store water. Some desert shrubs have thick, succulent leaves for water storage, while others shed their leaves during prolonged dry periods to conserve water. Desert animals are small, and many burrow in the soil. Certain species of lizards and insects are dominant. Warm-blooded animals are generally comparatively rare because of the shortage of water and the difficulty in maintaining a constant body temperature where daily air and land temperatures vary from hot during the day to extremely cold during the night. The absence of large bodies of water and the rapidity with which the land warms up and cools off result in extreme changes in temperature on a daily basis, sometimes as much as 100°F.

TROPICAL RAIN FOREST

The tropical rain forest biomes are found where there is abundant rain (80–200 inches annually) with no dry season and fairly high temperatures. This biome is the most complex in terms of species makeup. There is a dense growth of tall broadleaf evergreen trees and heavy vines. The dominant trees form a tight canopy over the rest of the forest. Beneath this canopy are other well-developed layers: the subcanopy, overstory, understory, and ground layers. This vertical stratification has different floral species dominating at each level. Direct sunlight and rain do not reach the forest floor, but the shaded lower levels are continually bathed by water dripping from the trees. Near the forest floor the temperature remains constantly high and it is exceedingly humid.

The fauna of the tropical forest biome is also stratified. Certain species live high up in the canopy, others just below in the large branches and along the tree trunks, while others are limited to the forest floor. Much of the fauna is largely nocturnal. This biome covers large areas of central Africa, south and central Asia, Central America, and the Amazon Basin of South America.

While the biomes are represented as clearly defined areas of characteristic flora and fauna, there will be overlapping where one biome merges into another. In fact, the changes tend to be gradual rather than sharply defined. The overlapping areas may be classified as minor biomes such as chaparrals, tropical scrub forests, Mediterranean scrub forests, and tropical semideciduous forests.

READING SELECTION

THE POETS OF WORLD WAR I

The outbreak of war in 1914 stirred many young soldiers to poetry, not to glorify its pomp and circumstance, still less to write hymns of hate, but to express their new-found sense of beauty and dearness of the homeland which they might never see again. Much of this war-poetry, born as it was of a temporary mood of exaltation, was evanescent, like the poetry men make when they fall in love; but Mr. Robert Nichols and Mr. Robert Graves were born poets, and the former's *At the Wars* and the latter's *Rocky Acres* express the feeling we have tried to describe in language that is likely to endure. These two survived to write much poetry after the war in other moods. Another true poet who survived the war was Mr. Maurice Baring. But who can estimate what English poetry lost by the deaths of Charles Sorley, Wilfred Owen, Julian Grenfell, Francis Ledwidge, Rupert Brooke, and Edward Thomas, and who knows how many others, inheritors of unfulfilled renown? The extraordinary promise of Sorley's *Marlborough Poems* was cut short before he was twenty-one. Grenfell, the English patrician, and Ledwidge, the Irish peasant, both turned to Nature for solace in the din of war. . . .

Brooke and Thomas, unlike these three, were already writers of established reputation. Nothing in Brooke's life became him like the last few months of it. He had outgrown the flippancies of youth but not its generous ardours when he died on active service at Scyros in the spring of 1915. . . .

Edward Thomas (1878–1917) impressed all who met him by his character and his profound knowledge of, and feeling for, the English countryside, of which he wrote charmingly in prose. Among those who met him was the American poet, Robert Frost, who was in England when the war began. It was Mr. Frost's example and advice that led Thomas to try his hand at verse; but he was killed in action before he had quite mastered the new medium. There is the stuff of poetry in all he wrote, but, as Emerson said of Thoreau's verses, "the thyme and marjoram are not yet honey."

The war revealed two remarkable poets in Mr. Siegfried Sassoon (b. 1886) and Wilfred Owen (1893–1918). Mr. Sassoon entered it, no doubt, in the same exalted spirit as many other young soldiers; but as it went on exaltation succumbed to horror and indignation, to which he gave passionate utterance in verse. Owen had written verse

Organizing the Details of a Theme

before the war with Gray, or Keats, or Tennyson for models; but it was his admiring friendship for Mr. Sassoon that made him a war-poet. The waste of war afflicted him even more than its horrors; it moved him less to indignation than to pity. The subject of his poems, he wrote, "is War, and the pity of War. The poetry is in the pity." His compassion extended to the foe. . . .

The war which touched these young poets to such different issues did not leave the older men unmoved. Hardy's old heart was stirred, as we have seen, to write "Men who march away"; Bridges compiled *The Spirit of Man,* a wonderful anthology which has an even deeper significance in this war than it had in the last. Only Yeats remained unaffected: it was not Ireland's war! Most of the middle-aged poets were too deep in some sort of war-work to have much time for writing verse. Mr. Gibson served in the ranks, and recorded his experience of trench warfare in verse so plain that it sounds almost prosaic. Mr. Masefield's *1914* is a noble example of patriotic poetry; other memorials of his public service, his *Gallipoli* and *The Old Front Line,* are in prose. Mr. de la Mare used such little leisure as his war-work left him to issue a small volume of poems, which he called *Motley.* The mark of the war is stamped deep on the title-poem, in which the "simple happy mad" fool in motley shrinks aghast from the foul Satan-mad fool of War,

> Who rots in his own head.

It is stamped too on the accompanying piece named *Marionettes,* the title and temper of which recall, and are probably meant to recall, the supernal machinery of Hardy's *Dynasts.* For the rest, *Motley* contains some of Mr. de la Mare's most delicate work. There are notes in it which were not heard, or were very faintly heard, in *The Listeners;* the unnamed shadow which loomed over *The Dwelling-Place* in *The Listeners* has a name now: it is Death. Yet the poet's last word is a prayer that when he is dust these loved and loving faces may please other men. But the poet on whom the war produced the most remarkable effect was Binyon. As a stretcher-bearer with the French armies he saw it at as close quarters almost as Mr. Gibson. The lyric fire, which seemed to us to have died down a little in his narrative poems, burned up again stronger than ever. His voice took on a deeper note; his verse broke into larger and more turbulent rhythms. He wrote, always in the same exalted strain, of the things he had seen with his own eyes in training or in service—of London defying the Zeppelins, guns sweeping round Stonehenge on parade, guns thundering at the front, the sower sowing behind the lines, Arras, Ypres, the patience of the French wounded, the lads in hospital blue. . . .

READING SELECTION

ADJUSTMENT MECHANISMS INDICATIVE OF POOR MENTAL HEALTH

The problem situations in the preceding sections have implied a need for action by the individual. The well-integrated individual will react both emotionally and rationally to

From *The School in American Society,* 3rd ed. Eds. Ralph L. Pounds and James R. Bryner, pp. 250–253. Copyright 1973. Reprinted by permission of Macmillan Publishing Co. Inc.

problem situations. It is only when emotional reactions become habituated as the major "solutions" to problems that poor mental health is indicated. In this section we shall list some of the better-known emotional reactions that are typical of most people. Individuals with good mental health use them sparingly and accompany or follow them with rational attacks upon their problems. Persons with poor mental health use them excessively and often employ them as their only response to problem situations. . . .

ANGER

We refer here to emotional outbursts of anger. When this anger is directed against people, it is referred to as aggression. When anger is vented against things, it is referred to as destruction. When anger is repressed, or when it is a constant, deep-seated feeling indicative of many unresolved frustrations, we refer to it as hostility. By whatever name, this emotional reaction and its accompanying behavior are ineffective techniques for solving problems and they accelerate mental illnesses. Levy emphasizes the fact that aggression is not a constructive form of tension release by noting that it is invariably followed by compulsive self-punishment, restoration (restitution), rationalization, or all three. These compulsive behaviors are indicative of the heightened level of tension that follows aggressive behavior. The aggressive behavior to which we are referring is not rational aggression in socially approved ways, but unadulterated anger which results in antisocial behavior.

WITHDRAWAL

Withdrawal from the conflict situation is a common response at the unconscious level. Tensions may be relieved through withdrawal techniques, but such withdrawal indicates either abandonment of the goal or postponement of goal-seeking activity. In either case the relief is only symptomatic; the immediate tensions are relieved, but the source of anxiety is unchanged. At best, withdrawal maintains a status quo of unresolved frustrations and a potential source of intense and prolonged anxiety.

Some of the common withdrawal techniques will be sketched very briefly. Physical withdrawal from the conflict area may be a perfectly rational action, if there is real physical danger and/or if there is no goal to be attained by remaining. It is the habituation of this response to frustrations that builds anxieties; unresolved frustrations mount in number, tensions multiply, and more severe withdrawal techniques are demanded. In psychological withdrawal the person lives in an inner world into which no conflict can intrude. Emotional equilibrium is maintained through emotional apathy. This is incipient schizophrenia, a psychosis perennially causing the greatest number of admissions to mental hospitals. Regression to less mature levels of behavior is another withdrawal defense against tension. The sick or younger person is not expected to be able to cope with adult problems. Occasional use of the regression technique does little harm. A good cry may relieve tensions and leave one more relaxed, which may aid in problem solving if one soon retackles the problem. Continued infantile behavior, however, neither solves perplexing problems nor builds confidence for meeting new ones. Psychosomatic illness is one form of withdrawal behavior. The inefficient bank clerk or bookkeeper may develop an upset stomach, backache, sleepiness, or other physical symptoms of distress as the time for the examination of the books approaches; if he is ill enough, he can stay away from work while his books are being examined. Postponement of decision and compulsive use of alcohol and narcotics are withdrawal techniques that have been discussed earlier. The use of fantasy is another withdrawal technique that has consequences all the way from beneficial effects on mental health to development of psychosis. Daydreams are common in childhood. The vicarious achievement of daring deeds through fairy tales, comic books, movies, radio, television, and adult fiction may serve a very real emotional need for recognition for most of us. It is when the individual resorts to fantasy in the compulsive fashion of the alcoholic, to escape reality, that we recognize the symptoms of serious mental illnesses.

RATIONALIZATION

Rationalization is an easy way out of difficult situations, because it involves merely inventing plausible statements as to the desirability of the status quo. This may mean attributing altruistic motives to selfish behavior, claiming insightful behavior upon the fortuitous resolution of an unwise decision, feigning indifference or dislike of a group by which one has been rejected, and the like. If the original goal was unrealistic, rationalization probably promotes better mental health. The danger is that rationalization involves fantasy. Such distortions of fact may make future goals even more unrealistic.

REPRESSION

Repression of our real reasons for behavior, while verbalizing rationalizations until we actually are unaware of our real motives, may lead to marked mental illness. The real motives usually are so socially unacceptable as to cause shame and humiliation if we admit them, even to ourselves. An example is that of the young man who has homosexual tendencies. He is so ashamed of them that he disavows all interest in sex, on the basis of moral precepts, until he himself actually has forgotten why he became so sexually moral. Such behavior involves tremendous tension, to the point of severe physical fatigue.

PROJECTION

Projection of our original motives on another is a mechanism that has its amusing as well as its tragic aspects. For example, a respectable businessman was standing at a bus stop, innocently reading his newspaper. A frustrated spinster was standing beside him. As the bus arrived and he moved to board it, he accidentally brushed against her. She had him arrested for indecent advances. The woman had so wanted to be touched, though not admitting it to herself, that she actually thought that he had run his hand caressingly over her body.

SUBLIMATION

Sublimation refers to the channeling of the energy generated by a primitive urge into culturally or ethically high patterns of behavior. According to some psychoanalytical theories of genius, some of the finest art and music is attributed to sublimation of the sexual drive into esthetic experiences. For some persons, in some situations, sublimation is the only possible positive adjustment.

IDENTIFICATION

Identification is one of the more important of the adjustment mechanisms. The importance of the adult model in shaping behavior patterns of children and youth can hardly be overemphasized. If a child likes an adult and is liked in return, the behavior and personality patterns of the child may show a striking similarity to those of the adult model. This can be one of the major forces contributing to sound mental health when the child selects wholesome models. It can be a most disrupting influence when the models are socially or emotionally deviant, or when two or more models adopted by the same child hold conflciting values or exhibit conflicting behaviors.

READING SELECTION

CLASSIFICATIONS OF DECISION MAKING
by Bettye B. Swanson

Not all decisions are alike. Nor is every decision made in the same manner. Although some actions you undertake derive their basis from newly made decisions, there are other instances when decision making does not really take place. The latter, according to Deacon and Firebaugh, may involve routine, programmed, impulsive or intuitive action.

When you wake up in the morning and prepare to attend class do you consciously make decisions about such things as which side of your hair to comb first, how to brush your teeth, or which shoe to put on first? Probably not. Although you may have made a conscious decision about what you were going to wear to class, you probably didn't spend any time in making a decision about how to get ready to attend class. Every individual has certain habits or routine behaviors. Although they originated from decisions made at an earlier time in your life, you no longer consciously make these decisions each time you undertake this type of action.

Routine plans or actions serve a useful purpose in your daily life and management. How long would it take you to get up, get ready, and walk to class if you had to make separate decisions for each action you take? You use routine plans or actions as a resource. Since they are applicable each day, you need not use your resources to make new decisions.

In addition to the habitual behaviors or routines you follow, you also have certain specific actions you undertake in a given situation. These are called programmed decisions. Programmed decisions are different from routines. Routine plans or actions are patterns of behavioral actions repeatedly undertaken on a consistent and regular basis. Programmed decisions, on the other hand, utilize your past experience in a similar sit-

From *Introduction to Home Management* pp. 64–70. Copyright 1981. Reprinted by permission of Macmillan Publishing Co. Inc.

uation. For instance, you know you are going to have a test. Your method of studying for this test will be done using your knowledge of a similar experience. The degree of success previously achieved will be a determinant in how, when, where, and the length of time you study for this test.

Programmed decisions, like routines, are a resource in your management. When the action undertaken proves to be successful you repeat the same action the next time a similar situation occurs. This successful achievement, measured by the satisfaction you received, determines when and the extent to which you modify the original decision before employing it again in other like situations.

Both routine and programmed decisions serve useful purposes. They act as resources by eliminating the need to make new decisions. They also evaluate managerial action. The success you achieve enables you to by-pass or minimize the use of the decision-making process.

There are, however, times when you undertake action without any real thought process, lacking prior experience as a base, or in the absence of conscious awareness. This action results from either impulse or intuition. In either case, the action taken is not necessarily a negative one.

As you think back over some instances in your life you can probably recall situations where you acted impulsively or upon intuition. Although it is true that some of these might not in the long run have been in your best interests, there are undoubtedly others that were. Many products purchased in the marketplace were obtained through impulsive decisions. There have probably been times when you have acted not on the basis of any knowledge but rather due to an inner sense or feeling you could not explain. Your intuition, in the absence of fact or logic, motivated you. Perhaps you have reviewed your notes just prior to going to class without really knowing why. When the class began, the instructor announced a "pop quiz." This is but one example of intuition. You can probably relate others that have happened to you.

Acting by intuition does not mean making a choice among alternatives. However, daily living does involve decision making. . . .

There are five categories of decision making . . . technical, economic, social, legal, and political.

TECHNICAL DECISIONS

Technical decisions are "actions undertaken for the sake of a given end." Decisions that fall into this category are goal oriented. The alternatives have some known degree of specificity as do the available resources. These decisions involve weighing the alternatives. This means selecting the alternative that has the highest probability of achieving the desired goal and reducing the degree of risk as much as possible. These are the easiest decisions to make.

An example of a technical decision might be whether to go to class or stay in your room. You know the probability of risk, the instructor may give a quiz, whether or not you can obtain the lecture notes from another class member, and any additional potential risk factors. The decision you make will be based on these known facts.

Economic decisions have two basic components: multiple goals and limited resources. In these decisions, you have a number of goals competing against each other. Each of these goals necessitates allocation of the established resources. Your decision involves determining which goals and what resources. Since the attainment of these competing goals necessitates the use of similar or like resources you will have to determine goal priority. Completing this you can allocate resources.

One fallacy that often occurs among students examing decisions is to think these resources can only be monetary. There are many resources other than money. Therefore all resources are involved in these decisions. Inherent in these decisions are the characteristics of exchange and allocation resources. In order to achieve your goals, resources are either allocated and/or exchanged. Keenan's representation of these decisions is as follows.

Assume your multiple goals are to

1. Achieve a high grade on a test to be given tomorrow.
2. Attend a party given at a friend's house this evening.
3. Get the laundry done and go shopping for a birthday present.
4. Clean your room by tomorrow morning.
5. Finish the library research for a term paper due at the end of the week.

Your established but limited resources are time and energy. You must begin by setting priorities for your goals. Following this you allocate your resources among the combination of goals that will bring about the greatest degree of satisfaction while maximizing the resources used.

What resources do you have which might be exchanged for your limited resources of time and energy? Although most college students would not do this, you could use a money resource to pay someone to clean your room and do your laundry. In this instance you are exchanging one resource (money) for another to achieve a goal. Can you think of other resources you might exchange? In making economic decisions you are seeking to allocate and/or exchange your established resources in the most effective manner to bring about the highest degree of satisfaction.

Although these decisions are not the easiest to make, in your daily life you continually make economic decisions. These decisions involve a greater degree of risk than do technical decisions. In the latter decisions you know the alternatives and their respective degrees of risk. This is not necessarily true concerning economic decisions.

Using the economic decision cited earlier what would be the risk factor if your highest priorities were to do the laundry and go shopping for the birthday present? Would the risk factor be the same if your highest priority was to attend the party?

What could you do to reduce the risk factors involved in economic decisions? Gathering factual information is one step you often undertake when the economic decisions involve your monitary resources. Another might be to rely on past experience. Talking with friends, examining the depth of the alternatives, or assessing resources are other ways the risk factor might be reduced.

In the two previous categories, your decisions involved goals and resources. Although social decisions are directed toward goal attainment resulting from the utilization of resources, they occur through interaction between individuals.

You have been involved in many social decisions. When you moved into your dorm room or off-campus housing you and your roommate(s) made several social decisions. Examples of these might well have been: where to place the furniture, which drawers and what part of the closet were to be used by each individual, or determining each person's responsibility for keeping the room clean and neat.

As you made these decisions, interaction took place between you and your roommate(s). Your values and role perceptions influenced your interaction. Whether you realized it or not, you had assigned a role not only to yourself but also to your roommate(s). Your roommate(s) also assigned a role to you. These roles and the values of each individual involved in the process affected the decisions made.

Social decisions differ from economic decisions in several ways. In the two previous categories resource allocation and choosing among alternatives were involved in the decision making process. Social decisions mean that interaction is taking place. Thus the values, goals, and standards of each person are involved. The communication taking place also has a bearing upon the process.

In the social decision just cited, you and your roommate(s) undertook the decision making process on the strength of your personal values, goals, and standards. Through communication you interacted. In the process of communication you decoded what was being said to you and the actions taken by your roommate on the basis of your values, goals, and standards. Your roommate(s) did the same thing . . .

Social decisions may involve conflicting values and role perceptions. Part of the decision making process in social decisions involves recognizing these and determining the cause. Therefore, social decisions may never be truly resolved to the ultimate satisfaction of all involved individuals. In the decision concerning your housing, were you totally satisfied with the results? Or did you and your roommate(s) compromise, allowing each person to have his own way part of the time?

In these decisions, too, there is a risk factor. The risk factor involves values and roles. Since each individual participates in these decisions using his values and on the basis of role perceptions, the risk factor includes value and role conflicts. You may not be aware of the values or role perceptions of the other person. Nor is that individual aware of yours. Both of you are seeking to make a decision when all of the factors involved are not really known. Since incomplete information is available, the risk factor is increased.

Within each of your spheres of interaction you have various rules, regulations, and/or policies (legal decisions) that pertain to you and your actions within society. These may have been established by law, an authority, agency, or organization, or by the common consent of a group of people. Regardless of the method of establishment, these rules, regulations and/or policies derive their basis in the common welfare of the total group. They are the basic structure by which society and the culture function for the common good of all.

When your decisions concerning these rules, regulations, and/or policies are made you are aware of the risks involved and the probability of the consequences should you elect not to observe them. For instance, if you drive 70 miles per hour on a highway you know that it is likely that sooner or later you will get a speeding ticket. You also know that should you get a speeding ticket you will probably have to pay a fine. If you continue to receive speeding tickets, in all probability you may lose your driver's license either temporarily or permanently.

Unlike other categories, you know the risk factors and the probable consequences. It is then a question of what is the degree of risk you are willing to incur. Are you willing to accept the consequences of the risk probablility?

POLITICAL DECISIONS

Political decisions are made by a group of individuals whose major purpose is to function as a single unit. Unlike social decisions, the emphasis here is placed upon the procedure of how the decision is made rather than the actual resolution of the problem or situation. Political decisions involve establishing an organizational structure within the group. This organizational structure is then employed to resolve a problem or make a determination.

Suppose your instructor assigned you and five other members of your class to research and make an oral report on any topic you choose. What would the six of you do first? In order to complete this assignment, your group would start by establishing an organizational structure. In so doing you and the other members of your group have been making political decisions. Can you cite other instances where you have been involved in political decisions?

Theme Revision Using Classification

The following theme is a deliberately mixed-up version of a well-organized original. Without the intended sequence of ideas, it becomes hard to understand. As you read the first and last sentences of each paragraph, try to decide whether the paragraph should precede or follow the paragraphs immediately preceding and following it.

Paragraph 1. If one considers the entire living world, other *more complex levels* of organization become apparent. It is obvious, for example, that *not all organisms are single-celled* units; in fact, most are not. Cells of multicellular organisms are organized into more complex levels called tissues. In most multicellular forms, the various systems are interconnected and constitute the total functioning organism.

Paragraph 2. Communities possess unique characteristics such as numbers, kinds of species, and patterns of behavior. A community is a dynamic organization and may be replaced by other communities over periods of time.

Paragraph 3. It has been shown that changes in the environment can affect *more than the level of a single ecosystem* or group of ecosystems within a given geographical area. There are certain relationships that more or less affect *all forms of life* on earth. The term biosphere is a collective designation for all forms of life that inhabit the globe.

Paragraph 4. The concepts of energy and order can be applied to *all levels* of organization that exist in the living world. The continuum of life consists of basic levels of biological organization, which range from an interaction of exceedingly small atoms to the entire living world, the biosphere. All these levels of biological organization are dynamic and interacting. Any given level is a part of all higher ones and contains all lower levels as part of itself.

Paragraph 5. Populations of several different species associate locally to form *a more complex level* of organization, the community. Communities always contain a variety of organisms. Representative communities would be all forms of life in a pond, in an evergreen forest, and in a city.

Paragraph 6. The smallest structural units of matter are atoms which are composed of subatomic particles — protons, neutrons, and electrons. Atoms interact in certain combinations to form molecules, which may be joined to form more elaborate units called macromolecules. Some macromolecules exhibit many properties characteristic of living forms. Aggregations of macromolecules result in structural entities termed organelles, specialized components of a cell that perform different life activities. *The next higher level* of organization, the cell, is the smallest structural and functional unit that may exhibit all properties of life.

Paragraph 7. As one moves up the scale toward *higher and higher levels* of organization, each level is more complex than the last. In terms of energy and organization, each higher level represents a unit that is more unstable than the preceding level. Each level requires a constant supply of energy to maintain its degree of organization. If a cell, for example, could no longer obtain or utilize energy in order to maintain its organization, it would break down into the molecules of which it is composed and these molecules would eventually break down further to the most randomly ordered state. Without a constant expenditure of energy, each level in the hierarchy would break down into successively less complex units until the least organized state was reached.

Paragraph 8. Although *the foregoing discussion* has dealt only with levels of biological organization, it should be noted that none of these levels can be separated from the physical environment of the organism.

Paragraph 9. The organismic level does not represent the highest organizational complex in the world of living things. *The next higher grouping* is the population, a relatively permanent association of organisms of the same kind that occur in a particular habitat. Populations may be local units such as families, tribes, and herds. Familiar examples of local populations are daisies in a field, earthworms in a garden, spruce trees in a forest, frogs in a pond, and people in a city. The sum of all populations of the same kind, and therefore, the sum of all organisms of the same kind, represents a species. Specifically, a species is a group of organisms with certain characteristics in common, which breed freely among themselves but are prevented from breeding indiscriminately with other species by one or several isolating mechanisms.

Paragraph 10. The ecosystem represents the highest level of organization and presents the greatest degree of complexity. It is a broad environmental unit consisting of a community of organisms interacting with each other and with the physical environment through interchanges of chemical nutrients and energy.

As it appears above, the theme classifies matter in terms of certain structures, but it is a randomly ordered collection of paragraphs with no clear sequence of ideas. However, the italicized words suggest a clearer organization: "smallest," "more complex," "the next highest," "more complex," "the highest level," and so on. Since "the smallest" units are part of larger ones, a progression from the smallest or lowest level to the highest would seem to be appropriate. This would reorder more than half of the ten paragraphs: 6, 1, 9, 5, 10, and 3.

Paragraphs 7 and 8 obviously should follow the other ideas to form the conclusion. Paragraph 7 summarizes the ideas of all the other paragraphs; paragraph 8 is merely a brief reminder that the discussion of biological organization does not include all the known information about organisms. Therefore, paragraph 8 should precede paragraph 7.

This leaves paragraphs 2 and 4. Paragraph 4 is quite general; it looks like a good introduction. Since paragraph 2 adds further details about communities, it should follow paragraph 5, which defines the word "community".

If the paragraph order is changed so the sequence is 4 6 1 9 5 2 10 3 8 7, the explanation is much clearer:

READING SELECTION

THE STRUCTURAL ORGANIZATION OF MATTER

The concepts of energy and order can be applied to all levels of organization that exist in the living world. The continuum of life consists of basic levels of biological organization, which range from an interaction of exceedingly small atoms to the entire living world, the biosphere. All these levels of biological organization are dynamic and interacting. *Any given level is a part of all higher ones and contains*

THESIS *all lower levels as part of itself.*

PARAGRAPH TOPIC *The smallest structural units of matter are atoms* which are composed of subatomic particles—protons, neutrons, and electrons. Atoms interact in certain combinations to form molecules, which may be joined to form more elaborate units called macromolecules. Some macromolecules exhibit many properties characteristic of living forms. Aggregations of macromolecules result in structural entities termed organelles, specialized components of a cell that perform different life

From Life Science, 2 ed. pp. 6–7. Eds. Gerard J. Tortora and Joseph F. Becker. Copyright 1978. Reprinted by permission of Macmillan Publishing Co. Inc.

TRANSITION TO NEXT
PARAGRAPH activities. The next higher level of organization, *the cell,* is the smallest structural and functional unit that may exhibit all properties of life.

PARAGRAPH TOPIC

TRANSITION FROM
PREVIOUS PARAGRAPH If one considers the entire living world, *other more complex levels of organization become apparent.* It is obvious, for example, that not all organisms are *single-celled units;* most are not. Cells of multicellular organisms are organized into more complex levels called tissues. Tissues are composed of cells, either similar or different types, that usually perform a single function, such as muscle tissue and nervous tissue. In the vast majority of organisms, tissues are intimately associated at a still higher level of organization into structures called organs. Organs are composed of structurally and functionally integrated tissues. Common examples of plant organs are roots, seeds, stems, leaves, and flowers; familiar animal organs are the heart, lungs, kidneys, stomach, liver, and brain. The further integration of organs constitutes an even higher level of organization, called systems. Systems are groups of functionally correlated organs that typically perform a specialized activity. In most multicellular forms, the various TRANSITION TO NEXT
PARAGRAPH systems are interconnected and constitute the total functioning *organism.*

TRANSITION FROM
PREVIOUS PARAGRAPH

PARAGRAPH TOPIC *The organismic level* does not represent the highest organizational complex in the world of living things. *The next higher grouping is the population,* a relatively permanent association of organisms of the same kind that occur in a particular habitat. Populations may be local units such as families, tribes, and herds. Familiar examples of local populations are daisies in a field, earthworms in a garden, spruce TRANSITION TO NEXT
PARAGRAPH trees in a forest, frogs in a pond, and people in a city. *The sum of all populations* of the same kind, and therefore, the sum of all organisms of the same kind, *represents a species.* Specifically, a species is a group of organisms with certain characteristics in common, which breed freely among themselves but are prevented from breeding indiscriminately with other species by one or several isolating mechanisms.

TRANSITION FROM
PREVIOUS PARAGRAPH
PARAGRAPH TOPIC

TRANSITION TO NEXT
PARAGRAPH *Populations of several different species* associate locally to *form a more complex level of organization, the community.* Communities always contain a variety of organisms. Representative *communities* would be all forms of life in a pond, in an evergreen forest, and in a city.

TRANSITION FROM
LAST PARAGRAPH
AND TO THE NEXT *Communities* possess unique characteristics such as numbers, kinds of species, and patterns of behavior. A community is a dynamic organization and may be replaced by other communities over periods of time.

PARAGRAPH TOPIC

TRANSITION FROM
LAST PARAGRAPH

TRANSITION TO NEXT
PARAGRAPH *The ecosystem represents the highest level of organization* and presents the greatest degree of complexity. It is a broad environmental unit consisting of a *community* of organisms interacting with each other and with the physical *environment* through interchanges of chemical nutrients and energy.

THE THEME

It has been shown that changes in the *environment* can affect more than the level of a single ecosystem or group of ecosystems within a given geographical area. There are certain relationships that more or less affect all forms of life on earth. The term *biosphere* is a collective designation for all forms of life that inhabit the globe.

Although the foregoing discussion has dealt only with levels of *biological* organization, it should be noted that none of these *levels* can be separated from the physical environment of the organism.

As one moves up the scale toward higher and higher *levels* of organization, each level is more complex than the last. In terms of energy and organization, each higher level represents a unit that is more unstable than the preceding level. Each level requires a constant supply of energy to maintain its degree of organization. If a cell, for example, could no longer obtain or utilize energy in order to maintain its organization, it would break down into the molecules of which it is composed and these molecules would eventually break down further to the most randomly ordered state. Without a constant expenditure of energy, each level in the hierarchy would break down into successively less complex units until the least organized state was reached.

Using classification to organize the ideas in a theme involves more than just deciding how a subject can be subcategorized and then writing a paragraph about each category. There should be a clear progression of relationships from one category to the next. In textbooks and other kinds of published material, the clear progression is not always apparent. (Even published authors are not always perfect.) In the two preceding selections on "Mental Health" and "Decisions", there are few transitions between one category and the next; the separate sections are like self-contained short essays. Similarly, in the following example, the three central paragraphs are related to one another only in that all refer to types of drugs.

READING SELECTION

CHEMOTHERAPY

Basically, in using the term chemotherapy, we are talking here about the use of chemicals to treat or alleviate emotional or mental problems. Technically, of course, a physician prescribing medication for the flu or pneumonia is also using chemotherapy.

Narcosynthesis involves the use of certain drugs like sodium amytal or sodium pentothol, so-called "truth serums," which release unconscious materials into the conscious mind. These drugs are sometimes used in the treatment of severely inhibited or repressed patients.

From *The Struggle for Significance*, 3rd ed., pp. 188-192. Editors John H. Brennecke and Robert G. Amick. Reprinted by permission of Glencoe Publishing Co. Inc.

Tranquilizers, the well-known "mother's little helpers" of song and story, have been around since time began in natural herbal, root, and bark forms. For instance, rauwolfia (snakeroot) was used for centuries in India as a general medication, but patients suffering psychotic symptoms were often aided by ingesting this drug. A derivative of rauwolfia, reserpine, was found to have a value in treating hypertension and some symptoms of psychosis as well. Other tranquilizing drugs are chlorpromazine, perphenazine, meprobamate, and librium.

Energizing drugs, or "mood elevators," are generally administered to people experiencing chronic states of depression. Among the most commonly used energizing drugs are iproniazid, phenelzine, imipramine, and amitripthyline.

Ours is close to being a "chemical age" and many people put their fullest confidence in the use of drugs. However, as Coleman points out, drugs alone are not the answer.

Chemotherapy is not a cure-all. Psychotherapeutic drugs are welcome adjuncts to the total treatment program, but it would be unrealistic to assume that mental disorders based on the gradual development of faulty frames of reference and response patterns could be permanently cleared up by such limited methods . . . Tranquilizers and energizers tend to mask symptoms rather than to come to grips with the actual causes of mental disorders.

EXERCISES

1. Rewrite the essay on "Chemotherapy," adding transitions between successive pairs of paragraphs. Parallel structure might be a more effective transitional technique than word or phrase repetition or the insertion of common transitional words like "first, next, than, another category/kind of drugs _____," and so on.

2. Remembering that a thesis statement should say something more specific than "I am going to write about_____," write a categorization theme of approximately six or seven well-developed and well organized paragraphs on one of the following topics:
   a. Family members (parents, brothers and sisters, aunts and uncles, cousins).
   b. The geographical areas of your country.
   c. Methods of coping with homesickness.
   d. Problems a non-native speaker has with English.
   e. Modes of transportation available to tourists.

3. Read over your theme to determine whether or not additional (or more subtle) transitions are needed, whether the introduction clearly states and generally discusses the thesis, and whether the conclusion generally summarizes the main ideas (without adding any extra ones).

4. Consider the possibility of organizing the ideas in your theme chronologically and spatially. If either model is possible, decide which organization model is best suited to your thesis. Be prepared to discuss your decision in class.

COMPARISON AND CONTRAST

Probably because rather than despite the fact that comparison and contrast are opposites, they are frequently linked. (Professors especially seem to like comparison and contrast questions for essay exams.) Comparison deals with the similarities between two subjects; contrast deals with differences. To organize the details of a comparison, the writer has two choices: she or he can fully discuss one of the subjects in one or more paragraphs and then discuss the other, pointing out the likenesses between the two (an item-by-item comparison); he or she can discuss each point of similarity between the two subjects in successive paragraphs (a point-by-point comparison). A theme contrasting two subjects can also follow either the item-by-item or the point-by-point approach.

A comparison of two subjects not usually considered alike is an *analogy*. Analogies are often used to describe or explain something unfamiliar in familiar terms or to provide a different way of looking at something familiar.

As is true of any theme, the content of the individual paragraphs in an analogy, a comparison, a contrast, or a comparison-and-contrast theme is vitally important. The writer must carefully consider what kinds of details to include, deciding which facts, statistics, examples, definitions, explanations, or descriptions would best clarify the similarities and/or differences between the two subjects. The writer also needs to consider the various models of paragraph organization and carefully choose the most effective way of presenting the details of each paragraph.

Only after initial decisions about the contents and organization of individual paragraphs have been made is the writer ready to consider overall theme organization, although she or he may later find that individual paragraphs need to be revised to fit into the general organization of the theme.

When a writer wants to explain both the similarities and the differences between two subjects, the similarities might be discussed first and then the differences (point-by-point); the similarities might be discussed alternately with the differences (also point-by-point); or one of the subjects might be fully discussed before the other is even mentioned (item-by-item). The choice depends somewhat on the subject matter and somewhat on the author's decisions about what points to emphasize. If one point is more important, interesting, or impressive than the others, it may have more impact on the reader if it is the last point discussed.

Item-by-item comparisons and/or contrasts are especially vulnerable to disunity. To avoid producing two mini-essays when a single, unified comparison/contrast essay is desired, the writer must be especially careful to include transitions between paragraphs. The most common transitional words and phrases are "similarly, also, likewise, in comparison, compared with, on the other hand, in contrast (to), opposed to, contrasted with, however, unlike," etc. Often, the most common transitions are not the most effective; parallel structure and the repetition of words or ideas often work better to unify this type of composition.

The previous section contains an essay on several biomes (pp. 184–187). If a writer wished to discuss two similar biomes, taiga and deciduous forest, for example, he or she might choose comparison and contrast as an organizing technique. A brief outline of the similarities and differences might look like this:

I. Similarities
   A. the presence of trees
   B. the presence of animals
   C. severe winters
   D. annual growing seasons
II. Differences
   A. kinds of trees
   B. kinds of animals
   C. length of winters
   D. length of growing seasons

The details might appear in precisely this sequence in a theme. After an introductory paragraph explaining that a taiga and a deciduous forest share some characteristics and differ in others, there could be two or three paragraphs about the similarities, followed by two or three paragraphs about the differences. Or an author might prefer to discuss the similarities of trees, animals, and seasons in the two biomes in one paragraph and continue with three more paragraphs about the differences between the kinds of trees, the kinds of animals, and the severity and duration of the seasons. The ideas would then follow this outline:

I. Both a taiga and deciduous forest have trees, animals, and changing seasons.
II. Some trees found in a taiga are not found in a deciduous forest.
III. Some animals found in a taiga are not found in a deciduous forest.
IV. A taiga has a more severe winter and a shorter growing season than a deciduous forest.

Instead of discussing similarities first and differences next, an author might choose to follow the introductory paragraph with a paragraph about the similarities and differences between the varieties of trees found in each biome, then a paragraph about the varieties of animals in each, and a paragraph about the seasons in each.

In the following example, the author has chosen an item-by-item comparison. After the introductory paragraph, he first presents the questions for which sociology seeks answers, then those that are the concern of psychology. His transitional technique is parallel structure. The first sentence of the third paragraph is identical to the opening sentence of paragraph two, with the exception of one key word: "psychology" replaces "sociology". Both paragraphs contain three questions, which differ in structure but are alike in content.

THE THEME

READING SELECTION

PSYCHOLOGY AND SOCIOLOGY
by Homayoun Jamasbi

Psychology and sociology are both categorized as social sciences, and both study human behavior. However, psychology is the study of individual behavior, whereas sociology is the study of group behavior. Psychology deals with the possible problems an individual might have in social interaction with other individuals, but the main concern of sociology is the ways that different societies with different cultures deal with each other.

Sociology asks and tries to answer questions like these: why does one society progress rapidly and another one remain primitive for centuries? what is the main reason for revolution in a society? what is the role of religion or art in a society?

Psychology asks and tries to answer questions like these: why does one individual adapt easily to a changing environment and another individual become mentally disturbed? what are the causes of antisocial behavior? what role does religion or art play in an individual's mental and emotional life?

Psychology and sociology often work together in their study of human behavior. It is assumed that by better understanding individual motivation and behavior, more will be learned about group motivation and behavior. The reverse is also assumed: if scientists can learn more about social groups, they will learn more about individuals.

A student theme, reprinted by permission.

Item-by-item comparison and contrast has also been used to organize the details of the following essay. Take careful note of the transitions as you are reading. What points are compared or contrasted? Are any points mentioned in the discussion of only one of the two subjects?

READING SELECTION

CAT KILLERS
by Terri McGinnis

There are two major infectious feline diseases for which safe and effective vaccines are available—rabies and feline panleukopenia (feline enteritis, feline distemper). Each of these diseases can easily cause death in an unprotected cat. We are very fortunate to be able to prevent such serious illnesses with a procedure as technically simple as vaccination. . . .

Feline panleukopenia is an extremely common, very contagious, often fatal viral disease which occurs in cats (both domestic and wild) and raccoons and other members of the raccoon family. Although this disease is commonly called *distemper,* it is not at all

From *The Well Cat Book,* pp. 76–81. Copyright 1975. Reprinted by permission of Random House.

related to *canine distemper,* which often occurs in young dogs. Other common names for panleukopenia are feline infectious enteritis, cat or show fever, and cat plague.

The incubation period (time from exposure to first signs of disease) for panleukopenia is usually about seven days, although it may vary from two to ten days. In young cats (under six months) in particular, the disease can be so severe and of such rapid onset that death occurs before an owner is truly aware that signs of illness are present. More often the first signs are fever (frequently 104–105°F), listlessness, lack of appetite and vomiting, usually accompanied by extreme dehydration. A cat may seem interested in drinking (some sit with their heads over or near their water bowls) but often will not drink or vomits soon after doing so.

Although panleukopenia is often fatal, there is no reason to give up at the first sign of disease. Many cats have survived severe cases to live out normal, healthy lives. . . .

Recovery from *rabies,* on the other hand, is so extremly rare that you might as well not even consider it. The rabies virus can infect any warm-blooded animal, including humans. It causes a disease of the nervous system manifested by changes in behavior preceding paralysis and death. Signs of rabies usually begin between about two weeks and two months following infection, but cases have developed after more than one year. . . . Rabid cats usually first show changes in their temperament. At this time rabies can be particularly difficult to diagnose because the signs are so variable. A cat may become restless, apprehensive, overly affectionate or shy. A cat will often have a tendency to hide at this stage. Some cats may be febrile (have a fever) and may have dilated pupils. Following these early signs the animal often becomes extremely ferocious . . . The *dumb* form of rabies may follow the furious form or may be seen by itself. It is mainly characterized by paralysis. A cat's mouth may hang open and saliva may drip from it. Since such cats cannot ingest food or water they become quite dehydrated. More often, however, cats with the dumb form of rabies develop difficulty walking and then paralysis of the rear legs. Eventually total paralysis occurs, followed by death.

Two statesmen are described in the following essay, which could be outlined as follows:

   I. Similarities between Churchill and Roosevelt *(item-by-item)*
      A. Roosevelt loves pleasure, appears carefree, is high-spirited, effectively solves problems.
      B. Churchill loves pleasure, appears carefree, is high-spirited, effectively solves problems.
   II. *(Transition sentence)* Churchill is not frivolous.
  III. Differences between Churchill and Roosevelt (point-by-point).
      A. Behavior.
         1. Roosevelt plays the game of politics.
         2. Churchill broods about the potentially tragic reality.
      B. Emotional depth: Roosevelt lacks deep emotion; Churchill feels deeply.
  IV. *(Conclusion sentence)* Both are great men.

READING SELECTION

CHURCHILL AND ROOSEVELT
by Isaiah Berlin

Roosevelt, as a public personality, was a spontaneous, optimistic, pleasure-loving ruler who dismayed his assistants by the gay and apparently heedless abandon with which he seemed to delight in pursuing two or more totally incompatible policies, and astonished them even more by the swiftness and ease with which he managed to throw off the cares of office during the darkest and most dangerous moments. Churchill too loves pleasure, and he too lacks neither gaiety nor a capacity for exuberant self-expression together with the habit of blithely cutting Gordian knots in a manner which often upset his experts; but he is not a frivolous man. His nature possesses a dimension of depth — and a corresponding sense of tragic possibilities, which Roosevelt's lighthearted genius instinctively passed by.

Roosevelt played the game of politics with virtuosity, and both his successes and his failures were carried off in splendid style; his performance seemed to flow with effortless skill. Churchill is acquainted with darkness as well as light. Like all inhabitants and even transient visitors of inner worlds, he gives evidence of seasons of agonized brooding and slow recovery. Roosevelt might have spoken of sweat and blood, but when Churchill offered his people tears, he spoke a word which might have been uttered by Lincoln or Massini or Cromwell but not Roosevelt, greathearted, generous, and perceptive as he was.

Excerpt from "Mr. Churchill" In *Jubilee*, Eds. Edward Weeks and Emily Flint.

Looking at the author's choice of words in the essay, we find that he rarely repeats a word; rather, he uses a synonym or a variant form or a direct or implied antonym:

pleasure-loving/loves pleasure
gay/gaiety
spontaneous, heedless abandon/exuberant self-expression
delight in pursuing . . . incompatible policies/blithely cutting Gordian knots
dismayed his assistants/upset his experts
effortless skill/agonized brooding
sweat and blood/blood, sweat, and tears (a phrase from a famous speech)

EXERCISES

1. Using a good dictionary, look up the meanings of unfamiliar words in the essay and be prepared to discuss them in class.
2. The author obviously respects both Roosevelt and Churchill; which of the two does he consider the greater man? How do you know?

3. Outline the following essay. What type of comparison-and-contrast model does it follow?

READING SELECTION

Botany and Zoology
by Eugenia C. Obi

Both botany and zoology are parts of a more general field of science, biology. The two are studies of living things, which share certain characteristics, whether they are plants or animals. Botany deals with plants, those organisms that can manufacture their own food by the use of sunlight. Zoology, on the other hand, deals with animals, those organisms that cannot manufacture their own food and are thus dependent on plants for their food.

Although plants and animals share many abilities, the extent to which plants can exercise some of those abilities is limited. For example, both plants and animals need food, water, and warmth for growth, but plants can move to acquire those needs only by the slow extension of their leaves and roots, while animals can move relatively large distances in relatively little time. When an animal is pricked with a needle, the animal will withdraw the part of the body being pricked. This ability to draw back from pain or irritation, called irritability, is found only to a very limited extent in plants.

If plants had the same mobility and irritability as animals, animals would have a more difficult time finding food. If animals were as limited as plants, they might have evolved a means of manufacturing their own food, as plants do now. The world would be a very different place than it is if the characteristics of plants and animals were reversed.

A student theme, reprinted by permission.

In the following essay, the contrasts between medieval and modern English poetry are implied, not stated. A careful reader, however, can draw conclusions about modern English poetry from the essay, even if he or she has no previous knowledge of its form. As you read it, make a list of the implied contrasts and be prepared to discuss them in class.

READING SELECTION

The Meter of Medieval Germanic Epic
by W. T. H. Jackson

The meter used in *Beowulf* and the Scandinavian poems is highly complex. . . . There was no rhyme in the modern sense, nor was the number of syllables in any line fixed.

From *The Literature of the Middle Ages*, pp. 179–181, Columbia Books, 1960.

Each line contained four main stresses, two in each half-line, and the first sound of the word bearing the third main stress had to alliterate with at least one other initial sound of a stress-bearing word in the first half-line. It was possible to have three, or, exceptionally, four such alliterating sounds in each line. Occasionally there were two alliterating pairs. The number of unstressed syllables was quite indefinite, and their method of inclusion in the rhythmic pattern has been the subject of much dispute. . . .

That the lines had, for listener and author alike, a basic rhythmic and musical beat pattern is highly likely. The poems were almost certainly sung or chanted to a rhythmical accompaniment and it is clear from the complexity of the schemes used that virtuosity in meter was appreciated. It should never be forgotten that the Germanic epic was essentially an oral form. Those who composed it could not write; those who could write usually despised it. . . .

A writer attempting to describe something unfamiliar to readers may use comparison and contrast to emphasize the details. In the following excerpt from a science fiction novel, the author's points of comparison create an analogy between something familiar to the reader (humans) and something unfamiliar (an alien species called "meszs"). The points of contrast reinforce the fact that meszs do not really look at all human.

READING SELECTION

The Inhabitants of Mestil
by Lloyd Biggle

As he drove, he talked about his animaloids. "The meszs," he said. "The original inhabitants of Mestil. Have you met them?"

"Only in pictures," Wargen said.

"They suffer the misfortune of looking almost human. They're highly intelligent, they're talented in the arts, and they make brilliant scientists, mathematicians, and philosophers. They're also competent technologists and engineers, even without training. Any one of them can build anything. Unfortunately, they're much too gentle and trusting to survive in this harsh universe. Until humanity arrived in Mestil their language had no words for 'war' or 'fight' or even 'quarrel.' They had a splendid civilization—in my opinion one vastly superior to what Mestil has now. The mesz tragedy is that they are similar enough to man to arouse his animosity and dissimilar enough so that he feels no obligation to treat them humanely."

. . . .

Jorno had been right—they suffered the misfortune of looking almost human. They were shorter than humans, slighter in stature, and they had long body hair on their arms but none at all on their heads. They seemed to have a profusion of fingers at the end of each arm and no hands at all. Their earless skulls were short and narrow and gro-

From *The Light That Never Was*, pp. 97–99, Daw Books, 1972.

tesquely elongated to a cranial capacity exceeding that of humans. Their eyes were wide set, their noses a smear of tissue with wide nostril gaps, and their mouths a repulsive, circular sucking device. Some animaloids possessed their own intrinsic beauty—Franff's species, for example, which was also different enough from humanity to be judged on its own merits. The meszs, at the same time startlingly similar and distortedly different, revolted and repelled. They were simply hideous. Wargen found himself wondering what further absurdities were concealed by their baggy clothing.

Based on this description, could you draw a picture of a mesz? On which features does the author concentrate? Which are left to the reader's imagination?

Comparison and contrast organization is often used simply to describe, explain, or define something. However, it can also be used effectively to reinforce an ethical, philosophical, historical, psychological, or sociological thesis. In the following excerpt from a book about American Indians, the author uses comparison and contrast to emphasize the tragic ignorance of Indian culture that led to both deliberate and unintentional cruelty to the Indians.

READING SELECTION

AMERICAN INDIANS
by Royal B. Hassrick

Life on the reservations during the last half of the nineteenth century was grim. Unable any longer to feed themselves, the Indians were given rations. Beef cattle were supplied, which when released from corrals were shot and butchered by the Indians—the whole affair having the semblance of a rodeo buffalo hunt. Rations were, however, often short; short because of the graft of Bureau of Indian Affairs agents and dishonest suppliers. But there were more fundamental problems than the mere sticky fingers of Indian Affairs agents and crooked traders. The philosophy on Indian affairs was based on the simplistic and determined assumption that by remaking of Indians in the image of white men, the Indian problem could be successfully solved. It was a policy formulated by well-meaning church groups, organizations devoted exclusively to the best interests of Indians, working with government policy makers. It contained all the basic elements of the Puritan ethic of the 1870s. It was essentially the American philosophy for success. Industriousness and frugality, thought to be easily achievable for the Indian through farming, made for self-sufficiency and prosperity. Fear of God through staunch adherence to Christian principles produced men of upright morality and unimpeachable integrity. It was an approach to life that was clear-cut and forthright. And today, from the Indian's point of view, hindsight indicates it was disastrously wrong.

Even with a policy designated by the best-intentioned people, forcing benighted sav-

From *The Colorful Story of North American Indians*, pp. 128–135. Copyright 1974. Reprinted by permission of Octopus Books.

THE THEME

ages into the alien culture of an enlightened and dominant society was about as logical as trying to transform a hawk into a dove.

From the white man's viewpoint, the Indians were savages. They scalped one another and white men too. They killed women and children. They practiced polygamy. The men did not work, rather had fun hunting or sat around the council lodge smoking the evil weed tobacco while their women carried the burdens, even did the back-breaking work of tilling the field. Rather than accumulating wealth for a rainy day, they splurged it on feasting, squandered it in gambling or just gave it away. And as if to confirm their savagery, not only did witch doctors and medicine men perform wild ceremonies with rattles and drums to cure the sick, but some men underwent cruel and inhumane self-torture in the Sun Dance, worshipping pagan gods, especially the Sun.

The white man conveniently overlooked the entire gestalt of Indian culture in their blind and determined self-righteousness. They also easily forgot that the English and the French had paid bounties for scalps and that the frontiersmen boasted of the "hair" they had taken. The Yankees were quick to condone the destruction of the Iroquois villages by General Sullivan's armies in the eighteenth century, were loud in their cheers at General Custer's killing of women and children at the surprise attack on the Cheyennes at the battle of the Washita a hundred years later. This, of course, was all done in the name of civilization and manifest destiny.

For the Puritanical Americans, polygamy was a frightening and evil thing. Not only was it immoral, it was unclean. Quite naturally, the Indians must be perverted. Some not only had two wives, but a good provider might well maintain six women. Yet the white man winked at men who supported a mistress, and surreptitiously upheld the institution of prostitution. And today, to frown on the Indians' practice of polygamy is even more preposterous. With easy divorce and quick remarriage, the Americans practice a form of both serial polygamy and polyandry, not in having two spouses at a time, but enjoying one after another. The consequences for the children of a broken home are devastating, which was not the case when divorce occurred in the Indian's consanguine family.

The whole idea that Indian men did not work was ridiculous. Hunting to insure enough food for the year-round supply was hard work, a task that required skill and patience, endurance and courage. It was not a sport as viewed by the white man, but difficult, arduous work. War, too, was a profession for which men trained diligently to become proficient both in the use of weapons and in strategem. To the white man, however, laboring long hours behind a plow, whose days were often spent in drudgery, an Indian's life appeared idyllic. The white man was jealous.

With the exception of the nomadic buffalo-hunting tribes of the Great Plains, the Indians living east of the Rocky Mountains were all farmers. And the women did the farming. They also carried the firewood, toted the water, shouldered the burdens. Theirs, too, was the strenuous work of tanning hides and the tedious job of making the clothing. When traveling or moving camp, the men led the procession empty-handed, save for their weapons, while the women trailed dutifully behind bearing the provisions. There was good reason for the men to take the lead unencumbered. They must be the scout, the armed protector of their family in the event of a surprise attack. They must be vigilant. In the eyes of the white man, however, the Indian women were relegated to the status of beasts of burden by men too lazy and arrogant to work.

The ceremonies of the Indians, including those involved with curing, were considered as pagan rites conceived by a savage mind. The shaman's antics, his rattling rattles, his singing, his trance appeared demented, childish and ineffective—this, despite the fact that they very often worked. The Sun Dance with its grueling self-torture epitomized the barbarity of Indian mentality. To worship the Sun and other deities was not only polytheism but antichristian, both of which were anathema to the Victorian consciousness. Yet strangely these very white men revered a Saviour who himself endured the torture of crucifixion for their sakes. The Indians were far more direct. They themselves forthrightly suffered to gain power for the benefit of others. Interestingly too, the missionaries who ridiculed the polytheistic beliefs held by the Indians, themselves acknowledged a Holy Trinity and in some instances a Virgin Mother.

The Indians' concept of property and wealth were diametrically opposed to that of the white men's. For the majority of the tribes, tangible items were accumulated only to be given away. In the Plains, the horse became a standard medium of exchange and a man with a large herd was considered rich. But to obtain respect and status, he had to give his horses away. Generosity was the sure path to social success. It seems that only in California was money, in the form of shells, accumulated for money's sake.

For the Indian, the route to prestige lay in one's ability to acquire property and then share it with others. The epitome of this concept was the Potlatch as practiced in the Northwest. Here the give-away reached the proportions of mayhem. But the point to be understood is that for Indians, property for property's sake, wealth for wealth's sake, had in itself no meaning. On the other hand, property and wealth, when shared, when given away, were vital to the individual's chance for gaining the respect of his fellow men, of achieving for himself status and prestige. The white man's approach to property and money was quite different. Earning money not only brought the comforts of life, but large amounts could bring especially desirable rewards. Wealthy men could afford mansions and servants, join exclusive clubs, bedeck their wives in emeralds. If they were to receive the accolade of public recognition, they had best contribute to the building funds for the new library or give heavily to the church. Yet the wealthy man's real status, the awe of the public's acclaim in the nineteenth century was and still is based upon the very aura of his being rich. His money brought him all the good things of life, he was envied, he was held in high regard. The rich man was reverently respected yet somewhat resented for the mere size of his bank account. In the nineteenth century, money was God. The Americans did not then, nor have not now, equated success with much else than the dollar sign.

Because of the white man's ignorance, misunderstanding, inconsistent thinking and blatant prejudice, national policy in the 1870s demanded that Indian culture be changed to conform with Christian standards of values, with the "white" methods of doing things. The Indians had been defeated militarily, now they were to be destroyed culturally.

EXERCISES

1. Write an outline summarizing the similarities between white and Indian customs.

2. Write an outline summarizing the differences between the white man's perception of Indian culture and the realities of that culture.

3. Outline two or three aspects of cultural behavior in your country that could be misunderstood by a person from a different culture. Be prepared to contribute to a class discussion of cultural differences.

As you read the following essay, make a list of the items and points that are compared and contrasted. When you finish, reorganize your list in outline form. Your instructor may ask you to write an in-class theme comparing and contrasting existentialism and stoicism, using only your outline as a resource.

READING SELECTION

EXISTENTIALISM
by Richard Paul Janaro

Coping with life, expecting disappointment, learning to accept what happens without disturbing one's inner tranquility—the major goals of Stoicism—presuppose one thing about the universe: it is perhaps incomprehensible, but there is a divine plan, a rationality behind it. It all makes sense ultimately would we but know it. Epictetus and Marcus Aurelius say this over and over again. In truth, almost anything is bearable if one is convinced it is not so much foolishness. The third-grader who must stay inside the classroom and write "I will not laugh behind teacher's back" may take a measure of comfort in the thought that a better character is being molded by his punishment. Then again, he may not, especially if he were not the one who snickered.

The philosophy of existentialism is also the basis of a life-style. It is one that can be most attractive to people who want very much to cope, to achieve happiness by an effort of will, to maintain their equilibrium no matter what happens around them—but who cannot believe there is ultimate wisdom at work behind existence. In some respects existentialism is a modern brand of Stoicism for people who will not be put off by faith of any kind. Existentialism appeals to unflinching realists who believe in the present, the existent moment, for whatever it is and for nothing besides what is there. If one is loved at that moment, then he is loved, and the world is beautiful for the time being. But he does not count on being loved tomorrow.

The existential life-style may at times borrow a little from the hedonist. One is not against pleasure. Even the most disciplined Stoic does not cross the street to avoid all forms of enjoyment. However, the existentialist, like the Stoic, does not go out of his way to court pleasure. He does not allow the experience of pleasure to be the indispensable test of life's goodness. He is too wise for that. He believes the hedonist is deceiving himself in his desperate quest for gratification. The existentialist cannot see how anybody can live for very long on this earth without understanding that love seldom

From *Philosophy: Something to Believe In*, pp. 303–309. Copyright 1975. Reprinted by permission of Glencoe Press.

lasts, fame is fleeting, friends are not always around when you need them, children grow up and move away and stop writing, and people die—sometimes when you least expect them to.

Is life, then, to be considered good in any sense of the word? That replies the existentialist, is strictly up to you. Life is nothing whatever in itself. It simply is. Like the Stoic, the existentialist believes the quality of life is not located outside or beyond us but within the emotions. Life is therefore good or bad or simply neutral, depending upon one's choice. The whole premise of existentialism . . . is one's freedom to make of his life whatever he pleases. Existence precedes essence.

In making one's life good, one must work very carefully. It is a little like crossing the rapids via slippery stones that refuse to stay in place. One false move, and it's all over. It is not all that simple to remain in the existent moment, to see what happens as it is, not in the light of what one had hoped, or dreaded. It is difficult never to feel that one has been a victim, that one is unfortunate, that one's luck has run out.

Hence feelings of anxiety or even anguish are all part of the normal course of things. The existentialist does not struggle to cope when events become overwhelming. He knows the value of releasing his feelings. Much existential expression is for this very reason released in the forms of poems, plays, novels, paintings, and songs. Edith Piaf, the cafe entertainer extraordinaire, with her throbbing voice and her tragic songs of broken loves and the cruelties we inflict upon each other, was the existentialist-as-performer. It scarcely mattered who wrote her songs; as she sang, they became her philosophy. But in the throb, in the electric vibrance of her voice, there is victory as well. The sufferer has cried out, and in the crying has survived the existent moment.

Existentialism is a strong, strident, bold life-style. One is adventurous even if he is precise and careful as he makes his way across the stones. He is not the Epicurean trying to remain as detached and uninvolved as possible. To avoid being hurt, he will not refrain from loving. As we listen to the dying notes of Piaf's account of her latest and most disastrous love affair, we somehow know she will go through the whole thing again next week.

The reason one is bold and adventurous is that one has an intuition of his importance. If life as a whole makes little sense, I know that I can make sense, quite as much as you can. You do not make more sense than I. I need not be ashamed of what I do—so long as I do it with the fullness of my integrity, so long as I am not consciously deceitful. I respect and love the humanness in you, but you must accord me the same honor and respect. In each one of us the universe is entirely reborn, and it gains whatever rationality it has from the things each of us does. For this reason each of us comes back again; he tries once more. Unlike the Stoic, he is not absolutely certain that he will always lose . . .

Have you ever rented an apartment or moved into a house that was brand new? If so, you can remember how different it looked when you first saw it: those empty rooms, that blankness, the smell of new paint or freshly laid carpeting. It is doubtful that you said to yourself, "Ah, this is my home." If you did, perhaps the reason was the fireplace or the view through a particular window. Something had to be specific. Normally we begin to feel "at home" only after we have collected and arranged furniture, paintings, bric-a-brac. After a time the experience of being at home takes on a special kind of quality impossible to define, yet unmistakable all the same.

Now picture yourself opening the front door one night, switching on the light, and sensing that everything seems different. You take a few minutes to absorb the scene, and suddenly you realize one of the paintings is missing from its customary place on the wall. Someone has broken in and stolen it. Will the experience of being at home be the same through the first night? No matter how you rearrange pictures so as to take away the gaping emptiness, you will no longer know the same home. That painting has been the cause of the existence of your home. . . .

To put one's faith in either nature, as the Stoic does, or God, as the religious person does, is, for the existentialist, to act out a play in a fantasy world. It is like pretending to live in another house, to be blind to what actually is. Many people will not face this. In order to bear what happens to them, they must delude themselves. "Everything happens for the best, and so there is a reason that my painting is gone." Or even, "My painting has left me in order to go to a more beautiful home where it will be far happier . . ."

It is precisely at the point of one's seemingly bleak and unflinching head-on confrontation with an illusionless reality that one discovers the true secret and the true joy of being. One realizes himself to be unique. If—to use my own metaphor—reality is ultimately an unfurnished house, one may, after all, do the furnishing. One is not a victim of life, since that which has no shape or form can pose no threat. The sense of victimization is all within us. If one is unique, how may he also be a sufferer of life's injustices? Justice and injustice imply standards, molds, and traditions. To believe that man has been persecuted by disappointments, bad luck, and finally death is to tie oneself with ropes of one's own devising . . .

Even to say that death is part of nature and must be tolerated is to suggest a pattern or purpose. Removing the pattern removes the unquestioning acceptance, but at the same time it enhances one's own meaning and power. One does without faith in a higher providence, whether God or nature; but one experiences a sudden feeling of personal strength.

Existentialism is thus a unique product of the Western mind, since it is that mind which has been especially involved with the issue of life's meaning and purpose. First Aristotle and then the Christian philosophers dealt with the reasons man is on this earth. Aristotle believed that each of us is here to reach perfection, to fulfill the human potential; thus the purpose of life is self-actualization. The Christians believed that each of us is here to earn God's love and so enter an afterlife of eternal happiness. Other philosophers in the West have agonized over the question of life's meaning. Not to have discovered it has meant philosophical suicide for some.

Existentialism does not, as you can see, abandon that quest. It merely places the responsibility on the individual. One does not discover the meaning of life; he asserts it . . .

EXERCISES

1. List two or three features of existentialism that are shared by another philosophy (Christianity, Islam, Buddhism, or some other) and list two or three

features that differ. Then write a comparison-and-contrast theme about the two philosophies.

2. Write an outline for an item-by-item comparison and contrast of two related fields of study. Reorganize the details in your outline for a point-by-point comparison and contrast. In your opinion, which outline would produce the more effective essay? Why? (Be prepared to defend your answer in class.)

3. Invent a comparison/contrast question for a report or an examination in one of your other courses and answer it in three or four paragraphs.

4. The following essay is not a comparison and contrast, but it contains sufficient information for a theme emphasizing the similarities and differences between the two men who are described. Pick out the relevant information and write an essay comparing John Gordy with Alex Karras.

READING SELECTION

TWO FOOTBALL PLAYERS
by George Plimpton

[John Gordy] was one of the offensive guards on the Detroit Lions, about the best in the league at that difficult position. During the time I had spent with the team, he had been a sympathetic friend and a lively source of information. He was called The Bear because his body was covered with a thick pelt-like thatch of hair, and on his way to the shower, a towel around his middle, one of his teammates would invariably lean out of his locker room stall and call out, "Hey, John, don't forget to take off your overcoat!"

Gordy's notion for the book was simple and practical. . . . He would devote himself to the text on offensive line play, and for the defense he suggested his training camp roommate, Alex Karras. . . .

In truth, Karras was an excellent choice. He was an All-Pro defensive tackle, relatively short for that position—being a massive hydrant-like figure of 245 pounds—but possessed of tremendous strength in the upper part of his body and a startling quickness of foot which carried him into opposing backfields in a savage bustling style of attack which caused some observers to refer to him as The Mad Duck. Since he was not overpowering, but relied on deftness and guile to get to the opposition, his theories on defensive lineman technique would be valuable; furthermore, his mind was freewheeling, full of fancy, and loved to drift into extemporized skits and monologues, which would help brighten the instructional text of the manual.

. . . .

When Karras and Gordy turned up in my New York apartment, shucking their coats, and coming down the steps into the living room, it seemed to me that a proper starting place for their book was to get them both to talk about that moment when they knew they were going to become football players. . . .

From *Mad Ducks and Bears,* by George Plimpton. Copyright © 1973 by George Plimpton. Reprinted by permission of Random House, Inc.

THE THEME

For Karras it was a shot he made on a basketball court when he was in high school in Gary. He was sent into a game against a team running third in the state. Karras had no particular wish to go into the game. He was a reserve; because of the athletic pro-ficiency of his older brothers, he lacked confidence; furthermore, the pressure on him was inordinate, the game being extremely close and in its final minute.

"I went down the court," he said, "and they threw me the ball. I don't know what made me do it, but I said to myself that for once in my life I was not going to pass the ball off. That's what I generally did—I'd get the ball and throw it to someone else quick, like a bomb was ticking in it. But this time I took a shot, pushed it up with one hand, and it went in, and we won the game." . . .

"And if the shot hadn't gone in?" I asked.

"I probably would have ended up as an elegant fop," Karras said expansively. "Maybe I would have learned the harpsichord. At this very moment I might be the Secretary of the Interior, lolling on a sofa in Washington with an ecology student, reach-ing out from time to time with a long arm and hitting a sad chord on the harpsichord, instead of sitting around with you bums. Of course, I could have turned out to be a bum, too."

. . . .

"What about you, John?" I asked.

"My freshman year in high school," Gordy told us, "I was five feet two and weighed one hundred and nineteen, and I played trumpet in the band. We marched at the games. I didn't care at all about football. I ate hot dogs and looked at the girls. Then I changed high schools. I didn't have any friends in the new place, . . . and I was lonely. Then one day a girl walked up to me in the corridor and told me that if I went and got a crew cut—this shows you how long ago it was—maybe some of them would start talking to me. A red-haired girl. Well, I high-tailed it down to the barbershop and came back with a crew cut that apparently made me acceptable enough so that I was invited to the weekend high school dance.

"Well, that night I got into a fight. I was leaving the place with a girl who was a cheerleader. A guy by the name of Joe Henderson came running out and wanted to know what I was doing taking his girl home. He was a *huge* guy, about six foot eight . . . He grabbed me. Out of fright I swung a punch at him, and down he went, right there on the street under the arc light. I reached down and grabbed his jacket, and he busted out crying and carrying on and asking me to leave him alone. This big guy, and all of a sudden there he was on the ground.

"Well, I got this tremendous surge of confidence. After that, I didn't play the trumpet anymore. I didn't even know that professional football existed then, but I would guess that knocking down that guy put me on the road to it."

CAUSE AND EFFECT

Cause and effect is the ideal organizational model for a writer who wants to discuss the reasons for an occurrence or the results of an event. There are many varieties of cause and effect theme order. A discussion of several effects of one cause may begin with an introductory paragraph explaining the cause and continue with several paragraphs discussing the effects. However, a writer who wants to dramatize the cause may reverse this order, using the introductory paragraph to discuss the effects in a general way, explaining each effect in each of the following paragraphs and concluding the theme by revealing the cause in the last paragraph.

A theme explaining several causes of one effect could also be organized at least two different ways: the author could begin by introducing the effect and then discussing its causes; he or she could wait until the end to reveal that effect. A discussion of the causes first, of course, will provide the reader with hints about the resulting effect.

The transitional words and phrases most frequently found in cause and effect themes are "because, for this reason, the reason for this is, as a result, consequently, due to." In the following short essay, one of the three paragraph transitions is from this list: the word "because" at the beginning of the third paragraph.

READING SELECTION

THE WORK-SIN ETHIC

The system of thought and action called the work-sin ethic continues to be an underlying philosophy of the capitalistic economy of the United States and most nations in Western civilization, and deserves some attention. The work-sin ethic has also been called the Protestant ethic and the Puritan ethic, because it has its roots in the theology of the followers of John Calvin, the fundamentalist reformer. Essentially, the idea is that "good" people (those who are predestined to be "saved" and go to heaven) can be recognized by their "good" life here on earth and by their material success. "Bad" people (those who are predestined to be damned to hell) show their evil nature in their unsuccessful and wasteful life-styles.

While few people today subscribe to this black-and-white concept of good and evil, the idea has somehow taken hold and continues to permeate the thinking of many people in Western civilization. This is only a theory, but it does help explain many of the abuses of human rights that have taken place in the Western world since the Industrial Revolution, and the justification of the exploitation of the workers and discrimination of all kinds.

Because people of all religious backgrounds (even those who call themselves atheists or agnostics) have been influenced by this viewpoint, and since the Puritan mentality dominated our country's early colonial history, we are all caught up in it. To signify that it no longer belongs exclusively to Protestants or Puritans, we call it the work-sin ethic: if you work, you are good; if you don't, you are bad!

In the minds of many people, economic success and affluence are equated with goodness or at least with rightness. Even though many affluent people also play and enjoy

From *The Struggle for Significance*, 3rd ed., pp. 274–74. Eds. John H. Brennecke and Robert G. Amick, Glencoe Publishers Inc., 1980.

THE THEME

themselves, there is still a tendency in our society to consider play less important than work, and this is traceable to Puritan ideas about the importance of hard work and relative worthlessness of leisure activities.

The first paragraph of this essay explains what "the work-sin ethic" is: a belief that hard work causes success and goodness (and an afterlife in heaven) and that leisure causes failure and badness (and an afterlife in hell). The second paragraph suggests that this work-sin ethic may have caused many abuses of human rights. The word "because" introduces the third paragraph, in which the general effect of the belief is traced back to its cause, the fact that all Western people have been influenced by it. Paragraph four summarizes the idea: the Western view that work is more important than play was caused by Puritan ideas about work and play.

These four paragraphs serve as the introduction to a much longer discussion of work and leisure. By themselves, they are not a good essay; they are too general. For a good theme, facts and examples would be needed to support and clarify the ideas of paragraphs two and three.

The following essay on humor makes good use of a lengthy example to support a basic point.

READING SELECTION

HUMOR

In the face of the tensions and pressures we all face every single day, a sense of humor can be a saving grace. The ability to laugh is crucial to our fullest development, to our "mental health." And if we can laugh at ourselves, we're even further along the road to self-fulfillment.

This is not to say that it isn't important to be able to stand back and objectively evaluate yourself at times, but too much self-criticism can interfere with the development of a healthy self-concept. If you continually expect too much of yourself, tear yourself down, and are dissatisfied with everything you do, you'll have trouble finding self-respect. It's not only a great tension reliever to be able to kid yourself; it also promotes a necessary objectivity. There is a delicate balance between objectivity and subjectivity. Consider the following example.

Gordon, who is nineteen, is hoping to become a professional singer. He has a good voice, is a good musician, and has performed in public a number of times. But he's very sensitive about his abilities. For instance, if his voice coach suggests that he practice a particular song a few more times until he gets it right, Gordon falls apart, absolutely certain that the coach is implying that he isn't any good and has no future in music.

He mentioned this sensitivity in a paper he wrote for a psychology class. The psychology professor called him in, ostensibly to talk about the paper, but hoping to give the boy a

From *The Struggle for Significance*, 3rd ed., pp. 188–192. Eds. John H. Brennecke and Robert G. Amick. Copyright 1980. Reprinted by permission of Glencoe Publishers Inc.

Organizing the Details of a Theme

chance to open up about the problem. The teacher rarely told her students what they ought to do, but she felt Gordon should know that such hypersensitivity would make it difficult for him in the entertainment field, where hecklers, stage personnel, critics, and fellow performers often are very hard on new talent. She asked Gordon if he felt he had the wherewithal to follow through in such a competitive and difficult business. He was being asked to stand back from his extreme sensitivity and evaluate some realities.

Three days later, Gordon came back to the teacher, pointed a brave finger at her, and told her she was "dead wrong" about him. Further, Gordon asked, what could she possibly know about music and the pressures of the profession? The teacher stood up and turned Gordon around, right in the middle of a sentence, asking him to continue, but to watch himself in the mirror on the back of the office door as he talked. Gordon tried to go on, pointing and gesticulating, but suddenly he saw the expression on his face.

As he talked, he nervously glanced in the mirror, then turned to confront the psychologist. When he got the phrase " . . . and I have guts enough to stick with it," he noticed a grin beginning to form on the teacher's face.

At this climax of his "tantrum," Gordon burst out laughing. He stopped his tirade and asked the teacher if he looked that ridiculous all the time. The teacher shrugged and suggested that he might want to find this out from people who knew him better than she did. Gordon continued to laugh.

Seeing himself "objectively" made Gordon realize how ludicrous it was for him to take himself so seriously. In other aspects of our everyday life, the ability to catch ourselves being too serious, bearing all the burdens of the world, and trying to save the human race helps us relieve some built-up tension through laughter.

Laughter serves many other useful functions. Sometimes it is a means of releasing tension when we realize the futility of trying harder. For example, we may beat our heads against the wall trying to communicate with another individual, only to realize we are getting nowhere. But we have to accept that sometimes and with certain people communication simply isn't possible. If we can learn to laugh at situations like these, we'll find ourselves better equipped to deal with similar situations in the future.

Laughing at the misfortunes of others is occasionally a form of sadism, wherein some pleasure is gained from observing their difficulties. More often, it's simply a crude acknowledgement of how much we identify and empathize with the other person.

Most laughter is a kind of reflex behavior that occurs when we recognize the irony in situations. Life is full of little ironies. Humor enables us to "safely" experience them. There are many incongruities in life. We laugh at them partly because they are humorous or absurd and partly because we really don't know what else to do. They are "unmanageable." We can't do very much to change or utilize them. Take environmental pollution. We construct a society that depends on industry for its survival. The industry converts raw materials into products and waste. The waste is disposed of, and it often clogs the very environment we're trying to improve. We take a fishing trip to try to get back to nature. But the waters are filthy and the fish are either diseased or dead. When we realize the vicious circle that has been created, we have to shake our heads and laugh at the folly of humankind. This point was illustrated when several New York City newspapers recently suggested in all seriousness that everyone in the city should, on a specified night, refuse to turn on their lights and use candles instead in order to force the city's electric power plant to consider cutting down on its air pollution. Many people were in favor of this dramatic boycott, yet almost no one saw the absurdity of over eight million burning candles cutting down on smog—even "smokeless" candles!

Maslow indicates that this type of humor, which acknowledges the absurdity of human behavior, is healthy and is the kind of humor that the Selfactualizing person enjoys. Such people shun the hostile, morbid humor that pokes fun at cripples, minorities, or the less fortunate. "Sick" and "cruelty" jokes don't make them laugh for they contain too much tragedy and sadness. It's in the absurd lengths to which some people carry their behavior that the Self-actualized person finds humor.

Some laughter is hostile. Many comedians today are capable of biting satire. They select a person or a stereotype as the butt of their humor. When we laugh at them, we are making a commentary on our own feelings about the object of the joke, about the situation in which we live, and about ourselves. Satire has always been an effective but fairly safe means of expressing hostility toward a person, a group, or a situation. For example, Jonathan Swift's "children's tale," *Gulliver's Travels,* is actually a biting satire on the British Empire that was accepted only because it appeared in fictionalized form. Many people have never been aware of Swift's original purpose. Nor are we aware of the political satire in most of the Mother Goose nursery rhymes we learned as children.

If the object of satire feels the sting and is tempted to retaliate or at least get angry, the satirist's easy response is "What's the matter? Can't you take a joke?" Being able to take a joke is an example of "good sportsmanship." Pity the satirist, though. He may be a person who is unable to openly express hostility and deal with it in a mature fashion.

This is not to say that satire isn't an effective way to bring about social change. Many political cartoonists get their point across to politicians better than all the constituent cards and letters ever could. But it's obvious that satire, however subtle it may be, is meant to express some kind of hostility or resentment toward what's being depicted.

Laughter, then, is a necessary part of mental health. Honest joy, open amusement, and pure childlike delight are all aspects of well-developed Selfhood. In Eric Berne's terms, we are letting the Child in each of us "come out to play." The Adult in us is too often serious, stuffy, and objective—busy with the data processing of daily existence. The Parent in us is often busy judging what we do as right or wrong, good or evil, appropriate or inappropriate. The Child, which is the remnant of simple, basic, sensual, open personhood, is vital to our fullest development. It's in the "play" activities—like sports, hobbies, art, lovemaking, eating, and dancing—that we experience this very important part of ourselves. Each of the three—Child, Adult, and Parent—is necessary, but none is more important than the others. Fortunate is the person who can watch a cartoon on TV and experience it as funny (Child), entertaining and diverting (Adult), and valuable (Parent).

Laughter is one of the ways in which we relax and recreate the Self. The things we find humorous may vary, but the experiences of humor, pleasure, and enjoyment are extremely important and must be cultivated for the fullest experience of living.

The first two paragraphs in "Humor" serve as an introduction, to state the thesis that humor causes mental health, progress toward self-fulfillment, and objective self-respect. The next six paragraphs support the points made in the introduction by providing an example of humor causing a healthy change in attitude. The rest of the essay explores some of the causes of laughter (sadistic pleasure at others' misfortunes, recognition of our own shortcomings, awareness of life's incongruities and human absurdities, and hostility toward certain people or situations) and implies the effect of most laughter: greater well-being. The conclusion summarizes the basic effects of laughter and humor: a healthy growth toward self-awareness.

In this essay the general subject, humor, is seen as both a cause and an effect, and the essay follows that mode of organization: cause-effect-cause.

The organization of the next essay, "Changing Managerial Roles," also follows a cause and effect model, but it follows a pattern of effect-cause-effect rather than cause-effect-cause.

READING SELECTION

CHANGING MANAGERIAL ROLES
by Bettye B. Swanson

A role is a set of related activities or behavior patterns that fulfill the expectations of others in given contexts. Roles result in a general degree of predictability of behavior in recurring, frequently encountered situations. Organizations prescribe official task roles through job titles and descriptions, but roles also have a more informal content consisting of the expectations of superiors, subordinates, peers, or even customers or suppliers. In a given society, people come to learn a number of socially acceptable roles, which are drawn upon almost automatically to meet frequently occurring situations; in the same way, people learn useful roles in organizations.

The complexity of the manager's role arises from the varied sources of expectations. Some of the demands come from the external environment, some from technical aspects of the work, others from internal associations and conditions, and still others from the manager's own view of his tasks. Moreover, the demands may be in substantial conflict with each other. Therefore, managers face the problem of synthesizing and rationalizing these role demands. They must also select appropriate roles, and shift from one to another to meet ongoing situations. Organizations as well as managers need the stability and predictability that derive from skillful role performance, but the formal and informal pressures of expectations dictate resilience and flexibility on the manager's part.

CHANGES IN BASIC ROLES

The external and internal conditions affecting managerial roles are continuously changing. Expectations, technology, and managers change; therefore roles also change. Some important roles have undergone substantial change over time. The role of owner was once very important in the business enterprise. The owner was closely involved

From *Introduction to Home Management*, p. 48–50. Copyright 1981. Reprinted by permission of Macmillan Publishing Co. Inc.

with the company's day-to-day activities. Now, in corporations at least, the ownership role is diffused among many stockholders who act through elected boards of directors. Direct owner influence is minimal in large organizations and in many small ones.

Like the role of the owner, the leader's role too has changed. Great leaders have been replaced by organizationally created leaders. Whereas such men as Ford, Rockefeller, Sloan, Chrysler, and others were few in number but prominent, powerful, wealthy, and influential, leaders today are more numerous, and they appear at every level. They are the product of corporate training programs and professional schools. Leadership is expected of the newest supervisor as well as of the highest executive.

As some roles change or disappear, others come into being. As "great leaders" were superseded by trained leaders, and as organizations grew in size and complexity, the manager's role became more bureaucratic. *Bureaucracy* refers to the highly rational, systematic, hierarchical organization structure, and to the accompanying assumptions that most organizations employ today. Managers occupy assigned positions in the hierarchy, with corresponding duties and rewards. The manager's primary role is to participate in the system according to its well-developed rules. The content of the manager's various roles is based on the logic of task requirements and on the demands of the hierarchical system. Roles typically involve considerable specialization of task or function. Bureaucratic roles tend to be somewhat independent of the role occupant, so that managers may change but the organization's needs continue to be met. Many organizations today are trying to reduce the emphasis on bureaucratic roles, replacing them with roles more oriented to innovation, employee participation, and involvement.

Male and female roles are changing rapidly in the light of society's pressure to achieve equality of status and treatment of men and women, and laws that seek to eliminate discrimination on the basis of sex. Roles that were traditionally male or female are now being redesigned to remove the male-female dimension from them. By law, with few exceptions, jobs may not be limited solely to men or women.

In addition to change, an important characteristic of roles is that they can be both learned and taught. A great deal of educational activity, both formal and informal, is centered upon the cultivation of appropriate roles. Many roles are learned through observation and imitation. The performance of a role is often automatic and subtle rather than consciously contrived. An example is the "bedside manner" of the physician.

Finally, it is important to note that managers play a number of roles all at once, or change roles to fit different situations. The existence of multiple roles is usually not a problem, because people have learned the roles that are the most useful in the typical situations they confront; thus an individual may take roles as a parent, a son or daughter, a teacher, a spouse, or a boss.

| **EXERCISES** |

1. Outline the causes and effects discussed in the essay on management roles and write a one-paragraph summary of the main ideas.
2. The traditional roles of women in the United States are changing. After

formulating a brief outline of two or three of the traditional roles of women, write a theme explaining them.

3. Using the same outline you used for exercise 2, write a theme discussing a man's ability to fulfill the traditionally women's roles.

As you read the following two essays, take notes on the thesis idea of each one and on the cause-effect relationships of the supporting ideas.

READING SELECTION

I WANT OUT
by Sheryl Coston

Twelve years ago, I made a deliberate and painstakingly objective decision regarding a career choice. I considered all my options, examined my capabilities and emotions, then chose nursing. It appeared to satisfy all of my needs and goals for an ideal profession. Today, however, like many of my colleagues, I want out!

Last year alone, more nurses left the profession than entered it. Their reasons ranged from nursing policies being made by non-nursing personnel to inadequate salaries. They named poor scheduling techniques and mandatory overtime as particular areas of conflict. They felt that their ideas and input were negated merely because they were women. Frustration is a word heard frequently among those of us who are leaving.

I have personally felt extreme frustration from these problems. My most recent experience involved changing jobs and finding that, as a Registered Nurse with nine years experience, I would make $2.00 less an hour than the housekeeping person who emptied the trash on the unit. I was told that this was due to the housekeeping staff being listed as specialists. I wondered what I was!

Nursing, as a typically female profession, must also deal constantly with the false impression that nurses are there to wait on the physician. We are licensed by the state in which we practice to provide nursing care only. We do not have any legal or moral obligation to any physician. Nurses provide health teaching, assess physical and emotional problems, coordinate patient related services, offer emotional support to patients and their families, and make all of our nursing decisions based upon what is best or appropriate for the patient. If, in any circumstance, we feel that a physician's order is inappropriate or unsafe, we have a legal responsibility to question that order or refuse to carry it out. We are independent practitioners under the law and we must be allowed to practice as such.

Nursing is not a nine to five job with every weekend off. All nurses are aware of that before they enter the profession. The emotional and physical stress, however, that occurs due to odd working hours is a prime reason for a lot of the career dissatisfaction. It is sometimes mandated that we work overtime and that we change shifts as many as four or five times in a two week period. That disturbs our personal lives, disrupts our

A student theme, reprinted by permission.

sleeping and eating habits and isolates us from everything except job-related friends and activities.

The quality of nursing care is being affected dramatically by these situations. Most hospitals are now staffed by new graduates, as experienced nurses finally give up trying to change the system or "bum out" from frustration. Consumers of medically related services have evidently not been affected enough yet to demand changes in our medical system. But if trends continue as predicted, they will find that most critical hospital care will be provided by new, inexperienced and sometimes inadequately trained R.N.'s. These nurses will be overworked, underpaid, and poorly prepared to care for patients and their families.

Because of my values, I can no longer conscienciously function in the sytem as it is today. I do not feel my standards are too high nor too idealistic. It is merely the fact that I still have them.

READING SELECTION

INFANTRY VS. TANKS
by Daniel John Bilodeau

On the eve of the Second World War, one could say that the allies could afford to be smug, because of their superior industrial capabilities, and, therefore, the ability to out-produce the Germans in tanks. Tanks were the weapon with which the Nazis hoped to win the war, but they had fewer tanks than the Allies. France alone had a slight supe-riority in numbers. Add to this the small, but growing contingent of British armored vehicles, and one definitely gets the picture of Allied superiority in numbers. Not only here did the West boast a lead. By and large the bulk of French armor was more heavily armored, better gunned than all but the heaviest of the German tanks. Rounding out this perspective, the Soviet Union alone (at worst a neutral, at best a potential ally of the West) had the potential to outproduce the Germans in tanks. Why, then, were the Germans able to achieve results which were obviously far beyond their industrial capa-bilities?

The answer lies in the technological edge which they had developed over the rest of Europe in the methods of conducting mechanized warfare. Whereas the Western Allied armies valued the infantry as the attacking weapon, the Germans used their tanks as the offensive spearheads. These traits from both sides would lead to peculiar charac-teristics from both armies. Because the West put the burden on their infantry, their tanks were relegated to a secondary role, usually mixed with the artillery, robbing this armor of its mobility. The ability of these armies to maneuver rapidly and plug up trouble spots quickly was also very poor, because everything depended on the speed of the foot sol-dier. The German armies' characteristic, however, was almost the converse of this. Because they relied on tanks as the weapons of their advance, two things were true. First, instead of dispersing their tanks, they massed them, because it was the tank, not the infantry, which made the breakthrough. The Western Allies' habit of dispersing their

A student theme, reprinted by permission.

tanks with artillery in support of the infantry played into the Germans' hands in that there were never enough tanks in the area of the breakthrough to have much of an effect on the onrushing German armor. In the cases where the Germans did run into trouble, their air force, which had swept the skies clean of Allied aircraft, was used as a highly mobile artillery to bail out the armor. The other characteristic that greatly facilitated the Germans' attack was their speed once they had broken through. Having a great mobile superiority over the Western infantry armies, once the Nazis had broken through they could quickly attack the West's undefended supply lines and choke off the supplies that would be needed for the fight in the field. Because of the slowness of the Allied armies, there was no hope of their getting to the breakthrough area quickly enough to intervene.

The common denominator in all these tactics that the German Army employed was quickness, so it should not be surprising that they began to take Europe in such a short period of time. Poland fell in two weeks, the "invincible" French (along with the Low Countries, Norway, and Denmark) in six weeks. Even in the difficult and mountainous terrain of Yugoslavia and Greece (which had the aid of a British military expedition), armed resistance was put down in less than a week. The mechanized revolution in warfare had burst like a storm out of Germany, and now Europe lay at her feet.

If indeed speed was Germany's weapon, then time must have been the weapon of her opponents. Up until now Germany had not given her enemies time to bring in the full potential of their resources. However, this changed somewhat with Great Britain. The Royal Navy kept the hungry Panzers away, and gave England time. England's being safe from Nazi attack would also give the United States time to build up the British Isles when the U.S. would finally enter the war.

Seeing that they could not invade England, and also seeing that time was now working against them, the Germans turned their finely honed mechanized weapon against the Soviet Union, in hopes of a quick victory and vast quantities of raw materials. The story was the same as the previous year in the West. Russian superiority in numbers was negated by the obsolete methods they employed. The Germans made rapid advances and destroyed much Russian equipment, with the loss of many Russian lives. There was one difference, though, from the previous battles with the West. The Soviet Union was a much larger area than the West, and because of this the Nazis found it impossible to overrun the country quickly enough to prevent the Soviets from mobilizing the full weight of their industry. In time, the Soviets would also begin to learn the methods of mechanized warfare.

Now that the war would be a long one, the Allies would be able to bring the superior weight of their industry to bear on Germany. Time would also mean that the technological gap would disappear and, along with it, Germany's choice of winning the conflict.

EXERCISES

1. List the transitional words and phrases in the preceding essays and compare the frequency of occurrence of each type. Discuss how a carefully placed "because" or "reason" or "result" clarifies the cause/effect relationship between sets of events.

2. Make a list of all the synonyms in the essays for "cause" and for "effect" and be prepared to discuss the authors choices of each one (e.g., to avoid repetition, to clarify the relationship between a cause and its effect, or to emphasize an event or occurrence, etc.)

3. Be prepared to write and discuss an outline of each essay that shows how cause and effect organization supports each thesis statement.

4. Write a theme on one of the following subjects, beginning with an introduction that discusses, defines, exemplifies, or illustrates a cause and continuing with carefully developed paragraphs which examine various effects of that cause. A pointedly worded thesis statement will effectively narrow the subject and provide a central focus for all the paragraphs.

    a. a professor's teaching methods
    b. a question on an exam
    c. a chapter in a book
    d. a term paper assignment
    e. a required course

MIXED ORDER

Many themes follow more than one model. Chronology and space order frequently occur together; categorization may appear with comparison and contrast or with cause and effect; and a comparison/contrast may help to explain a cause and effect discussion. ("If cause x had not occurred, effect y would/should not have happened.") Also, a particular model of organization may be interrupted at various points by paragraphs of example, illustration, definition, and so on. Planning a theme by considering the numerous possibilities for organizing the ideas makes the difference between a mixed-order theme and a jumble of paragraphs lacking coherent order.

In the paragraphs of the following essay, examples provide the supporting details, and they are organized within each paragraph according to a comparison-and-contrast model. The organization of the essay as a whole mixes categorization with cause and effect. An outline of the essay looks like this:

   I. Introduction. "My home town has changed."
  II. Categorization of the changes
     A. Sights
     B. Sounds
     C. People (two paragraphs)
     D. Food and clothes
     E. Distance and time
 III. Technology as a cause of change
     A. Introduction
     B. Transportation (two paragraphs)

C. Business

D. Electricity

IV. Material changes as a cause of social change

A. Release

B. Discipline

C. Escape (two paragraphs)

D. Good will

V. Conclusion. Thesis: "It is personal freedom that makes us better persons. . . . There is no real freedom without privacy, and [now] a resident of [Velva, North Dakota] can be a private person much more than he could before."

READING SELECTION

VELVA, NORTH DAKOTA
by Eric Sevareid

Paragraph 1. My home town has changed in these thirty years of the American story. It is changing now, will go on changing as America changes. Its biography, I suspect, would read much the same as that of all other home towns. Depression and war and prosperity have all left their marks; modern science, modern taste, manners, philosophies, fears and ambitions have touched my town as indelibly as they have touched New York or Panama City.

Paragraph 2. Sights have changed; there is a new precision about street and home, a clearing away of chicken yards, cow barns, pigeon-crested cupolas, weed lots and coulees, the dim and secret adult-free rendezvous of boys. An intricate metal "jungle gym" is a common backyard sight, the sack swing uncommon. There are wide expanses of clear windows designed to let in the parlor light, fewer ornamental windows of colored glass designed to keep it out. Attic and screen porch are slowly vanishing and lovely shades of pastel are painted upon new houses, tints that once would have embarrassed farmer and merchant alike.

Paragraph 3. Sounds have changed; I heard not once the clopping of a horse's hoof, nor the mourn of a coyote. I heard instead the shriek of brakes, the heavy throbbing of the one-a-day Braniff airliner into Minot, the shattering sirens born of war, the honk of a diesel locomotive which surely cannot call to faraway places the heart of a wakeful boy like the old steam whistle in the night. You can walk down the street of my town now and hear from open windows the intimate voices of the Washington commentators in casual converse on the great affairs of state; but you cannot hear on Sunday morning the singing in Norwegian of the Lutheran hymns; the old country seems now part of a world left long behind and the old-country accents grow fainter in the speech of my Velva neighbors.

Paragraph 4. The people have not changed, but the *kinds* of people have changed: there is no longer an official, certified town drunk, no longer a "Crazy John," spitting

From *This is Eric Sevareid*, pp. 215-219. Copyright © 1964 by Eric Sevareid. Reprinted by permission of Harold Matson Company, Inc.

THE THEME

his worst epithet, "rotten chicken legs" as you hurriedly passed him by. People so sick are now sent to places of proper care. No longer is there an official town joker, like the druggist MacKnight, who would spot a customer in the front of the store, have him called to the phone, then slip to the phone behind the prescription case, and imitate the man's wife to perfection with orders to bring home more bread and sausage and Cream of Wheat. No longer anyone like the early attorney, J. L. Lee, who sent fabulous dispatches to that fabulous tabloid, the *Chicago Blade,* such as his story of the wild man captured on the prairie and chained to the wall in the drugstore basement. (This, surely, was Velva's first notoriety; inquiries came from anthropologists all over the world.)

Paragraph 5. No, the "characters" are vanishing in Velva, just as they are vanishing in our cities, in business, in politics. The "well-rounded, socially integrated" personality that the progressive schoolteachers are so obsessed with is increasing rapidly, and I am not at all sure that this is good. Maybe we need more personalities with knobs and handles and rugged lumps of individuality. They may not make life more smooth; more interesting they surely make it.

Paragraph 6. They eat differently in Velva now: there are frozen fruits and sea food and exotic delicacies we only read about in novels in those meat-and-potato days. They dress differently. The hard white collars of the businessmen are gone with the shiny alpaca coats. There are comfortable tweed now, and casual blazers with a touch in their colors of California, which seems so close in time and distance.

Paragraph 7. It is distance and time that have changed the most and worked the deepest changes in Velva's life. The telephone, the car, the smooth highway, radio and television are consolidating the entities of our country. The county seat of Towner now seems no closer than the state capital of Bismarck; the voices and concerns of Presidents, French premiers and Moroccan pashas are no farther away than the portable radio on Aunt Jessey's kitchen table. The national news magazines are stacked each week in Harold Anderson's drugstore beside the soda fountain, and the excellent *Minot Daily News* smells hot from the press each afternoon.

Paragraph 8. Consolidation. The nearby hamlets of Sawyer and Logan and Voltaire had their own separate banks and papers and schools in my days of dusty buggies and Model T's marooned in the snowdrifts. Now these hamlets are dying. A bright yellow bus takes the Voltaire kids to Velva each day for high school. Velva has grown—from 800 to 1,300—because the miners from the Truax coal mine can commute to their labors each morning and the nearby farmers can live in town if they choose. Minot has tripled in size to 30,000. Once the "Magic City" was a distant and splendid Baghdad, visited on special occasions long prepared for. Now it is a twenty-five minute commuter's jump away. So P. W. Miller and Jay Louis Monicken run their businesses in Minot but live on in their old family homes in Velva. So Ray Michelson's two girls on his farm to the west drive up each morning to their jobs as maids in Minot homes. Aunt Jessey said, "Why, Saturday night I counted sixty-five cars just between here and Sawyer, all going up to the show in Minot."

Paragraph 9. The hills are prison battlements no longer; the prairies no heart-sinking barrier, but a passageway free as the swelling ocean, inviting you to sail home and away at your whim and your leisure. (John and Helen made an easy little jount of 700 miles that weekend to see their eldest daughter in Wyoming.)

Paragraph 10. Consolidation. Art Kumm's bank serves a big region now; its assets are $2,000,000 to $3,000,000 instead of the $200,000 or $300,000 in my father's day. Eighteen farms near Velva are under three ownerships now. They calculate in sections; "acres" is an almost forgotten term. Aunt Jessey owns a couple of farms, and she knows they are much better run. "It's no longer all take out and no put in," she said. "Folks strip farm now; they know all about fertilizers. They care for it and they'll hand on the land in good shape." The farmers gripe about their cash income, and not without reason at the moment, but they will admit that life is good compared with those days of drought and foreclosure, manure banked against the house for warmth, the hand pump frozen at 30 below and the fitful kerosene lamp on the kitchen table. Electrification has done much of this, eased back-breaking chores that made their wives old as parchment at forty, brought life and music and the sound of human voices into their parlors at night.

Paragraph 11. And light upon the prairie. "From the hilltop," said Aunt Jessey, "the farms look like stars at night."

Paragraph 12. Many politicians deplore the passing of the old family-size farm, but I am not so sure. I saw around Velva a release from what was like slavery to the tyrannical soil, release from the ignorance that darkens the soul and from the loneliness that corrodes it. In this generation my Velva friends have rejoined the general American society that their pioneering fathers left behind when they first made the barren trek in the days of the wheat rush. As I sit here in Washington writing this, I can feel their nearness. I never felt it before save in my dreams.

Paragraph 13. But now I must ask myself: Are they nearer to one another? And the answer is no; yet I am certain that this is good. The shrinking of time and distance has made contrast and relief available to their daily lives. They do not know one another quite so well because they are not so much obliged to. I know that democracy rests upon social discipline, which in turn rests upon personal discipline; passions checked, hard words withheld, civic tasks accepted, work well done, accountings honestly rendered. The old-fashioned small town was this discipline in its starkest, most primitive form; without this discipline the small town would have blown itself apart.

Paragraph 14. For personal and social neuroses festered under this hard scab of conformity. There was no place to go, no place to let off steam; few dared to voice unorthodox ideas, read strange books, admire esoteric art or publicly write or speak of their dreams and their soul's longings. The world was not "too much with us," the world was too little with us and we were too much with one another.

Paragraph 15. The door to the world stands open now, inviting them to leave anytime they wish. It is the simple fact of the open door that makes all the difference; with its opening the stale air rushed out. So, of course, the people themselves do not have to leave, because, as the stale air went out, the fresh air came in.

Paragraph 16. Human nature is everywhere the same. He who is not forced to help his neighbor for his own existence will not only give him help, but his true good will as well. Minot and its hospital are now close at hand, but the people of Velva put their purses together, built their own clinic and homes for the two young doctors they persuaded to come and live among them. Velva has no organized charity, but when a farmer falls ill, his neighbors get in his crop; if a townsman has a financial catastrophe his personal friends raise a fund to help him out. When Bill's wife, Ethel, lay dying so long in the Minot hospital and nurses were not available, Helen and others took turns driving up there just to sit with her so she would know in her gathering dark that friends were at hand.

Paragraph 17. It is personal freedom that makes us better persons, and they are freer in Velva now. There is no real freedom without privacy, and a resident of my home town can be a private person much more than he could before. People are able to draw at least a little apart from one another. In drawing apart, they gave their best human instincts room for expansion.

EXERCISES

1. The comparisons and contrasts in the preceding theme are implied, rather than stated directly. Make a list of the sights, sounds, people, food, and clothes of the past which are contrasted with those of the present in paragraphs 2–6.
2. In paragraph 16, the author states, "He who is not forced to help his neighbor for his own existence will not only give him help, but his true good will as well." What does he mean? How do the examples in the paragraph support the statement?
3. The thesis statement does not appear until the final paragraph of the essay. Why didn't the author state the main idea in the introductory paragraph?
4. The author chose to present his ideas by mixing the two models of organization. Is this effective? How could the first six paragraphs be altered to follow a cause/effect model? What would be lost or changed if they were altered?
5. Which organizational models are mixed in the following theme?

READING SELECTION

TRADE NEEDS MONEY

In the cradle of Western civilization, around the Mediterranean Sea, many early civilized people used cattle as a measure of wealth. When seaborne commerce became increasingly important with the rise of merchant nations on the Mediterranean shore, something more portable than cattle was needed to carry on the thriving commerce. Furthermore, in such an expanded market system not every commodity used as money in a local self-sufficient tribal economy would be acceptable by merchants of different nations.

Although many of these Mediterranean civilizations displayed warlike tendencies, others were interested in expanding their wealth and influence through trading. The first of these merchant, or shopkeeper, nations was averred by the ancient historian Herodotus to be Lydia. Inasmuch as merchants needed a medium of exchange to carry on their commerce, it is not surprising that King Midas of Lydia was the first sovereign to put his imprint on ingots of gold, thus giving civilization its first coins. These early gold

From Money, Banking, and The Economy, 4th ed. pp. 20-21 by John A. Cochrane. Reprinted with permission of Macmillan Publishing Co. Inc. Copyright © 1979 by John A. Cochrane.

coins possessed all the characteristics of desirable money and became widely accepted in trade.

It has been said that gold is the "natural standard of merchants." Certainly, gold was used very early in trade among merchants; but among the common people, silver or baser metals were more likely to serve in hand-to-hand circulation. Alfred Marshall, the great English economist of the nineteenth century, suggested that silver and money were almost synonymous terms throughout most of history and that silver was the dominant basis of currency in most of the world prior to the discoveries of gold in Australia and California in the nineteenth century. Some nations alternated between a monetary system based on one or the other of these two precious metals, or a system combining them in some manner.

Nations often resorted to gold or silver, or both, as their monetary base, because these precious metals possessed in great measure certain basic monetary characteristics needed by a commodity used as money in an expanded market. These desirable characteristics of money are (1) portability, (2) durability, (3) divisibility, and (4) general acceptability.

The earliest forms of money did not always possess all these characteristics. Soft commodities obviously were not as durable as gold, silver, or stones. Larger stones, however, were not very portable. Only through much trial and error did crude forms of money evolve into more sophisticated monetary systems that were suitable for widespread production and trading activities. The evolution of different forms of money in England illustrates some of the stages through which money has changed its form, as economic organization itself has developed into a more elaborate market system.

The title of the following essay, "Population Trends and Education," suggests that the author is concerned with the effect of population shifts on education. The reader expects to find cause/effect organization, and in fact does, but cause/effect is not the only model used: the author has mixed cause/effect with chronology and categorization.

READING SELECTION

POPULATION TRENDS AND EDUCATION

EFFECT OF INCREASED BIRTH RATE ON AMERICAN SCHOOLS

Changes in population will naturally change or influence the schools. The babies of yesterday become the pupils of today and tomorrow. The lower birth rate during the 1930's produced smaller classes, just as the booming birth rate following World War II brought about a flood that engulfed the schools. The tidal wave hit the high schools in the early 1960's; by 1965 it had pressed on the colleges. Merely to maintain the style

From *The School in American Society*, 3rd ed. pp. 416–420. Copyright 1973, Eds. Ralph L. Pounds James R. Bryner. Reprinted by permission of Macmillan Publishing Co. Inc.

THE THEME

of education of the immediate past more classrooms and more teachers had to be provided. The current oversupply of teachers is due in part to limited finances, which prevent expansion. We must consider greater possibilities in adult education and expansion of educational services in quantity and diversity even if our population were stabilized.

Of great importance to educators and to all citizens is the number of children who are of school age. Nonpublic institutions are quite sensitive to economic conditions, and so the continuing rise in their enrollments depends upon continuing prosperity and their ability to meet rising education unit costs.

By 1978 the high school enrollment will increase to 87 per cent more than that of 1958. Today over 90 per cent of the adolescents of high school age are actually in school; about 88 per cent will graduate. It is estimated that college enrollment will be 232 per cent more in 1978 than in 1958, with 68 per cent of all high school graduates going on to college! Over half of these will complete their college degrees.

All of these facts show clearly that the schools must provide more classroom space and more teachers, and this takes more tax money. The problem has been heightened by past troubles. From 1930 to 1940 the schools did not keep up their building pace because of economies needed during the Depression; from 1940 to 1946 they fell behind because of the increased birth rate.

The problem is complex. With more people over sixty-five years of age, there may be competition for public support. As indicated earlier in this chapter, the population is highly mobile. The population of the West Coast increased 49 per cent in one decade, from 1940 to 1950; many rural areas have gone down 12 per cent in the same length of time. This, of course, affects the school population directly. One-fourth of all school children moved from at least one county to another. Besides the trend to the West, there is a strong one from the South to the North. Suburban industrial areas have grown greatly, with the result that schools in some sections are more hard pressed than those in others.

In 1970 teacher supply caught up with demand for elementary and secondary school teachers in most fields. This was due to a slackening of demand as well as an increased supply because of expanded university enrollment.

IMPLICATION OF POPULATION PROBLEMS FOR EDUCATION

The first and most obvious implication of the population problems for education grows out of the effect of the birth rate on the elementary and secondary schools. The problem of providing an adequate number of teachers from the young adult population, at low ebb because of the reduced birth rate of the 1930's, was extremely difficult during the late 1950's and early 1960's. By 1955 the increase in number of persons in college made it much more easy to solve this problem, but there were other factors that contributed to the lack of teachers in a great number of areas of teaching, such as elementary education and mathematics and science. One of these was the competition for the college graduates in areas that were more remunerative than that of teaching.

By far the most difficult implications for the period of the late 1960's and on into the era of 1970's related to the problem of the expanding college. The amount of money necessary to build the buildings, to enlarge the campuses, to provide the additional equipment, and so forth, for the large number of students entering college is enormous. The colleges and universities had expanded greatly between 1950 and 1965 because an increased percentage of the population had become interested in going to college. Then the "population bulge" hit the colleges, thereby necessitating even more expansion.

The problem of getting adequate and competent staff at all levels remains great. However, in 1970 the teacher supply and demand situation had reversed at the elementary and secondary levels and, at least at the Ph.D. level, was much less critical for colleges and universities.

Another implication arises from the kind of education to be given in the world of the future. One of the things that makes the educational problem much more acute is the extent to which people desire more schooling. From less than 10 per cent of persons going to college before 1930, the figure had risen to more than 40 per cent in 1965 and will eventually go higher than the over 50 per cent of the population in 1970. Similarly, the percentage going to high school has risen to more than 90. This demand for education is proper in the light of the greater complexity of our world and the necessity of training to live in it and cope with its problems. The unbelievable expansion of human knowledge in the past few years and the inability of people to secure this knowledge merely from casual contacts with their culture present an unanswerable argument for the necessity for more education.

Still another implication arises from the necessity of providing schooling for a much longer period of time. The population trends point toward a need for additional educational or quasieducational facilities for persons aged sixty-five or over. In many cases there may be a necessity for reeducating these people to live a different kind of life after their work period has passed, to help them face the many additional years of life in which, under our present family structure, they must depend largely upon their own resources. The challenge for this kind of education for the aged is very great.

The challenges faced by the schools seem unsurmountable: rapidly swelling enrollments, limited teacher supply, inadequate numbers of classrooms, inadequate facilities in classrooms, the need for the extension of education, a challenge to improve education better to fit the conditions of the changing world, and an immediate need to improve the high school to meet the needs of the great heterogeneous mass of individuals now presenting themselves for education. The situation seems to be an almost impossible one to meet, even for a country as wealthy as the United States. It certainly means that we must put an increasing amount of our energies, money, and time into the enterprise of education.

EXERCISE

The preceding essay was written a decade ago. The main problem facing educators in the U.S. today is too few students for the available facilities, personnel, and financial support from state and federal government. The baby boom discussed in the essay has now graduated from college and there are fewer students of college age than there were ten years ago. Another factor affecting enrollment in educational institutions is the economy: rising inflation and unemployment have raised the cost of education while simultaneously lowering the number of people who can afford to pay for it. Write an outline for a theme that would mix cause and effect organization with comparison and contrast organization to discuss the similarities and differences between the challenges of education ten years ago and those of today.

Both of the following essays mix organizational models, using chronology, cause and effect, and categorization to clarify the main idea. The first one explains a term familiar to mathematicians, prime numbers. Non-mathematicians may prefer to ignore it and read just the second essay, which discusses college families.

READING SELECTION

THE PRIMES
by Sherman K. Stein

When there were only 48 states in the Union, the United States flag had 6 rows of 8 stars. Forty-nine states could be represented by 7 rows of 7 stars. Fifty states could be shown in a rectangular array of 2 rows of 25 stars or 5 rows of 10. Fifty-one could be shown as 3 rows of 17; 52 as 2 rows of 26 or as 4 rows of 13. But 53 would be quite troublesome. The only flag of 53 stars in which each row has the same number of stars is a 1 by 53 flag. The number 53 is troublesome because it is not the product of two smaller natural numbers; it is an example of a "prime number." So is 47. This chapter is devoted to the prime numbers, which are important both in theory and in practice.

In order to define the primes formally, we shall need the notion of the divisors of a natural number. A natural number A divides a natural number B if there is a natural number Q such that B is the product of Q and A,

$$B = QA$$

If A divides B, we call A a divisor of B and B a multiple of A. Thus 6 has four divisors, 1, 2, 3, and 6; and the multiples of 2 are precisely the even numbers. Any natural number A is a divisor of O, since $O = O \times A$. The only natural number with precisely one divisor is the number 1. Any other natural number has at least two divisors, namely itself and 1. The natural numbers with only two divisors are called the primes. The reader may check that the first twenty primes are

2, 3, 5, 7, 11, 13, 19, 23, 29, 31, 37, 41, 43, 47, 53, 59, 61, 67, 71

and may easily extend this brief list. A prime can also be described as a natural number (larger than 1) that is not the product of two smaller natural numbers.

From *Mathematics: The Man-Made Universe* by Sherman K. Stein. W. H. Freeman and Company. Copyright © 1976.

As we compute more and more primes, various questions may come to mind. How many primes are there? Calling two primes adjacent if there is no prime between them, we may ask, "How far apart can adjacent primes be?" (In the above list the largest gap between adjacent primes is 6.) How many pairs of primes differ by 1 (for examples, 2 and 3)? How many pairs of primes differ by 2 (for examples, 3 and 5, 5 and 7, 11 and 13)? How many pairs of primes differ by 3 (for example, 2 and 5)? How many pairs of primes differ by 4 (for example, 3 and 7, 7 and 11)? Some of these questions can be answered easily, but others are so hard that nobody knows the answers. Let us take them up one by one.

The first question—"How many primes are there"?—was answered by the Greeks some 2,300 years ago. Their solution, which appears as Proposition 20 in Book 9 of Euclid, is based on a theory that they developed, which we will call the Prime-manufacturing Machine. When anyone feeds primes into this machine, it spews out brand new primes—primes that are different from those fed into it. First watch it in operation; we will explain afterward why it always works.

Let us feed the machine the primes 3, 5 and 11, which are chosen at random. The machine multiplies them all together, getting 165. Then it adds 1 to this result, getting 166. Then it produces all the primes that divide 166; namely, 2 and 83. We see that 2 and 83 are indeed brand new, being different from the three primes fed into the machine.

The reader may check that when the machine is given the primes 2, 3, and 5 it produces just the one new prime, 31. That the primes manufactured by the machine are indeed different from those fed into it is the content of Theorem 1, which depends on the first part of the following lemma.

Lemma. If a natural number D divides each of two natural numbers A and B, then D divides their difference, $A - B$, and their sum, $A + B$.

Proof. By the definition of "divides," there are integers Q_1 and Q_2 such that

$$A = Q_1 D \text{ and } B = Q_2 D.$$

Thus

$$A - B = Q_1 D - Q_2 D + (Q_1 - Q_2)D.$$

Since $Q_1 - Q_2$ is an integer and $A - B = (Q_1 - Q_2)D$, we conclude that D divides $A - B$. (A similar argument shows that D divides $A + B$.)

Theorem 1. Any prime dividing the natural number that is 1 larger than the product of several primes is different from any of those primes.

Proof. Let us, like Adam naming the creatures, give names to the several primes in question so that we can speak of them. If we called them $A, B, C, \ldots Z$, then we would limit ourselves to feeding the machine at most twenty-six primes. We can avoid this artificial limit by naming the first prime fed into the machine F_1 (the letter F standing for Feed), the second prime fed into the machine F_2, and so on. When we feed the machine twenty-seven primes we name them

$$F_1, F_2, \ldots, F_{27}.$$

Now let us feed the machine N primes,

$$F_1, F_2, \ldots, F_N.$$

The machine forms their product $F_1, F_2, \ldots F_N$ and then adds 1 to this product to obtain the natural number

$$1 + F_1 F_2 \ldots F_N,$$

which we call M. Thus

$$M = 1 + F_1 F_2 \ldots F_N.$$

We must prove that none of the primes $F_1, F_2, \ldots F_N$ divides M. To do this, we first observe that no natural number larger than 1 can divide two natural numbers that differ by 1, for as the lemma shows, when a natural number divides two natural numbers it also divides their difference. Now, each of the $F_1, F_2, \ldots F_N$ clearly divides the product $F_1 F_2 \ldots F_N$. Hence none of the F's can divide the natural number M, which is one larger than $F_1 F_2 \ldots F_N$. Thus the machine produces only new primes. Our proof is complete.

READING SELECTION

THE COLLEGE FAMILY
by Bettye B. Swanson

Following World War II many college and university administrators found that in order to meet the housing needs of their students, a different type of housing unit had to be constructed. The veterans from World War II were returning to the college campuses and they were bringing with them their families. The need for married student housing began with these veterans and has continued.

Many college campuses, particularly urban and community colleges, along with specialized training schools, have a high percentage of married students. An ever increasing number of young couples are choosing to combine parenthood with the attainment of their college education. Although the vast majority of these students are under twenty-five, many colleges and universities are finding an ever-increasing number of older women who are returning to or entering college for the first time.

The college family may consist of two full-time students, one full-time student who is being financially supported by the other partner, or a student who enrolls in classes to increase personal knowledge. These students may be enrolled in graduate or undergraduate programs. Regardless of their status within the educational institution, there are inherent problems which exist and therefore set them apart from the other family units. Some are full-time students throughout the academic year. Others attend only evening or summer session courses. The actual status of the college student will have a direct bearing upon the management taking place. Regardless of the enrollment status

From *Introduction to Home Management*, pp. 280-281. Copyright 1981. Reprinted by permission of Macmillan Publishing Co. Inc.

of the college student, each is striving to meet the demands of being a student and the demands of a family member.

Categorization and space order provide the unity of the following essay describing primitive money.

READING SELECTION

PRIMITIVE MONEY

Even before metals were available in sufficient quantity to provide a crude monetary system, primitive man found it necessary and desirable to have money of sorts. Each primitive group's distinctive money often depended upon the nature of its livelihood. Useful commodities common to a particular culture were often used, so that a hunting society would use the skins of wild animals for money. A pastoral culture often used livestock, whereas agricultural communities often used grain and foodstuffs. Almost every useful commodity was probably used by some group somewhere as money. These early moneys are not completely forgotten, as evidenced by the fact that a number of modern money terms derive from some of the ancient forms of money. For example, the modern word *pecuniary* comes from the Latin *pecus* for cattle. Similarly, *salary* derives from the Latin word for salt, *salarium.* Both salt and cattle were used as money at different times in ancient Rome.

On the American continent, certain Indian tribes used wampum, a beaded belt of seashells, as money. Some Indian tribes even used woodpecker scalps as money, and among the plains Indians, buffalo hides were common currency. Horses were also used as a measure of wealth and for trading purposes among many Indian tribes.

In Africa cattle were most commonly regarded as a store of wealth and were available to buy other useful commodities, such as wives. In the Pacific islands of Melanesia, pigs were the desired form of wealth. Snouts and ears of animals were used as currency in early Russia, whereas even in the twentieth century, squirrel skins have continued to be used as a medium of exchange in Mongolia. Shells and beads of all sorts and colors have been used in various regions of the world, although certain tribes have had a marked preference for particular shapes and colors. Another tribe, even close by, might have a different monetary preference. Feather money was used in the South Banks Islands of the Pacific. Cubes of salt and animal skins were often used by different cultures for exchange purposes. Spears, fishhooks, bits of wire, and many other useful articles have also served in various parts of the world in place of direct barter of goods.

Whatever useful commodity is used as money in a given primitive society, some form of money is needed to fulfill commercial or trade needs and non-commercial needs, such as those required to make payments for marriage purposes. In either case, the emphasis is on money as a medium of exhange . . . The noncommercial uses of money, which some anthropologists say first developed in early primitive societies, included not only

From *Money, Banking and the Economy,* 4th ed. pp. 19-20 by John A. Cochrane. Reprinted with permission of Macmillan Publishing Co. Inc. Copyright © 1979 by John A.Cochrane.

THE THEME

marriage payments but payments for taxes or tribute, in sacrifices, in other religious ceremonies, in festive gifts, in blood money, in fines, in peace offerings, in funerals, in payments for skilled or sacred labor, and in ornaments and prestige tokens. As trade developed, particularly "foreign trade," the benefits of using money, rather than barter, greatly increased, particularly among the early Mediterranean peoples, some of whom settled rather early into trading cities.

Often when mixed order is used, one model is predominant. As you read each of the following three essays, note the author's method of organizing the ideas and consider its effectiveness. In "Existential Morality," the first essay, chronology is the primary mode of organization, although the essay is an extended definition of existentialism, not a history of it. Chronology is also the major, but not the only organizing device for the second essay, "Atomic Structure and the Quantum Theory." (Students who have not had a basic course in physics may prefer to skip this; it is rather technical.) The third essay mixes classification, chronology, and cause and effect to discuss recent studies of a once taboo subject, death.

READING SELECTION

EXISTENTIAL MORALITY
by Richard Paul Janaro

The philosophy of existentialism is rooted in the belief that people are free in a sense that most of them cannot or do not wish to comprehend. It maintains that a person, like a plant or tree or any other natural object, is what he is; it maintains that each of us is unique, activated by some inner law of being that is to be accepted rather than explained; it maintains that the expectations of family, society, or governments regarding the developments of each of us are not nature's laws. If we allow ourselves to be conditioned or molded by forces outside our own nature, we have consigned ourselves unnecessarily to enslavement. The natural condition of any man cannot but be freedom in the same sense that the way a flower grows cannot be determined by anything but what is taking place inside it. When we cry out that we are trapped by society's laws, by required conformity, we must realize that it is we who make that decision. Jean-Paul Sartre (b. 1905), one of the foremost contemporary existentialists, points out that the majority of people prefer not to be free; it is easier to flow with the onrushing tide and blame it for the misfortunes one suffers than to shoulder the full responsibility for one's life.

To the existentialist it is clear that true liberation of the self comes with the understanding that it is really possible. As soon as one says "I am," as soon as one learns to accept himself, to know that he is not alive to measure up to any particular ideal or

From *Philosophy: Something to Believe In*, pp. 268–273. Copyright 1975. Reprinted by permission of Glencoe Publishers Inc.

norm except which his own nature has decreed, he finds the strength and courage to follow the direction he must.

Hence the label existentialism, which means "existence precedes essence." One's "essence" is whatever he is and is to become for whatever mysterious, not-to-be-accounted-for reason of his inner nature. "Existence" is the fact of being here at all. It precedes "essence" in the sense that no one is born for the attainment of any preconceived direction or norm. One first exists, then achieves whatever essence is possible to him. . . .

Modern existentialism has its roots in those nineteenth-century developments in philosophy which seriously challenged the domination of Socratic and Judeo-Christian moral absolutes. German idealism, in particular, as embodied in the dynamic and controversial writings of Friedrich Nietzsche, insisted upon the right of the individual to steer his own destiny, unfettered by outmoded moral precepts. Values, said Nietzsche, are what we create. Each person interprets reality as he sees fit. Each person is free to impose himself upon reality, to alter it, and if he is powerful and courageous enough, even to direct the course of history as he wishes. Nothing is right or wrong except what is able to prevail, and Nietzsche's constant message is that you have as much right to prevail as anyone else. . . .

The existentialist reasons thus: if one consigns himself to being the slave of somebody else's values, then he must accept those values; if he will not and wishes instead to create his own values, then if there are unforeseen and unfortunate consequences, he must not hide behind a mask, pretending he has had no part in the act of creation. The existentialist seldom supports spontaneous, instinctive, unreflected deeds. Rather, he tends to be hyperconscious of the moment-by-moment continuum of living, the choices he must make as he goes, and reasoning out the possible consequence of each choice.

Sartre's monumental work, *Being and Nothingness,* while exhorting the courageous to act and to create, is heavily concerned with the defense of moral responsibility. The basis of Sartre's morality is the existence of "the Other." We live in this world side by side with other people, and each choice we make necessarily involves them. Acting only to please ourselves involves a hazard for "the Other."

. . . . In one sense we have here a modernization of the Golden Rule, which, as it turns out, has provided a solid foundation for moral systems in cases where a philosopher is seeking to justify moral absolutes without appealing to the authority of revelation or tradition.

Another forerunner of the existential movement, but one who moved in a different direction from that of Nietzsche, was Immanuel Kant. Kant's primary aim in philosophy was to make a strong case for reason as the valid instrument of knowledge in an age leaning increasingly toward scientific empiricism (the position that all knowledge comes directly and solely from sense experience). As a moralist Kant has appealed to many modern existentialists who are unwilling to uphold what they consider the recklessness of a totally self-directed moral system, who still seek a foundation of binding moral principles without turning the individual into a slave of the establishment. Kant offers moral absolutes that are both practical for the individual and binding upon everyone.

. . . . Kant presents a series of examples. One concerns a man who, having experienced a reversal of good fortune, decides he must borrow money. He knows he has no way of ever repaying it, but he decides to say he intends to do so; otherwise who would lend him what he needs? The urgency of the man's plight does not, says Kant, make his intended deceit morally justifiable. . . .

Kant agrees that man's will is free, but he adds that the very definition of will implies a necessary commitment to its sense of reason. Will, in other words, is not equivalent to narrow self-interest. At heart the will recognizes that it does not endorse wrong deeds for everyone, even as it knows that it cannot logically be the one exception existing in all the universe.

Many moral philosophers have further contended that the wrongdoer always acts on the assumption that others will uphold their part of the bargain and do the right thing. The thief who plans to hold you up in the park will approach you and pretend to want a match. He will not advertise his intentions; he will count on your goodwill and lack of distrust in your fellowman and on your general honesty. In this sense he is morally inconsistent, expecting one kind of behavior but exhibiting another kind.

The preoccupation of the existentialist with morality is an indication that modern philosophy is acutely sensitive to the enduring need for moral sanctions other than the erratic, unpredictable, and irresponsible wishes of the person who argues that this is a "dog eat dog" world in which "everything goes" or that "if it feels good, do it."

READING SELECTION

ATOMIC STRUCTURE AND THE QUANTUM THEORY

It was on October 19, 1900, that Max Planck (1858–1947), a professor of physics at Berlin, presented to the Berlin Physical Society the explanation of the distribution of radiation from a blackbody and in the process shook the science of physics to its very foundations. Planck's explanation was revolutionary because it rejected what was considered an ancient truth. All scientists at that time believed that change takes place in a continuous fashion. Nature does not make jumps. If a body is heated, it can absorb all possible energies sent to it and can re-emit all possible energies.

Planck's explanation broke with this idea by postulating that electromagnetic radiation (including visible light) is emitted in small packages called *quanta*. The energy of the quantum of radiation is directly proportional to the frequency of the radiation. The proportionality constant is called *Planck's constant*. . . .

. . . Using this new concept, Planck was able to reproduce the experimental spectral distribution curves from a blackbody. . . .

[Planck's explanation also indicated that the] amount of energy of light (or any other electromagnetic radiation) is proportional to its frequency. *The higher the frequency, the greater the energy.* Thus, ultraviolet light has more energy light. Also, blue light has a higher energy than green light, which in turn has a higher energy than red light. . . .

The energy of visible light, and some radiation with lower frequencies than that, is enough to cause some harm to human beings. Skin cancers have been produced by

From *General Chemistry*, pp. 365–361. Eds. Jerry March and Stanley Windwer. Copyright 1979. Reprinted by permission of Macmillan Publishing Co. Inc.

overexposure to sunlight. This effect may take many years of prolonged exposure. High-frequency radiation has much greater energies and these, for example X-rays and gamma rays, can cause genetic damage, radiation sickness, and even death. . . .

At about the same time that blackbody radiation was causing such a problem for physicists, another phenomenon was emerging. This was the *photoelectric effect,* discovered by Heinrich Hertz and Philipp Lenard (1862–1947) around 1890. When light of the proper frequency range is allowed to shine on certain metal surfaces, electrons are emitted. The following two observations can be made using a typical photoelectric apparatus. . . .

1. When light of low frequency is allowed to shine on the metal surface, no effect occurs. As the frequency is raised, a point is reached when current flows. Any higher frequency will also produce a current.
2. One can determine the kinetic energy of the emitted electrons. This kinetic energy increases with increasing frequency of the light shining on the metal surface. Keeping the frequency of the light constant while increasing the amount (or intensity) of the light shining on the metal surface increases the number of electrons being emitted from the electrode but does not increase the kinetic energy of the emitted electrons. This, too, was contrary to the laws of nineteenth-century physics, since these laws predicted exactly the opposite: that the energy of the electrons emitted should depend on the intensity of the light and not on the frequency.

In 1905, Albert Einstein (1879–1955) applied Planck's theory of the quantization of light to explain the photoelectric effect. Einstein reasoned that electrons are constituents of all matter. When a quantum of light (also called a *photon*) strikes a metal surface, it imparts its energy to the electrons in the metal. In order for an electron to escape from the surface of the metal, it must overcome the attractive force exerted on it by the positive ions in the metal. Since, for example, a photon of blue light contains more energy than a photon of red light, it would not be surprising to find electrons emitted when blue light shines on the metal surface, whereas red light may not produce emission. Upon being struck by the blue light, the electron would have enough energy to overcome the attractive potential and escape. The energy absorbed by the electron would be equal to the attractive potential of the surface plus the kinetic energy of the emitted electron. . . .

Not only did Einstein's explanation of the photoelectric effect lend major support to Planck's hypothesis concerning the nature of light, it also provided physicists a novel method for determining Planck's constant. . . .

. . . when any object is heated to a high enough temperature, it gives off light. In 1860, Robert Bunsen (1811–1899) and Gustav Kirchhoff (1824–1887) decided to analyze the light given off by hot objects by passing it through a prism. Isaac Newton had shown, almost 200 years earlier (around 1665), that when ordinary sunlight is passed through a prism, we get the now-familiar ROYGBIV spectrum. Bunsen and Kirchhoff made the surprising discovery that when they volatilized an element (for example, H_2, Cu, Zn) by heating it in a flame and passed the light given off through a prism (the device they invented for doing this is called a *spectroscope*), what they got was not a continuous spectrum, but rather a series of lines . . . Even more surprising, *each element gave a different pattern of lines.* This discovery had at least three major consequences for the progress of science:

1. It greatly facilitated the discovery of new elements, since if one suspected that a certain rock, say, contained a new element, all one had to do was to analyze its spectrum and look for unknown lines.
2. It provided an excellent analytical tool, which is still used today to analyze for the presence of various elements.
3. However, the third consequences was the most important of all: the discovery of spectral lines was to lead (as we shall see) to our present knowledge of atomic structure.

As with blackbody radiation and the photoelectric effect, nineteenth-century physics had no explanation for these spectral lines.

It was soon discovered that atoms and molecules will also *absorb* light as well as emit light. In fact, it was Kirchhoff who stated the general law governing emission and absorption of electromagnetic radiation. This law states that *if a body emits light of a certain wavelength, it will also absorb light of the same wavelength.* . . . The pattern obtained during absorption is called the *absorption spectrum* of the material and the emission pattern is termed the *emission spectrum* of the material. Each substance, not only elements, has its own *characteristic* absorption and emission spectrum. A spectrum of a substance is a fingerprint of that substance; it is not surprising that a great deal of attention was paid to the emission spectrum of atomic hydrogen. . . .

In 1885, J. J. Balmer (1825–1898) discovered that the lines in the visible region of the spectrum of atomic hydrogen were not just randomly placed. There was a mathematical relationship which governed the position of these lines. . . . This proved that nature did not put the lines in at random, although the reason for the pattern could not be guessed at that time.

READING SELECTION

DEATH AND DYING
by Hedeel Al-Mansoor

For thousands of years death has been a taboo topic. During the last few years, however, as a result of clinical research with terminally ill patients, people have become aware that death, like all developmental events, is part of an ongoing process. A better understanding of this process has enabled a new group of professionals to help terminally ill patients and their families deal with the dying process.

Perhaps the best-known examination of the stages the dying person passes through is that by Elisabeth Kubler-Ross. Through extensive interviews with terminally ill individuals, she has concluded that the dying process consists of a series of five distinct stages. The first stage, denial and isolation, is that in which the news of a fatal illness

A student theme, reprinted by permission.

results in a denial of the fact. Kubler-Ross believes this first stage acts as a type of insulator, giving the individual time to adjust to the shock. After a period of time denial leads to an aggressive anger in which the person (and sometimes also members of the family) is outraged that it is himself or herself (or loved one) and not some other "less valuable" person who is going to die. The resentment is often directed toward others. The third stage, bargaining, is an attempt to postpone the inevitable. It frequently takes the form of "a deal" between the individual and God. For instance, someone might ask God to keep him alive longer in exchange for being a better person. In the fourth stage — depression — the individual feels tired, upset, and sick of almost everything. The individual realizes that little can be done to change the situation.

Finally, the last stage is acceptance. At this point the patient understands the finality of the situation and begins to adjust both psychologically and emotionally. This is the time when most people who have been guided and supported through the four previous stages fully accept death with dignity. Kubler-Ross stresses that hope is present throughout all five of these stages. Regardless of the condition, or the stage of dying, most people hope and believe, for example, that a miracle drug might be the answer or that the dying process itself may be reversed. These are not delusions, but a form of self-support and sustenance during this difficult time.

The traditional notion that stages of development are significant only during the early years of life is losing favor. Our attempts to understand death as a process raise the question of when development stops, if in fact it ever does.

EXERCISES

1. What is the thesis of "Existential Morality"? Discuss how the major ideas support the thesis and how the organization of individual paragraphs complements the overall organization.
2. Using well-chosen examples from your own experience, write an essay supporting or refuting the statement on page 237, "it is easier to flow with the onrushing tide and blame it for the misfortunes one suffers than to shoulder the full responsibility for one's life."
3. "Atomic Structure and the Quantum Theory" mixes chronology and cause and effect to present the ideas. Outline the chronological progression of ideas first and then indicate how each chronological step became a cause of the next step.
4. Write an essay explaining how the world of the 1980's would be different from the way it is if none of the discoveries in "Atomic Structure and the Quantum Theory" had occurred.
5. A mixed order of classification, chronology, and cause and effect has been used by the author of "Death and Dying." Outline the theme, showing the interlocking of the three types of organization.
6. Write an essay explaining the importance to a dying person of the continuing love and support from others.

SUMMARY

A theme is a set of paragraphs that consider, examine, analyze, discuss, or explain a general subject by presenting information about different aspects of that subject. The thesis statement provides the framework for unifying the theme's ideas. The model of paragraph organization selected by the author provides the framework for unifying the theme's structure. When the details for the discussion of a subject answer the questions "What happened?" or "How?" chronological order is the obvious choice. "Where?" suggests space order. "What kinds?" probably calls for classification. "How alike/different are *x* and *y*?" implies comparison/contrast. "Why?" asks for cause and effect. If the details answer more than one question, mixed order may be necessary. Before a writer begins to discuss a subject, he or she should consider the kinds of questions a potential reader might have about the subject and should organize the theme according to the model that will best present the answers.

EXERCISES

1. Discuss which organizational model(s) would best present the supporting paragraphs for each of the following thesis statements:
    a. For four reasons, Americans are buying smaller cars than they did ten years ago.
    b. Jorge decided to become an engineer so that he would be better off financially than his father, who was a farmer.
    c. After each of the European wars in the eighteenth and nineteenth centuries, many Europeans migrated to the U.S.
2. Write a specific thesis statement for each of the following general subjects and then state which organizational model(s) would be suitable.
    a. A presidential election.
    b. A promising career.
    c. Public parks.
    d. The benefits of physical exercise.
    e. A plan for peace.
3. Write a two- to four-page theme on one of the subjects in Exercise 2, developing the idea of your thesis statement according to the most suitable organizational model.

CHAPTER 13

Revising
the Rough Draft
of a Theme

Writers approach theme revision in many different ways. One person may begin to revise a rough draft by carefully expanding, cutting, reorganizing, and rewriting each paragraph; then later he or she may rearrange the order of some of the paragraphs, making sure there are transitions linking them. Another person may begin with the theme as a whole, changing the sequence of the paragraphs and revising the first and last sentences so each main idea progresses clearly to the next and then later he or she may work on the supporting sentences of each paragraph. Another writer may produce a rough draft that contains carefully linked two-sentence paragraphs and revise it by adding the supporting ideas needed by each paragraph.

The important point is that composition requires more than taking an hour or two to write some sentences on a piece of paper. Composition requires working with those hastily written sentences, revising each phrase, each sentence, and each paragraph to make them better and then revising the first revision, revising the second revision, and ultimately revising the next-to-last revision. A well-known modern poet, Dylan Thomas, realized the importance of revision: he rewrote one poem, "Fern Hill," more than two hundred times. Some revisions were major; others involved only changing a mark of punctuation, but the poet felt that each change improved the poem. Thomas had an important idea he wished to share, and he took the necessary time to express that idea artistically. That is the key to good writing.

The author of "Bring Back the Sheepdog" began with the following rough draft:

> Shepherds and coyotes have been feuding since they first met. Because of a federal law prohibiting the shooting and trapping of coyotes, shepherds must use other methods to protect their sheep.

To understand the problem, one must know something about the coyote. It is easier for a coyote to catch and kill a sheep than a rabbit, mouse, or deer.

The first shepherds fought coyotes any way they could. Now, laws allow only poisoned bait to be used to kill them.

Other animals are often killed or maimed by the methods intended for coyote control. And those methods are incredibly inhumane.

A well-trained sheep dog is both more effective and less expensive than other means of protecting sheep.

This rough draft is similar to an outline: all the main ideas are stated, but there are no supporting details. To revise this draft, the author first added some explanatory data to each paragraph. The introductory paragraph indirectly suggests that coyotes attack sheep, but it raises more questions than it answers. The second paragraph gives some information about coyotes, but not very much. The third paragraph refers to numerous ways of killing coyotes, but specifies only one. The fourth paragraph is also too general, needing some specific details to support the general statements. The final paragraph, which should be a conclusion, introduces a new idea, which is not supported by additional information.

In her first revision, the author added some explanatory data to each paragraph. She realized that the first paragraph involved a rather complex cause-and-effect relationship that needed careful development, so for the first revision she added details explaining that relationship:

Shepherds have been waging a war on coyotes since the early settlers first began moving into the western United States with their herds of cattle and flocks of sheep. Coyotes quickly acquired a taste for mutton because the slow-moving, passive sheep were easy prey. Shepherds began to poison, trap and shoot coyotes, almost to extinction. In 1975, a federal wildlife law was passed which prohibited the shooting and trapping of coyotes. Over the past several years the coyote population has risen considerably. The problem of what method to use to protect the sheep is now being investigated.

This is more information than the original paragraph, but the author realized that there were still a few problems. The second sentence included details that seemed to belong in the next paragraph. The third sentence seemed to imply that coyotes were near extinction within a short time; in fact, nearly a century elapsed between the arrival of the sheep herds and the extreme decimation of the coyotes. At the end of the paragraph, the cause-and-effect relationships between the Federal Wildlife Law, the increase in the coyote population, and the problem of coyote control needed to be made clearer. In the second revision of the introductory paragraph the author tightened up the organization, carefully mixing chronology and cause and effect.

Shepherds have been waging a war on coyotes since the early settlers, with their herds of cattle and flocks of sheep, first began moving into the coyote's domain, the western United States. The coyotes quickly acquired a taste for mutton. To protect the sheep, herders began to poison, trap and shoot the four-footed predators. Slowly, the numbers of coyotes dwindled until the species was almost extinct. In 1975, a Federal Wildlife Law was passed which prohibited shooting or trapping coyotes. As a result, the coyote population has increased considerably, causing sheep herders to look again for an effective, legal method of protecting their sheep.

At this point, the author felt that the first paragraph was a good general introduction to the subject. The past history had been reviewed, the problem had been stated, and the author was ready to proceed to the second paragraph. The first sentence of the draft version was rather too wordy, but it functioned well as a transition, referring back to the first paragraph ("the problem") and telling the reader what the new topic would be ("some knowledge of the coyote"). What this second paragraph needed was more details. The author added descriptive information about the coyote's appearance and habits, explained why sheep were so attractive to these predators, and ended with a sentence that provided a transition to the ideas of the next paragraph, organizing the ideas chronologically.

To understand the problem, one must first know something about the coyote. *Canis latrans*, the coyote's scientific name, is a small, grey cousin of the wolf and, like the wolf, a native of North America. Before the days of men and their sheep, a coyote's diet consisted mainly of rodents, rabbits, or an occasional sick deer. But after the sheep herds arrived, the coyotes quickly discovered that domesticated sheep are slower-moving and more passive than wild animals and much easier to kill. They began to prefer this new, easily obtained food supply to their traditional prey.

The author next added a transitional sentence to the beginning of paragraph three and included more specific details in that paragraph about the methods used to kill coyotes:

The early sheepherders soon realized that the coyotes were threatening their livelihood. Coyotes were trapped, poisoned, and shot on sight. Men tried to annihilate the coyotes, but the coyotes proved themselves to be very crafty. The coyotes left the tainted meat alone, learned to avoid men, and discovered quickly where traps were set. In today's world (before the federal law), the poisoned bait cannot be smelled, airplanes and helicopters are used for hunting, and the traps are much more ingenious. At the present, only the poisoned bait can be used.

The sequence of events in this first revision was not as clear as the author wanted it to be, so she omitted the last sentence, rewrote parts of some sentences, and arranged the sequence of others, in chronological order:

> The early sheep herders soon realized that the coyotes were threatening their livelihood. Men tried to annihilate the species by trapping them, poisoning them, and shooting them on sight, but the coyotes proved to be very crafty. They left the tainted meat alone, learned to avoid people, and learned to identify traps. So the shepherds got crafty, too. They invented bait in which poison cannot be detected, used airplanes and helicopters to hunt their prey, and produced more ingenious traps.

Reading over these three revised paragraphs, the author did not like the way the second and third paragraphs seemed to repeat ideas in the first paragraph without really developing them. Her solution was to recombine the sentences of these three paragraphs into two new paragraphs, each with a more clearly stated topic:

> Shepherds have been waging war on coyotes since the early settlers first began moving their herds of cattle and flocks of sheep into the coyote's domain, the western United States. The coyote, a small, grey cousin of the wolf, had previously preyed upon rodents, rabbits, and an occasional sick deer. But when the coyotes discovered that sheep are slower, more passive, and easier to kill than wild animals, they quickly acquired a preference for mutton.
>
> Realizing that the coyotes were threatening their livelihood, the shepherds tried to annihilate the four-footed predators by trapping them, poisoning them, and shooting them on sight. However, the coyotes proved to be very crafty. They left the tainted meat alone, learned to avoid people, and learned to identify traps. So the shepherds got crafty, too. They invented a poison which could not be detected, used airplanes and helicopters to hunt their prey, and produced more ingenious traps. Gradually the numbers of coyotes dwindled until the species was almost extinct. In 1975, a Federal Wildlife Law was passed which prohibited shooting or trapping coyotes. As a result, the coyote population has increased considerably, causing shepherds to look again for an effective, legal method of protecting their sheep.

The author initially revised the next paragraph by adding details to support the main idea:

> Unfortunately, coyotes are not the only animals affected by man's traps, poisons, and guns. Birds, rodents, and other animals (including pet

dogs and cats) will often encounter a baited carcass meant for a coyote. Naturalists have been in an uproar since several endangered bald eagles have died after consuming tainted coyote bait. Rabbits, foxes, deer, and dogs have been found in steel-toothed bear traps meant for coyotes. Animals poisoned or caught in traps do not die quickly, but have horrible convulsions and go into shock before slowly and agonizingly dying.

After she had written this revised version the author decided to add a paragraph reminding the reader that present laws do not allow trapping or shooting coyotes, but do allow poisoning. She then decided to combine the two paragraphs, first discussing the effect of traps and guns on other creatures, then noting that traps and guns are now illegal and discussing the horrors of poison. The examples above are loosely organized according to two categories (poison and traps); in the revision, examples of all three categories are discussed.

Unfortunately, coyotes are not the only animals affected by man's guns, traps, and poisons. Frequently, a hunter armed with a gun has fired at a poorly seen target and later discovered that he has shot a deer, a cow, a dog, or one of his own children. Guns at least kill quickly. Traps do not. They usually snap onto the victim's leg, crushing blood vessels and bones, causing a slow death from shock and loss of blood. Poison is the worst of the three, causing its victims to die in convulsions of agony, yet it is now the only legal means of controlling the coyote population. Unfortunately, coyotes are not its only victims. Birds, rabbits, and other animals (including people's pet dogs and cats) often encounter poisoned bait meant for a coyote. Naturalists began demanding a ban on poison when they discovered that bald eagles were dying after consuming tainted coyote bait. To protect the bald eagle, our national symbol which is on the endangered species list, the government may add poison to guns and traps as prohibited means of coyote control. If so, what protection will sheep have?

The author's intent, up to this point, was to persuade the reader that the most common methods of coyote control were inhumane, and to prepare the reader for an alternative method of protecting sheep from coyote attacks. The remainder of the first version of the essay discussed that alternative, the use of sheepdogs.

The solution to the problem has been available all along. A well trained sheepdog is smart enough to keep the sheep together, strong enough to intimidate even the largest coyote, and loyal enough to stay with the sheep at all times. Dogs can be bought fully trained at a cost of anywhere between four hundred dollars and five thousand dollars. The cost difference depends on size, pedigree, and amount of training. Compared to the cost of poison, traps, guns, and innocent lives, the cost of a good sheepdog is small.

This paragraph assumes that the reader knows that sheepdogs were used in the past. However, this information has not been stated previously. It should have been. To remedy this problem, the author revised the first sentence of the second paragraph, adding more details. She also added a few other references to sheepdogs in the first several paragraphs, including the information that gradually shepherds had relied more and more on artificial methods of control and less and less on sheepdogs. With these additions, the paragraph above, suggesting that sheepdogs should be used more, is less of a surprise to the reader.

The author then wrote a new conclusion:

> We must put an end to the cruel and inhumane ways that we destroy our wildlife. Government, shepherds, and naturalists must work together to stop the horrible murders of innocent animals. The Federal Wildlife Law is necessary to prevent the mistake of overkilling and causing the extinction of many animals in the world. At the present, I believe the only viable method for protecting a sheepherder's flocks is to begin to use the loyal sheepdog again. Other wild animals will not be adversely affected by the presence of a dog. Poisons, traps, and other coyote control devices will become obsolete. Until a better method is invented, the reliable sheepdog is a sound choice.

Reading the new conclusion carefully, the author realized that it was repetitious and not very well organized. She decided that a chronologically organized review would make a more effective conclusion. The result was this:

> In Europe centuries ago, sheepdogs and shepherds successfully protected the flocks against predators. When sheep were brought to North America, a new predator was waiting, the coyote. Gradually, shepherds depended less on sheepdogs and more on guns, traps, and poison to protect the sheep from the coyotes. These methods not only nearly eliminated the coyotes, they also cruelly tortured and killed harmless animals. The Federal Wildlife Law of 1975 outlawed guns and traps, but poison is still legally used to kill predators and pets indiscriminately. A stronger wildlife law is needed, banning poison as well. If sheepdogs are once again used as they were successfully used for centuries, the flocks will be well protected without the current high cost in terms of unnecessary suffering for dumb animals.

The author's original draft was loosely organized in terms of cause and effect. During the revision process the basic organization was not changed, but it was considerably tightened to clarify the progression from the first cause (the arrival of sheep in the United States) to the first effect (the coyotes' sheep killing), which became the cause of the next effect (the shepherds' defense), which became another cause, and so on. The final version of the theme appears below.

READING SELECTION

BRING BACK THE SHEEPDOG
by Cynthia Huber

Shepherds have been waging war on coyotes since the early settlers first began moving their herds of cattle and flocks of sheep into the coyote's domain, the western United States. The coyote, a small, grey cousin of the wolf, had previously preyed upon rodents, rabbits, and an occasional sick deer. But when the coyotes discovered that sheep are slower, more passive, and easier to kill than wild animals, they quickly acquired a preference for mutton.

Realizing that the coyotes were threatening their livelihood, American shepherds used sheepdogs to protect their flocks, as shepherds have done for centuries. However, they wanted not only to protect the sheep, but also to annihilate the coyotes. Coyotes were trapped, poisoned, and shot on sight, although they proved to be very crafty. They left the poisoned bait alone, learned to identify traps, and avoided people with guns. So the shepherds got crafty, too. They invented a poison which could not be detected, used airplanes and helicopters to hunt their prey, and produced more ingenious traps. They also abandoned their former companions, the sheepdogs. Gradually, the numbers of coyotes dwindled until the species was almost extinct. In 1975, a Federal Wildlife Law was passed which prohibited shooting or trapping coyotes. As a result, the coyote population has increased considerably, which is one of the reasons shepherds are looking for additional methods of protecting their sheep.

Another reason is the fact that coyotes have not been the only animals affected by man's guns, traps, and poisons. Frequently, a hunter armed with a gun has fired at a poorly seen target and later discovered that he has shot a deer, a cow, a dog, or one of his own children. Guns at least kill quickly. Traps do not. They usually snap onto the victim's leg, crushing blood vessels and bones and causing a slow death from shock and loss of blood. Poison is the worst of the three, causing its victims to die in convulsions of agony, yet it is now the only legal means of controlling the coyote population. What was true of guns and traps is still true of poison: coyotes are not its only victims. Birds, rabbits, and other animals (including people's pet dogs and cats) often encounter poisoned bait meant for a coyote. Naturalists began demanding a ban on poison when they discovered that bald eagles, which are on the endangered species list, were dying after consuming tainted coyote bait. To protect the bald eagle, our national symbol, the government may prohibit poison as well as guns and traps as means of coyote control. If so, what protection will sheep have?

A student research paper, reprinted by permission.

The solution to the problem has been available all along. A well-trained sheepdog is smart enough to keep the sheep together, strong enough to intimidate even the largest coyote, and loyal enough to stay with the sheep at all times. Dogs can be bought fully trained at a cost of anywhere between four hundred dollars and five thousand dollars. The cost difference depends on size, pedigree, and amount of training. Compared to the cost of poisons, traps, guns, and innocent lives, the cost of a good sheepdog is small.

In Europe centuries ago, sheepdogs and shepherds successfully protected the flocks against predators. When sheep were brought to North America, a new predator was waiting, the coyote. Gradually, shepherds depended less on sheepdogs and more on guns, traps, and poison to protect the sheep from the coyotes. These methods not only nearly eliminated the coyotes, they also cruelly tortured and killed harmless animals. The Federal Wildlife Law of 1975 outlawed guns and traps, but poison is still legally used to kill predators and pets indiscriminately. A stronger wildlife law is needed, banning poison as well. If sheepdogs are once again used as they were successfully used for centuries, the flocks will be well protected without the current high cost in terms of unnecessary suffering for dumb animals.

The author of the essay "The Years of Segregated Baseball" (pages 257–259) began with a lengthy draft, full of details:

It would be hard to imagine baseball without players like Frank Robinson, Reggie Jackson, Bob Gibson, and "Sweet Lou" Whittaker. We, as fans, owe a lot to the brave pioneers of integrated baseball. Before 1945, there were no black players on the major leagues, although there were some all-Negro teams.

The first Negro team was formed in 1885 in Babylon, Long Island, by the waiters of the Babylon Argyle Hotel. They chattered a bizarre dialect on the playing field, hoping to pass themselves off as Cubans. Most of the Babylon players later turned professional, creating the first great black team in history, the Cuban Giants. By 1886, the Cuban Giants were beating some of the most powerful teams in the National and American leagues, in exhibition games.

Any hopes the black players might have had of breaking into the majors were dashed on an April morning in 1887 in Newark, New Jersey. Newark, of the Eastern League, was scheduled to play the Chicago White Stockings. Pitching for Newark was thirty-five-game winner George Stovey, a light-skinned black man. Chicago's captain Adrian "Cap" Anson, prided as being the greatest player of his day, stomped off the field rather than face Stovey. The walk set a precedent that continued for the next sixty years. The decades of segregated baseball had begun.

The turn of the century brought many interesting attempts to integrate the major leagues. In 1902, John McGraw, owner of the Baltimore Orioles, signed Charley Grant, a black second baseman, to his team, trying to pass Grant off as an Indian, "Chief Tokahoma." The masquerade was working well until the Orioles rolled into Chicago for a series with the White Sox. White Sox manager Charley Comiskey's suspicions were aroused when the black fans greeted the "chief" with cheers of "our boy Charley Grant." So much for Indian lore; Charley was once again back in the Negro league.

By 1906, black baseball was loaded with talent. One team completed an incredible season of 108 wins and only thirty-one losses. The owner challenged the Chicago White Sox, the winner of the World Series, to play his club "and thus decide who can play baseball best, the white or black Americans." Chicago refused to accept the challenge.

Contests between the white and black players took place after the regular season was finished. For two years, the black ballplayers teamed up with the Cuban club for winter ball. The white pros met competition that they could not handle, being beaten 75 per cent of the time. Ty Cobb, of the Detroit Tigers, stomped off the field and vowed never to play blacks again.

In the pre World War I years, New York became the black baseball capital. Harlem's Lincoln Giants had two of the best pitchers in black baseball history, "Cyclone" Joe Williams and "Cannonball" Dick Redding. Thanks to these two, the Harlem team won 60 per cent of the postseason games against teams like the New York Giants, the New York Yankees, and the Philadelphia Phillies.

The West was also coming into its own. In Chicago, the great Rube Foster had formed his own club, the Chicago American Giants, challenging the Cubs and White Sox to an attendance war. On a Sunday when all three teams were playing, the Cubs drew 6,500, the White Sox 9,000, the Foster's Giants 11,000 spectators. But still there was no confrontation on a baseball field during the regular season. Some people wanted to see just that, but the owners of the white ball clubs remained silent and noncommittal. Regardless of what the owners did or did not say, the October barnstorming between the black and white players continued. In 1917 "Smokey" Joe Williams faced off against the World Champion New York Giants and nearly beat them. The final score was 1 to 0, the one run coming on an error. The black pitcher had pitched a no-hitter, striking out twenty of the opposing players.

After the war, there seemed to be a glimmer of hope that black players would be admitted to the all-white teams. The scandal surrounding the 1919 World Series had discouraged fans, and some owners thought that the fans might be attracted back to the ball parks if black players were on the teams. But nothing came of the idea.

In February, 1920, a meeting was held at which Rube Foster proposed a Negro National League, to minimize mutual raiding and maximize regular scheduling and paydays for the players, and also to create an atmosphere of mutual support among the teams and to compete directly with the major leagues for attendance. Foster's American Giants held the pennant for the first three years of the new league, winning games with their superior speed and bunting ability.

Meanwhile, the Eastern teams were becoming increasingly competitive, partly because they raided the Western teams for top players. In 1923 the decision was made to create the Eastern Colored League. Foster was enraged and would not agree to a World Series between the two top Negro Leagues. So once again, post-season play centered around the white teams.

In 1925, after the Hilldales repeated as the Eastern champs, Foster made peace and arranged for the first black world series. After ten games, the Kansas City Monarchs won the series. A disappointing 45,000 fans turned out to watch the games.

1926 brought tragedy to black baseball: Rube Foster, one of the earliest and greatest black players and promoters, was institutionalized after suffering a severe mental breakdown.

Joining the Negro National League in 1927 came a team of coal miners from the South, the Birmingham Black Barons, with a skinny young rookie named Leroy "Satchel" Paige, fresh out of reform school. Post-season barnstorming continued, with the non-league Homestead Grays cleaning up their big-league opponents.

In 1929 Baltimore defeated the big-leaguers seventy-four victories to forty-one losses, a decade record.

An era of black baseball ended in 1930 with the death of Rube Foster. A new era began, thanks to lighted ball parks, of night games. The 1930's were hard on black and white baseball alike, and again it seemed that perhaps the time was right for integrated teams. In 1932 black athletes were bringing gold medals home from the Olympics; pro football had just signed its first black players; Clark Griffith, the owner of the Washington Senators, gave tryouts to two or three black players; and the fans continued to fill the bleachers at black baseball games.

Life in the thirties became more and more difficult for the black baseball players, bounding from town to town, playing two or three games a day, and hustling for every penny.

In the spring of 1936, the Dominican Dictator Trujillo's well-financed call for a championship team brought Paige, Gibson, and Cool Papa Bill, to name a few, hurrying south to take advantage of the offer. When they returned to the U.S., Greenley suspended them all. Satchel Paige headed West. Bill went to Mexico, and Josh Gibson went back to the Maverick Homestead Grays, pounding home runs and leading the team to the next nine straight pennants.

Josh Gibson, like many black players, came up short, due to the lack of "official" record, but many people believe he had a lifetime record that has never been touched, even by the achievements of Babe Ruth or Henry Aaron. In 1931 and 1932, Josh hit 143 unofficial home runs.

Satchel Paige's records from the mound were similar. He is now said to be one of the world's greats, with credit for winning over two thousand games.

The thirties were hard times, but still the finest decade ever. In 167 games, against the major leagues, the black league teams won 112, lost 52, and tied three.

Satchel Paige made a comeback from arm trouble in the early 1940's, helping the Kansas City Monarchs to their second straight pennant. He pitched a three-hit, 3–1 victory against Dizzy Dean's All Stars in front of 30,000 fans.

By the 1940's, some of the major league owners were beginning to consider hiring some of the talent of the Negro League to improve their own teams. In 1945, Bill Branch, owner of the Brooklyn Dodgers, hired Jack Roosevelt Robinson, a talented black college graduate.

Many of the great black baseball players were never to play in the major leagues, Josh Gibson for one. He died in 1967 from a massive brain tumor. Satchel Paige played in the majors as did Roy Campanella and others.

There was much speculation whether Jackie would succeed or fail. If he succeeded, the decades of segregation would end. If he failed, segregation would continue. He succeeded, and major league baseball has benefited greatly from the many fine black players on its teams in the past four decades.

This draft is interesting, thanks to the wealth of details, but it is imbalanced.

It presents the information chronologically, but not clearly. Only readers knowledgeable enough about the history of baseball to write about it themselves would fully understand it. One of the problems is faulty inference.

The introductory paragraph suggests that Frank Robinson and the others are "pioneers of integrated baseball" (which they were not) and does not make it clear that they are black athletes. Furthermore, the topic idea of the paragraph — the fact that for sixty years America's national sport was racially segregated — is not emphasized. In the author's second revision, these problems were avoided. The introductory paragraph was rewritten as follows:

Modern baseball fans take for granted the appearance of black players on major league teams. Yet before 1945, baseball was totally segregated. There were the all-white major league teams, and there were some all-Negro teams. They met in competition only after the regular season was concluded, and the names of the winners never appeared in the official record books.

The author then looked at the second paragraph of the revised draft and decided that the information about the early history of Negro baseball did not really fit into a theme about the gradual shift of attitudes which finally ended segregation in professional baseball. So she omitted that part of the first revision. She realized that the second paragraph should develop one or two of the ideas introduced in the first paragraph, so she consolidated all the references to the achievements of the black players and wrote two new paragraphs.

For decades, the black teams won more post-season games than their white opponents. In 1886, the Cuban Giants beat some of the most powerful teams in the major leagues. In the early 1900's, a Cuban team made up primarily of black Americans won 75 per cent of its games against big league teams. Prior to World War I, Harlem's Lincoln Giants had two of the best pitchers in baseball history, Joe Williams and Dick Redding. Thanks to these two, the Harlem team won 60 per cent of its post-season games against teams like the New York Giants, the New York Yankees, and the Philadelphia Phillies. "Smokey" Joe Williams faced off against the 1917 world champion New York Giants and pitched a no-hitter; the Giants' winning run in the 1–0 game was the result of an error. A decade record was set in 1929 when Baltimore defeated the major league teams seventy-four times, with only forty-one losses.

The black athletes were also setting other records. Josh Gibson hit 143 home runs in 1931 and 1932. The current major league record for a single season (established by Roger Maris in 1961) is sixty-one, ten less than Gibson's average. A modern major-league pitcher is considered outstanding if he can win twenty or more games a season; he would have to play for a century to match Satchel Paige's career record of over two thousand wins. But these as yet unmatched records are not "official"; only the records set by the white major league players and teams during the years of segregated baseball are officially recognized.

At this point, since specific details about the abilities of the black players have been included, the author felt she could state her belief that segregated baseball was absurd. Again, she consolidated previously scattered details. The next four paragraphs discuss different attitudes toward black players.

Impressive as their talents were, the black players were repeatedly scorned by white baseball players. In 1887, a black team from Newark was scheduled to play Chicago's major league team. Pitching for Newark was thirty-five-game winner George Stovey. Chicago's captain Adrian "Cap" Anson, acclaimed as the greatest player of the time, stomped off the field rather than face Stovey. About twenty years later, Anson's behavior was repeated by the Detroit Tigers' star, Ty Cobb, who marched off the field vowing he would never compete against a black team.

Some people felt that the segregation policy of the national leagues was hurting baseball. Many of the best players in the country, just because they were black, were barred from teams looking for new talent. There were several attempts to remedy the situation. The players on the first Negro team, formed in 1885 by a group of waiters from a hotel on Long Island, chattered a bizarre dialect on the playing field, hoping the owners of the white teams would mistake them for Cubans. It did not work. The black players had to settle for their own all-black professional team, the Cuban Giants.

In 1902, John McGraw, owner of the Baltimore Orioles, hired Charley Grant, a black second baseman, announcing to the public that Grant was an Indian Chief. The masquerade was working well until the Orioles rolled into Chicago for a series with the White Sox. Charley Comisky, the White Sox manager, got suspicious when Chicago's black fans greeted "Chief Tokahoma" with cheers of "our boy Charley Grant." So much for Indian lore; Charley was returned to the Negro League.

After World War I, there seemed to be some hope that black players would be admitted to the all-white teams. The scandal surrounding the 1919 World Series had discouraged fans, and some owners thought that the fans might be attracted back to the ball parks if black players were on the major league teams. However, nothing came of the idea. There were similar hopes in the 1930's. In 1932 black athletes were bringing gold medals home from the Olympics; professional football teams had just signed their first black players; the owner of the major league Washington Senators gave tryouts to two or three black players; and the fans were filling the bleachers at black baseball games. But again, nothing happened.

As you have probably noticed the author has kept the chronological organization of the first revision to a certain extent: she has organized individual paragraphs and sets of paragraphs developing one central idea chronologically. What she has done in the second revision is to follow the chronology of the events that provide the details for one main idea (the achievements of black players prior to 1945), and then she has gone back to the starting point of the chronology to provide the details that support another main idea (attitudes about segregated baseball). After presenting those two main ideas and the support for them, she was ready to continue with the next chronological step, the change from segregation to integration in major league baseball. In neither the rough draft nor the first revision was any reason given for the decision to integrate the major leagues. In the next revision, the author included a possible explanation.

World War II finally weakened some of the long-standing racial barriers. Perhaps people felt that if a white man and a black man could fight together they could play baseball together. In the early 1940's, major league owners publicly talked about the possibilities of hiring the talented players of the Negro League to improve their own teams, although it seemed that each owner was waiting for someone else to make the first move. Finally, in 1945, the owner of the Brooklyn Dodgers broke the sixty-year-old "whites only" rule and hired Jack Roosevelt Robinson, a talented black college graduate.

The final revisions involved switching the order of the last two paragraphs of the first revision, and adding more details to what would be the concluding paragraph. The author realized that the paragraph providing additional information about Jackie Robinson should immediately follow the paragraph that first introduces him, and the conclusion to the theme should focus on the black players whose talent in the decades of segregated baseball contributed to the decision to end segregation on the baseball field. The last two paragraphs were changed to these two:

> There was much speculation about Jackie Robinson. If he succeeded as a major league baseball player, the decades of segregation would end. If he failed to play as well as his white teammates, segregation would continue. The fact that many of the outstanding players on the major league teams in the past four decades have been black proves that he succeeded.
> Although some of the athletes from the Negro League, including Satchel Paige, eventually played on major-league teams, most of the great Negro ballplayers never had a chance to show their talents in the major league ballparks. It was, however, their lifelong dedication to baseball which finally ended the years of segregated baseball. Today's fans owe a lot to these pioneers.

The final version of the theme earned the author an "A", which pleased her, and also evoked the reaction, "that is really fascinating," from a classmate, which delighted her. Compare the rough draft on pages 251–254 with the final version below.

READING SELECTION

THE YEARS OF SEGREGATED BASEBALL
by Gayle Roberts-Walker

Modern baseball fans take for granted the appearance of black players on major-league teams. Yet before 1945, baseball was totally segregated. There were the all-white major-league teams, and there were some all-Negro teams. They met in competition only after the regular season was concluded, and the names of the winners never appeared in the official record books.

For decades, the black teams won more post-season games than their white oppo-

A student research paper, reprinted by permission.

nents. In 1886, the Cuban Giants beat some of the most powerful teams in the major leagues. In the early 1900's, a Cuban team made up primarily of black Americans won 75 per cent of its games against big league teams. Prior to World War I, Harlem's Lincoln Giants had two of the best pitchers in baseball history, Joe Williams and Dick Redding. Thanks to these two, the Harlem team won 60 per cent of its post-season games against teams like the New York Giants, the New York Yankees, and the Philadelphia Phillies. "Smokey" Joe Williams faced off against the 1917 world champion New York Giants and pitched a no-hitter; the Giants' winning run in the 1-0 game was the result of an error. A decade record was set in 1929 when Baltimore defeated the major league teams seventy-four times, with only forty-one losses.

The black athletes were also setting other records. Josh Gibson hit 143 home runs in 1931 and 1932. The current major league record for a single season (established by Roger Maris in 1961) is sixty-one, ten less than Gibson's average. A modern major-league pitcher is considered outstanding if he can win twenty or more games a season; he would have to play for a century to match Satchel Paige's career record of over two thousand wins. But these as yet unmatched records are not "official"; only the records set by the white major league players and teams during the years of segregated baseball are officially recognized.

Impressive as their talents were, the black players were repeatedly scorned by white baseball players. In 1887, a black team from Newark was scheduled to play Chicago's major-league team. Pitching for Newark was thirty-five-game winner George Stovey. Chicago's captain Adrian "Cap" Anson, acclaimed as the greatest player of the time, stomped off the field rather than face Stovey. About twenty years later, Anson's behavior was repeated by the Detroit Tigers' star, Ty Cobb, who marched off the field vowing he would never compete against a black team.

Some people felt that the segregation policy of the national leagues was hurting baseball. Many of the best players in the country, just because they were black, were barred from teams looking for new talent. There were several attempts to remedy the situation. The players on the first Negro team, formed in 1885 by a group of waiters from a hotel on Long Island, chattered a bizarre dialect on the playing field, hoping the owners of the white teams would mistake them for Cubans. It did not work. The black players had to settle for their own all-black professional team, the Cuban Giants.

In 1902, John McGraw, owner of the Baltimore Orioles, hired Charley Grant, a black second baseman, announcing to the public that Grant was an Indian Chief. The masquerade was working well until the Orioles rolled into Chicago for a series with the White Sox. Charley Comiskey, the White Sox manager, got suspicious when Chicago's black fans greeted "Chief Tokahoma" with cheers of "our boy Charley Grant." So much for Indian lore; Charley was returned to the Negro League.

After World War I, there seemed to be some hope that black players would be admitted to the all-white teams. The scandal surrounding the 1919 World Series had discouraged fans, and some owners thought that the fans might be attracted back to the ball parks if black players were on the major-league teams. However, nothing came of the idea. There were similar hopes in the 1930's. In 1932 black athletes were bringing gold medals home from the Olympics; professional football teams had just signed their first black players; the owner of the major league Washington Senators gave tryouts to two or three black players; and the fans were filling the bleachers at black baseball games. But again, nothing happened.

World War II finally weakened some of the long-standing racial barriers. Perhaps people felt that if a white man and a black man could fight together they could play baseball together. In the early 1940's, major league owners publicly talked about the possibilities of hiring the talented players of the Negro League to improve their own teams, although it seemed that each owner was waiting for someone else to make the first move. Finally, in 1945, the owner of the Brooklyn Dodgers broke the sixty-year-old "whites only" rule and hired Jack Roosevelt Robinson, a talented black college graduate.

There was much speculation about Jackie Robinson. If he succeeded as a major-league baseball player, the decades of segregation would end. If he failed to play as well as his white teammates, segregation would continue. The fact that many of the outstanding players on the major league teams in the past four decades have been black proves that he succeeded.

Although some of the athletes from the Negro League, including Satchel Paige, eventually played on major league teams, most of the great Negro ballplayers never had a chance to show their talents in the major league ballparks. It was, however, their lifelong dedication to baseball which finally ended the years of segregated baseball. Today's fans owe a lot to these pioneers.

SUMMARY

Revising the rough draft of a theme requires several things:

1. Each paragraph must be expanded, cut, reorganized, and rephrased so that it both expresses a single idea and presents supporting examples, explanations, and other details to clarify that idea. (See Chapter 10 to review paragraph revision.)
2. Care must be taken each time a sentence or part of a sentence is added or changed to ensure that the grammar, spelling, punctuation, and other mechanics are correct.
3. The progression of ideas from one paragraph to the next must be considered, the method of organization carefully selected to ensure that the main idea is presented in the most effective way possible, and each successive paragraph analyzed to ensure effective transitions from one to the next.

Like other art forms, writing is a careful process. Like a painter, sculptor, or musical composer, a writer begins with an idea which is to be expressed in the appropriate raw materials. For a writer, those materials are words. Like paint, clay, or musical notes, the words a writer works with are combined and shaped; then the effect is critically examined, and the words are recombined, reshaped, and restructured many times before the composition expresses the original idea in a way that is pleasing to both the writer and the audience, the readers.

EXERCISES

1. Write a one- or two-page draft of a theme on the following topic: Some of the old ways of doing things are better than the new ways.

2. Consider the possible ways of organizing the main ideas in your rough draft. Would a chronological progression from one main idea to the next be effective? Would comparison and contrast present the ideas more clearly? Or would classification or cause and effect be preferable? Rewrite your draft as an outline, following the organizational model you have selected.

3. Expand each item in your outline into a paragraph, adding examples, explanations, definitions, descriptions, etc., that will clarify and support the topic idea.

4. Consider the possible ways of organizing the supporting ideas of each paragraph. Rewrite those paragraphs that need a more effective method of organization.

5. Reread your entire revision, paying particular attention to the first sentence of each paragraph. If the transition from one topic to the next is too abrupt, rephrase the beginning of the paragraph by repeating a word, phrase, or idea from the previous paragraph or add some other well-chosen transition.

6. Trade your rough draft and final revision with a classmate. Read his or her rough draft and revision critically, evaluating the effectiveness of individual paragraphs, noting transitions (or their lack), and assessing the models of organization that have been used to present the main idea of the theme and the supporting ideas of the paragraphs. Write an evaluation of your classmate's theme, noting the good features and the problems. Return the draft and the revision to the original author and reclaim yours.

7. Read your classmate's evaluation of your revision. Rewrite your theme, making any changes which seem to be necessary.

SECTION FOUR

CITING
AUTHORITY

INTRODUCTION

Many ways of developing ideas have been discussed earlier, but there is another effective way that has not yet been mentioned. It involves briefly quoting or paraphrasing what someone else has said about the subject and then discussing that person's ideas. Ideally, quotations should be short, no more than a sentence or two. Care must be taken to copy the quotation exactly as it appears (even if it contains errors). Long quotations should usually be paraphrased, that is, restated in your own words. Unless you are quoting a long passage to save your reader the trouble of having to go to a library to read it, such as a poem, a complex hypothesis, or a case history, avoid quoting long passages written by someone else.

Contrary to advertisers' practice, a football player is not necessarily an expert on mouthwash, nor is a movie star an expert on oven cleaners. Quotations should be statements made by acknowledged experts on the subject being discussed.

Whenever a writer uses someone else's words or ideas, credit must be given to the original author. Taking someone else's words or ideas without acknowledging that they are borrowed is like stealing. It even has a name: *plagiarism*. In the Middle Ages, no one considered plagiarism to be wrong. Poets often borrowed phrases or entire lines from other poets without acknowledging that they had done so. They can be partly excused on the grounds that they did not know the original authors; most medieval literature is anonymous. Today, however, plagiarism is considered sufficient reason to give a student a failing grade on a plagiarized paper, to fail a student in a course in which he or she plagiarized, or, in extreme cases, to expel a student from a college or university. Plagiarism is a risky business, not worth the penalties if one is caught.

CHAPTER 14

Footnotes
and Bibliographies

FOOTNOTES

There are conventional ways for a writer to acknowledge that she or he has borrowed the words or ideas of an expert. One way is to use a footnote. Footnotes are so named because formerly they always appeared at the foot of the page on which the borrowed material appeared, and still do so in many books. Now, however, most professors and some publishers (but not mine) prefer that all footnotes appear together on a separate page at the end of a composition. Sometimes they are called "endnotes," for this reason.

Each quotation in a composition should be marked with a number, starting with number [1] for the first quotation. The number goes at the end of the quotation, outside the quotation marks, slightly above the line. The following essay contains three quotations, numbered in sequence.

READING SELECTION

SAY WHAT YOU MEAN—IF YOU CAN

A noted semanticist once stated, "It is a common experience for a reader to learn the meaning of a word through seeing it often enough in print, without ever having heard it spoken, and even, in a language so unphonetically spelled as English, with a very mistaken notion of its accepted pronunciation in the spoken language."[1] If one reads the following three sentences, one meaning of the word "slough" becomes clear.

1. Snakes must slough their skin periodically, since their bodies grow, but their skin does not.

J. A. Johnson, unpublished essay.

2. The actor sloughed off the negative comments about his performance, claiming that the critics did not understand the play.
3. The game of bridge requires the skillful sloughing of useless cards.

The word "slough" in these examples is apparently a verb meaning "to discard, reject." In the next three examples, the word obviously has a very different meaning:

4. The children learned to swim in a nearby slough.
5. Our neighbor's slough is full of mud and stagnant water.
6. What Ivan called a slough looked like a little lake to Shakiba.

In these sentences, the word "slough" is apparently a noun referring to a small body of water.

The next question is, how is the word pronounced? The "-ough" words of English are notorious for their wide-ranging pronunciations. Consider the differences among "bough," "rough," "through," "cough," "plough," and "enough," just to mention a few. The noun "slough" is pronounced "slew," rhyming with "blew," "flu," and "true." The verb "slough" is pronounced "sluff," rhyming with "enough."

Another word referring to a body of water is "creek," which is pronounced "kreek" in some parts of the United States and "krick" in other parts. Its meaning also varies, as a well-known linquist has observed: "In parts of Ohio and Pennsylvania, for example, the term *creek* is applied to a much larger body of water than in Michigan."[2]

One last comment about words and their meanings: when a writer says "Everything is wet,"[3] he is not necessarily saying that everything is covered with a liquid of some sort. He may simply be saying that everything is, in his view, wrong.

On the footnote page of an essay, the source of each quotation is given in the sequence in which the quotations appear in the text. The footnote page for the essay "Say What You Mean—If You Can" would look like this:

Footnotes

[1] Louis B. Salomon, *Semantics and Common Sense* (New York: Holt, Rinehart and Winston, 1966), p. 7.
[2] Albert H. Marckwardt, "Regional Variations" in *Language: Introductory Readings*, 3rd ed., Virginia P. Clark, Paul A. Eschholz, and Alfred F. Rosa, Eds. (New York: St. Martin's Press, 1981), p. 482.
[3] P. B. Newman, "Indian Creek," *Kansas Quarterly*, VII (Fall, 1975), p. 66.

A careful examination of these footnotes indicates what information a footnote should provide. If the quotation is from a magazine, journal, or newspaper, the footnote should provide the following information, in the following order, with the indicated punctuation handwritten:

Author's first name/initial and second name/initial and last name, "Title of article," Name of the magazine, journal, or newspaper, volume number of a journal (date of publication), page number on which the quotation appears. Footnote 3 above illustrates this form.

If the quotation is from a book, the sequence of information is as follows:
Author's first name/initial and second name/initial and last name , " Title of chapter, section, or selection of book " (if the general source is not the entire book but only a part of it), <u>Name of the book</u>, volume number (if any), edition (if not the first) editor's name (if any)(Place of publication: name of publishing company, date of publication), page number(s) on which the quotation appears. Footnote 2 above carries all this information except a volume number. Footnote 1 cites the entire book as the source, so there is no quoted title.

Let's look at each of the items.

1. (a) In a book that is not a collection of selections from numerous authors, the author's name is on the title page of the book. The title page, at the beginning of the book, gives the title of the book, the author's or editor's name, the place of publication and the name of a publishing company.

    (b) For an article in a magazine, newspaper, or journal or a chapter or selection in a book which has many authors, the author's name is either given with the title of the chapter or article, at the beginning, or it appears at the end of the chapter or article. Sometimes, in magazines or newspapers especially, it is not given at all. In this case, the title of the article becomes the first item in the footnote.

2. The title of an article or chapter is put in quotation marks, to mark it as a title and to differentiate it from the name of the book, magazine, journal, or newspaper in which it appears.

3. The name of the book, magazine, etc. is underlined to differentiate it from the title of the article or chapter. If the paper containing the footnote is to be published, the underlining becomes an instruction to a printer to use italic type for the name.

4. Sometimes a book may be one volume in a set. When this is so, the volume number follows the name of the book. Scholarly and professional journals also have volume numbers.

5. Some books contain several chapters or selections, each written by a different author and put together by an editor. When this is the case, the editor's name is given, after the name of the book (and volume number if any). All magazines, journals, and newspapers have editors, but their names do not appear in footnotes.

6. For books only — never for magazines, newspapers, or journals — the place of publication and then the name of the publishing company are given in footnotes. This information, followed by the date of publication, is set in parentheses.

7. The date of publication is very important, because it enables the readers of the footnote to find the book or article from which the quotation was taken and to read the whole thing, if they wish. The date of publication of a book appears on the page following the title page and looks something like this: Copyright © 1976. If there is more than one copyright date, the most recent

one is listed in the footnote. What more than one date means is that the book has been reprinted and possibly revised since it first appeared, and the page numbers in the newest edition may not correspond exactly to the page numbers in earlier editions. Publication dates for magazines, journals, and newspapers appear on the cover and/or first page.

8. The final term in a footnote tells the reader on what page(s) of the source the quotation appears.

EXERCISES

A. Each of the following footnotes is missing one necessary piece of information. Identify the items which are included and those which are missing. *Two hints: Saturday Review* is a magazine; *America's Needs and Resources: A New Survey* is a book.

1. Abraham Ribicoff, "The Healthiest Nation," August 22, 1970, p. 18.
2. *Population Bulletin*, pp. 7–8.
3. *World Almanac*, 1971.
4. Carl M. Cobb, *Saturday Review*, August 22, 1970, p. 25.
5. Frederick Dewhurst and Associates, *America's Needs and Resources: A New Survey*, p. 61.

B. Using the following information about the sources of three separate quotations, write correct footnotes.

1. Quotation from p. 11 of "Oklahoma," an article that starts on page 10 and ends on p. 14 of Travel magazine. Gina Passarelli wrote the article in 1979.
2. "Investments" from The New York Times newspaper on page F 12, November 21, 1977.
3. Quotations from page 71 of the book, *My Life: Sally Gimelli Remembers*, published in 1980 by Avon Books, New York.

C. The following footnote page contains several errors. Find them and re-do them.

1. *National Ed. Review* 39, "How Much Can We Boost I.Q. and Scholastic Achievement," by A. Jensen, 1969, p. 17.
2. N. J. Block and G. Dworkin, eds. *The I.Q. Controversy*, p. 90, "Heredity, Intelligence, Politics, and Psychology," by J. Kaplan, 1969.
3. Cambridge, Mass. Teaching English as a Second Language; Winthrop Publishers, Inc., 1976, C. B. Paulston and M. N. Bruder, p. 3.
4. 1961, New York, The Macmillan Publishing Company, *Common Sense about Race*, p. 118, by P. Mason.

When numerous quotations in a composition are taken from the same source, each one requires a separate number, but it is not necessary to provide all the source information in every footnote. The first one must be complete, but successive ones need to give only enough information to refer the reader back to the full reference. Usually all that is needed is the author's last name and the page reference if it is different from the page reference in the full footnote. Footnote 4 in the following example illustrates this principle:

1. Leonard Bloomfield, *Language History* (New York: Doubleday & Company, Inc., 1962), p. 282.
2. Albert C. Baugh, *A History of the English Language* (New York: Appleton-Century-Crofts, Inc., 1957), p. 201.
3. Robert A. Hall, *Linguistics and Your Language* (New York: Appleton-Century-Crofts, Inc., 1957), p. 197.
4. Bloomfield, p. 289.

You may have seen footnotes containing the abbreviations *Ibid.* or *op. cit.* or *loc. cit.* These are rarely used nowadays. *Ibid.* is an abbreviation for a Latin word, *ibidem,* which is translated into English as "in the same place." What it means as a footnote is that the source is the same as the one given immediately before. *Op. cit.* translates as "in the work cited previously," *loc. cit.* "in the place previously cited." What they mean in a footnote is that a previous footnote contains the full source reference, so only part of the information is being repeated. The following pair of sample footnote lists shows these older types of footnotes and their more modern counterparts.

Older Forms

[1]Wilfred Funk, *Word Origins and Their Romantic Stories* (New York: Grosset & Dunlap, 1950), p. 7.
[2]*Ibid.*
[3]John W. Clark, *Encyclopedia Americana,* International Edition, Vol. 10, (New York: Americana Corporation, 1973), pp. 646.
[4]Funk, *op. cit.,* p. 11.
[5]Clark, *loc. cit.,* p. 648.
[6]*Ibid.*

Modern Forms

[1]Wilfred Funk, *Word Origins and Their Romantic Stories* (New York: Grosset & Dunlap, 1950), p. 7.
[2]Funk.
[3]John W. Clark, *Encyclopedia Americana,* International Edition, Vol. 10, (New York: Americana Corporation, 1973), pp. 646.
[4]Funk, p. 11.
[5]Clark, p. 648.
[6]Clark.

Footnotes are useful not only for acknowledging sources, but also for including information that otherwise would interrupt the flow of the essay. For example, a footnote is an excellent place for the definition of a word that some readers might not recognize.

Some writers use footnotes to acknowledge both borrowed words and borrowed ideas that they have rephrased in their own words. The author of "A Discussion of the Possibility of a World Language" (pages 277–281), trying to be very careful to acknowledge source material, has 37 footnotes for a seven-page paper (and yet one quotation lacks documentation). If all the borrowed ideas in a paragraph have the same source, it is sufficient to put one footnote number at the end of the paragraph and document the source in a footnote like this:

#For further discussion, see . . .

If a paragraph contains borrowed ideas from several sources, there is a better way to acknowledge those sources, as we shall see in the next section.

The footnote forms presented here are not the only ones used. In fact, there are many variations, some of which are published as "style sheets." (The Modern Language Association — MLA — style sheet is one that is frequently recommended by publishers and professors.) Most of the variations involve punctuation differences: periods in place of the commas and/or parentheses in the discussion above. Sometimes the name of the publishing company is omitted. The important thing to remember when writing a composition that requires footnotes is to be consistent. Sometimes a professor or a publisher will specify what footnote form is expected, or will require that a particular style sheet be used.

EXERCISE

Go to the library and look at half a dozen different journals in your major field. Compare the footnote forms used in each, and be prepared to report your findings to the class.

BIBLIOGRAPHIC ENTRIES

A *bibliography* is a list of sources consulted by a writer before (or during) the writing of a composition, whether or not the writer quotes anything from any of those sources. Writers who consult numerous sources may decide to list only the most important ones, in which case they do a "selected bibliography." A bibliography may also be referred to as "Sources," "References," "Additional Readings," or "Further Readings." A selected bibliography may be called "Selected Sources," "Selected References," etc.

The bibliography for a composition begins on a separate page at the end of the composition, after the footnote page, if there is one. The page carries a title ("Bibliography," "References," etc.) and is numbered consecutively, as part of the composition. If the composition ends on page 10 and page 11 is the footnote page, page 12 is the first page of the bibliography. The page number goes at the bottom of the title page.

Bibliographic entries look somewhat like footnotes; they contain most of the same information, as comparison of the following sample bibliographic entries with the sample footnotes on page 264 will illustrate.

Marckwardt, Albert H. "Regional Variations." *Language: Introductory Readings,* 3rd ed. Virginia P. Clark, Paul A. Eschholz, and Alfred F. Rosa, Eds. New York: St. Martin's Press, 1981, pp. 473-483.
Newman, P. B. "Indian Creek." *Kansas Quarterly,* VII, Fall, 1975, p. 66.
Salomon, Louis B. *Semantics and Common Sense.* New York: Holt, Rinehart and Winston, 1966.

However, there are important differences. Since the bibliographic entries do not refer back to footnotes in sequence in the composition, they are not usually numbered. A different method of organization is used in a bibliography. The last names (surnames) of the authors appear first, followed by the first and second names or initials. The last names of the authors are then arranged in alphabetical order, as in the sample bibliography above.

There is another difference: all footnotes include a page reference for a quotation. Bibliographic entries do not, since they refer to complete articles or books, not just to short quotations. Bibliographic entries include page numbers only if the reader is being advised that reading the source does not entail reading the entire magazine, journal, newspaper, or book. The third bibliographic entry above tells the reader that further information can be found in Salomon's entire book. The second entry tells the reader that Newman's work (a poem) appears on page 66 of the journal, the *Kansas Quarterly.* The first entry tells the reader that the specific essay referred to begins on page 473 and ends on page 483 of the book.

Let's examine these three sample bibliographic entries in more detail.

The Marckwardt essay is listed first because the last names of the authors of the other two sources begin with *N* (Newman) and *S* (Salomon), which follow *M* in the alphabet. If we had a source by someone whose last name was Mussen, that source would be listed between Marckwardt's essay and Newman's poem. (*Mu-* would follow *Ma-* because *u* comes after *a* in the alphabet.) The sequence of information for the Marckwardt essay is as follows (punctuation is indicated in ink; you will notice that parentheses are not used in bibliographic entries, although they are used in footnotes):

Last name (Marckwardt), first name (Albert) middle initial or name (H). "Title of article." ("Regional Variations.") <u>Title of book</u>, edition. (*Language: Introductory Readings,* third edition.) Editors' names in normal order. (Edited by Virginia P. Clark, Paul A. Eschholz, and Alfred F. Rosa.) Place of publication (New York): Publishing Company (St. Martin's Press), date (1981), pages on which article begins and ends (pp. 473–483).

The entry for Newman's poem differs somewhat from the entry for Marckwardt's essay:

Last name (Newman), first and middle initials (P. B.) "Title of poem." ("Indian Creek.") <u>Title of journal</u>, volume number (*Kansas Quarterly* VII), date (Fall, 1975), page (p. 66).

Because the poem is from a journal, the place of publication, the name of the publishing company, and the name(s) of the editor(s) have been omitted.

Some publishers and professors prefer different forms for bibliographic entries. Compare the following bibliographies, which have been taken from different publications:

Example 1[1]

References

Allwright, Richard. 1975. Problems in the study of the language teachers' treatment of learner error. In *On TESOL '75*, M. Burt and H. Dulay (Eds.). Washington, D.C.: TESOL.

Blatchford, Charles H. 1977. *Directory of teacher preparation programs in TESOL and bilingual education 1976–1978*. Washington, D.C.: TESOL.

Cathcart, R. and J. Olsen. 1976. Teachers' and students' preferences for correction of classroom errors. In *On TESOL '76*, J. Fanselow and Ruth Crymes (Eds.). Washington, D.C.: TESOL.

Chaudron, Craig. 1977a. A descriptive mode of discourse in the corrective treatment of learners' errors. *Language Learning 27*, 1:29–46.

Chaudron, Craig. 1977b. Teachers' priorities in correcting learners' errors in French immersion classes. *Working Papers in Bilingualism 12*. Toronto: Ontario Institute for Studies in Education.

Fanselow, John. 1977a. The treatment of error in oral work. *Foreign Language Annals 10*, 4.

Fanselow, John. 1977b. "I can't, I'm talking with the lady"—Feedback in teaching and non-teaching settings. *MEXTESOL Journal 11*, 4:1–29.

Hatch, Evelyn. 1977. A historical overview of second language acquisition research. In *Proceedings of the Los Angeles Second Language Research Forum*, Carol Henning (Ed.). UCLA.

Krashen, S. and T. Terrell. n.d. The natural approach: Language acquisition in the classroom. Unpublished manuscript.

Long, Michael. 1977. Teacher feedback on learner error: Mapping cognitions. In *On TESOL '77*, H. Douglas Brown, Carlos Yorio, and Ruth Crymes (Eds.). Washington, D.C.: TESOL.

Naiman, N., M. Frölich, H. Stern, and A. Todescu. 1978. *The good language learner*. Toronto: Ontario Institute for Studies in Education.

Paulston, C. B. and M. N. Bruder. 1976. *Teaching English as a second language: Techniques and procedures*. Cambridge, Mass.: Winthrop Publishers, Inc.

Ramirez, A. and N. Stromquist. 1979. ESL methodology and student language learning in bilingual elementary schools. *TESOL Quarterly 13*, 2:145–160.

Example 2[2]

1. JENSEN, A. 1969. "How much can we boost I.Q. and scholastic achievement." Harvard Ed. Review 39 (1):1–123.

[1]Jacquelyn Schachter, "The Hand Signal System." *TESOL Quarterly* 15:2 (June, 1981), pp. 137–138.

[2]Alain Corcos, "Genetics, Race, and Intelligence," *Michigan Academician* XII:2 (Fall, 1979), pp. 190–191.

2. KAGAN, J. 1969. "Inadequate evidence and illogical conclusion." Harvard Ed. Review 39:274-277.
3. KAMIN, L. 1976. "Heredity, intelligence, politics, and psychology." The I.Q. Controversy. N. J. Block and G. Dworkin, Editors.
4. LEWONTIN, C. 1970. "Race and intelligence." Science and Public Affairs, The Bulletin of the Atomic Scientists, March, pp. 2-8.
5. MASON, P. 1961. Common sense about race. McMillan.
6. SCARR, S., PAKSTIS, A. J., KATZ, S. H., AND BARKER, W. B. 1977. "The relationship between degree of white ancestry and intellectual skills within a black population." Human Genetics 857:1-18.
7. SCARR, S. AND WEINBERG, R. A. 1976. I.Q. test performance of black children adopted by white families. American Psychologist 31:726-739.
8. SHUEY, A. 1966. The testing of Negro intelligence. Social Science Press.
9. STERN, C. 1954. The Biology of the Negro, Sci. Amer. 191:81-85.

Example 3[3]

Bellugi, Ursula, and Edward S. Klima. 1973. "Formational Constraints on Language in a Visual Mode." Proposal to National Science Foundation from the Salk Institute for Biological Studies.
Bender, M. Lionel. 1973. "Linguistic Indeterminacy: Why You Cannot Reconstruct 'Proto-Human,'" Language Sciences 26:7-12.
Black, Mary B. 1973. "Ojibwa Questioning Etiquette and Use of Ambiguity," Studies in Linguistics 23:13-19.
Brown, Roger W. 1973. A First Language: The Early Stages (Cambridge, Mass.: Harvard University Press).
Chafe, Wallace. 1970. Meaning and the Structure of Language (Chicago: University of Chicago Press).
Darwin, Charles. 1913. The Expression of the Emotions in Man and Animals (New York: Appleton).
Foster, Mary LeCron. 1975. "The Symbolic Structure of Primordial Language," in Sherwood Washburn and Elizabeth R. McCown (eds.), Perspectives in Human Evolution IV (New York: Holt).
Gardner, R. Allen, and Beatrice T. Gardner. 1969. "Teaching Sign Language to a Chimpanzee," Science 165:664-72.
Hewes, Gordon W. 1971. Language Origins: A Bibliography. Department of Anthropology, University of Colorado.
———. 1973. "An Explicit Formulation of the Relationship Between Tool-Using, Tool-Making and the Emergence of Language," Visible Language 7:101-27.
Jakobson, Roman. 1969. "Linguistics in Its Relation to Other Sciences," in Actes du Xe Congrès International des Linguistes, Bucarest, 28 Août-2 Septembre 1967 (Bucharest: Editions de l'Academie de la République Socialiste de Roumanie).
Kuipers, A. H. 1968. "Unique Types and Typological Universals," in Pratidānam: Indian, Iranian and Indo-European Studies Presented to Franciscus Bernardus Jacobus Kuiper on His Sixtieth Birthday (The Hague: Mouton).
Lamendella, John T. 1975. Introduction to the Neuropsychology of Language. (Rowley, Mass.: Newbury House). Page references are to the manuscript.
Lieberman, Philip. 1972. The Speech of Primates (The Hague: Mouton).
———. 1974. "On the Evolution of Language: A Unified View," Cognition 2:59-94.

[3]Dwight Bolinger, "The Origins of Language" in Language: Introductory Readings, 3rd ed., Virginia P. Clark, Paul A. Eschholz, Alfred F. Rosa, eds. (New York: St. Martin's Press, Inc., 1981), p. 43.

In all three examples, each publication date immediately follows the author's name. In the first example, there are no quotation marks around the titles of articles. In the second example, the place of publication for books is not given, and although quotation marks are used for article titles, book and journal titles are not italicized. Discuss other differences among the various forms.

Although the forms differ somewhat, a person who is familiar with one form can quickly learn another. As with footnotes, bibliographic entries documenting the sources used in a theme should all follow the same form, and the writer should determine whether or not the professor or publisher for whom the theme is being written prefers a particular style.

EXERCISES

1. Rewrite the footnotes you did for Exercise B on page 266 as bibliographic entries.
2. Determine what has been omitted from the entries in the following sample bibliography.

Allen, Harold B., Ed. *Readings in Applied English Linguistics*, 1961.
Bloomfield, Leonard. New York: Henry Holt, 1933.
Chomsky, Noam. "Phrase-Structure Grammars." Mouton and Co., 's Gravenhage, The Netherlands.
Hughes, John. *The Science of Languages*. Random House, 1962. "Indian Verb Forms." New York, 1972, pp. 260–273.

3. Correct the errors in the following sample bibliography.

"A New Television Set" in *An Introduction to Visual Aids*, edited by EJP Devereux, 1962. Mathews, Drew and Shelbourne of London.
Bach, Emmon. Holt, Rinehart and Winston, New York, 1963 *An Introduction to Transformational Grammar Games for Second Language Learning*, 1966, by Gertrude Dorry. New York: McGraw-Hill.

4. For an essay about research on language variation, a student writer read several articles, including "Language Choice in Bilingual Classrooms", "The Situation of the Narrator in the Old English *Wife's Lament* " and "N.I.H. Beset by Budget Uncertainties, to Cut 12 Pct. from Research Projects." The following four pages show the contents page of one source, a journal, the title page and first page of the essay from the second source, another journal, and part of the front page of a news publication. Using the appropriate information from the illustrated pages, write a sample bibliography for the student writer's essay.
5. Write a bibliography for the essay (pages 277–281), "A Discussion of the Possibility of a World Language" and discuss how many footnotes the essay would then need.

TESOL QUARTERLY

| Volume II | March, 1977 | Number 1 |

Table of Contents

SPECULUM

A Journal of Medieval Studies

Vol. 56   JULY 1981   No. 3

published quarterly by

The Medieval Academy of America

Cambridge, Massachusetts

SPECULUM 56.3 (1981)

The Situation of the Narrator
in the Old English *Wife's Lament*

By Karl P. Wentersdorf

Although *The Wife's Lament* (*WL*) is one of the most frequently discussed pieces in the Old English poetic corpus, critics are still far from reaching agreement on the nature of the basic story conveyed by this elegiac monologue. Recent years have seen a flare-up in the old debate as to the identity of the narrator: Is the speaker a man or a woman? Detailed reexamination of the linguistic evidence regarding this question has confirmed the now traditional interpretation, that *WL* is indeed a woman's lamentation. This outcome has done nothing, however, to answer another question: Is the female speaker referring to one man (her husband or her lover), to two men (a first and then a second husband), or even to three men (two husbands and a kinsman of the second who accuses the wife of an offence deserving punishment)? There are several semantic and syntactic problems in *WL*, so that it has been possible to advance arguments, not equally convincing, for all three theories.[1] Today's reader seems compelled, as one editor has put it,

---

[1] See W. W. Lawrence, "The Banished Wife's Lament," *Modern Philology* 5 (1907–1908), 387–405; Svet Stefanovic, "Das angelsächsische Gedicht *Die Klage der Frau*," *Anglia* 32 (1909), 399–433; Ernst Sieper, *Die altenglische Elegie* (Strassburg, 1915), pp. 136–37, 215–23: Rudolf Imelmann, *Forschungen zur altenglischen Poesie* (Berlin, 1920), pp. 1–38, 73–117; B. J. Timmer, "The Elegiac Mood in Old English Poetry," *English Studies* [*ES*] 24 (1942), 33–44; Emily D. Grübl, *Studien zu den angelsächsischen Elegien* (Marburg, 1948), pp. 137–62; Stanley B. Greenfield, "*The Wife's Lament* Reconsidered," *PMLA* 68 (1953), 907–12; J. A. Ward, "*The Wife's Lament*: An Interpretation," *Journal of English and Germanic Philology* [*JEGP*] 59 (1960), 26–33; Robert D. Stevick, "Formal Aspects of *The Wife's Lament*," *JEGP* 59 (1960), 21–25; R. F. Leslie, *Three Old English Elegies* (Manchester, 1966 [1961]), pp. 1–12, 53–58; Kemp Malone, "Two English Frauenlieder," *Comparative Literature* 14 (1962), 111–17; A. C. Bouman, *Patterns in Old English and Old Icelandic Literature* (Leiden, 1962), pp. 43–89; Rudolph C. Bambas, "Another View of the Old English *Wife's Lament*," *JEGP* 62 (1963), 303–9; Robert P. Fitzgerald, "*The Wife's Lament* and 'The Search for the Lost Husband,'" *JEGP* 62 (1963), 769–77; Frank Bessai, "Comitatus and Exile in Old English Poetry," *Culture* 25 (1964), 130–44; M. J. Swanton, "*The Wife's Lament* and *The Husband's Message*," *Anglia* 82 (1964), 269–90; Thomas M. Davis, "Another View of *The Wife's Lament*," *Papers in English Language and Literature* [*PELL*] 1 (1965), 291–305; Jane L. Curry, "Approaches to a Translation of the Anglo-Saxon *The Wife's Lament*," *Medium Ævum* 35 (1966), 187–98; A. N. Doane, "Heathen Form and Christian Function in *The Wife's Lament*," *Neuphilologische Mitteilungen* [*NM*] 28 (1966), 77–91; Stanley B. Greenfield, "The Old English Elegies," in *Continuations and Beginnings: Studies in Old English Literature*, ed. E. G. Stanley (London, 1966), pp. 142–43, 165–69; Martin Stevens, "The Narrator of *The Wife's Lament*," *NM* 69 (1968), 72–90; Matti Rissanen, "The Theme of 'Exile' in *The Wife's Lament*," *NM* 70 (1969), 90–104; Fritz W. Schulze, "Die altenglische *Klage der Frau*," in *Festschrift für Edgar Mertner*, ed. Bernhard Fabian and Ulrich Suerbaum (Munich, 1969); W. F. Bolton, "*The Wife's Lament* and *The Husband's Message*: A Reconsideration Revisited," in *Archiv für das Studium der neueren*

THE CHRONICLE

of Higher Education.

November 25, 1981 • $1.25
Volume XXIII, Number 13

News Summary

Articles on inside pages

Despite his "pseudo-retirement" 30 years ago, the University of California chemist Joel. H Hildebrand continues his scholarly contributions at the age of 100. Story on Page 3.

Students from Gallaudet College interpret "America the Beautiful" through dance. Photo story on Pages 5-7.

Salaries of female faculty members average 85 per cent of those that male academics receive, the Chronicle Survey finds. Story and table on Page 8.

A faculty union in New Jersey is challenging the state higher-education board's rules for "reductions in force" at public colleges. Story on Page 9.

Freshman enrollment at private colleges and universities is down, but overall enrollment at the institutions is up by 1.1 per cent over last fall, new estimates show. Story and Fact-File on Page 10.

NIH, Beset by Budget Uncertainties, to Cut 12 Pct. from Research Projects

Agency complying with Reagan's order to lower spending until Congress acts on funds

By JANET HOOK

WASHINGTON

More than 1,300 biomedical researchers scheduled to receive grants from the National Institutes of Health next month have been told that they will get about 12 per cent less money than they expected.

The agency has decided to cut support for continuing research projects and make fewer new grants—at least until Congress decides how much money it will finally provide for the health institutes in the fiscal year that began October 1.

The decision to cut spending affects only grants scheduled to be made in December. The move could be reversed if an appropriations bill were enacted that provided more money for the institutes than the $3.3-billion President Reagan has requested.

However, if uncertainty about the institutes' final budget is not resolved quickly, N.I.H. officials say, similar reductions will be made in spending for grants in January and possibly in subsequent months.

Case-by-Case Decisions

Most immediately affected by the cutback are 1,384 recipients of multiyear N.I.H. grants who are due to receive an annual installment of funds on December 1.

Although many such researchers were given tentative notices earlier this year of how much money they would receive, the institutes have now said that such continuing grants will be cut by 12 per cent.

William F. Raub, associate director of N.I.H. for extramural research and training, said the exact amount to be cut from each grant would be determined on a case-by-case basis.

"It is neither practical nor sensible to reduce every grant 12 per cent," Mr. Raub said. "In some cases, there may be compelling reasons to make less than a 12-per-cent cut. In others, there may be good reason to cut more.

The institutes have trimmed their grants to comply with a White House order, issued last month, that requires federal agencies to keep spending down to the levels recommended by President Reagan when he called for a 12-per-cent across-the-board reduction in his 1982 budget request for all nondefense programs. That spending level was mandated even though, for most programs, Congress has provided more money for the programs in a continuous effort to save

Continued on Page 19, Column 1

READING SELECTION

Language is a form of life. There is probably no human institution which is so close to our life as our language.[1] In the world today there are at least three thousand natural tongues with only about one hundred of these extensive enough to have over one million speakers.[2] Because of this fact, many people have tried, throughout the years, to come up with a common means of communication for international use. It has been estimated that six hundred schemes have been proposed for a world language, but of these only a few have had any mass success whatsoever, the most appealing being the synthetic language of Esperanto.[3]

The problems of creating a world language are many, which accounts for the fact that none has been successfully adopted for international use as yet. It is interesting, however, to look at the schemes which have been proposed. Only three have made a dent in the field: Esperanto, Volapuk, and Interlingua.

Esperanto, the language invented by a young Polish eye doctor named Ludwig Zamenhof, has been the most successful and enduring of the artificial languages. This is due to the very simple structure of the language, and the ease with which it can be learned. The language is free of duplications, has no irregular verbs, no silent letters, and only sixteen rules to follow.[4] There are no exceptions to these rules (which is difficult for a native speaker of any natural tongue, such as English, to comprehend), and it is spoken and pronounced as it is written. It may be learned in a matter of a few hours by most persons, with Oriental people having a bit more difficulty because of the many sound combinations borrowed from English, German, and the Romance Languages.[5] Esperanto's basic vocabulary consists of about one thousand root-words, but an infinite variety of new words can be built from this base because of the regularized system of affixes. "There are no limitations, circumlocutions, or floundering among definitions, such as characterize Basic English."[6]

Zamenhof invented Esperanto at the age of eighteen because he was very disturbed about the constant bickering and misunderstanding which abounded in the city of Bialystok, Poland, where he lived. Four languages were in use there: Russian, Polish, German, and Yiddish, causing friction among the inhabitants.[7] He envisioned harmonious co-existence, not only in his city, but all over the world, with the acceptance of his clear, easily learned new language. He proclaimed that:

> Wars will be impossible if all men become brothers, overcoming language barriers and getting to know each other. A truly universal language is the only hope for mankind.[8]

A research paper by a student who asked not to be identified.

This, of course, was quite a strong statement and many people regarded him as a visionary, if not a crackpot. Because of this motive, Esperanto is felt, by some, to be more of an idealistic movement than a language.[9] The "brotherhood" of Esperanto, which it is often called, deplores prejudice and national rivalry. For example:

When Dr. Walter Lippman, a Leipzig scholar, had to flee from the Gestapo, he was spirited into Switzerland with the help of Esperantists with whom he had corresponded in this strange but precise language.[10]

The first description of this new language was published in 1887, in pamphlet form, written in Russian.[11] The publication caused quite a stir in Europe and America and slowly Esperanto societies began forming.[12] Under the Czar, Russia had its own society for the promotion of Esperanto. It flourished until the Reds seized power. They tried to subvert the language to their own political purposes, so most Esperantists in non-Communist countries gave up writing to their former Russian friends. In the 1930s, Soviet citizens were forbidden to speak or to receive letters written in Esperanto.[13] Dr. George Springer, of the Center for International Studies at M.I.T., says that, "Stalin himself decreed that Russian would be the future international language and exiled Esperantists to Siberia in large numbers."[14] In recent years the University of Leningrad broke a long-standing ban on Esperanto. It announced after-hours classes in the language and there was a rush by applicants.[15]

In Germany, before the Nazi's regime, Esperanto was eagerly being learned by many people. The Esperantists once planned an "Esperanto City" to be located on the outskirts of Munich and there were three hundred and thirty-five schools teaching Esperanto. "But with the advent of Hitler, who abhorred Esperanto, and feared the possibility of international friendship fostered by Esperantists, the German members of the movement had to use only German or face imprisonment."[16]

It was estimated in 1943 that 7,000,000 people in forty-seven lands used Esperanto as an auxiliary language.[17] Today, almost seventy-five years since its origination and fifty-seven years after the first Esperanto World Congress, which ushered in the period of its practical use, it is still quite widely used. There is still an Esperanto Congress held annually, where a wide range of programs in cultural and social activities are presented in Esperanto.[18] Henry W. Hetzel was greatly impressed with an Esperanto Congress he attended and had this to say:

Every world conference of the usual kind experiences the same linguistic chaos; a Congress using Esperanto stands out in refreshing and inspiring contrast. During the whole of the eight days the International Language is the only one heard, and no interpreters are seen or needed. Many of the participants have come literally from the ends of the earth, having learned their Esperanto entirely from a textbook, without as much as a phonograph record to give the pronunciation, and yet here is complete and immediate understanding. To cap the climax of this linguistic paradise, so uniform is the pronunciation that it is impossible to tell the nationality of the speaker, so far as his speech is any indication.[19]

At many places in the world, the wearer of the Esperantist emblem can rely upon fellow members for assistance in getting around. The green badge, (for hope), worn by speakers of Esperanto the world over, signifies the five continents in which this man-made language has devotees.[20]

As civilization advances, it also brings together the different peoples in contacts more numerous and more intimate. "Since the middle ages when Latin was the language of culture there has never been held a single world conference, truly international, in which any national tongue was used solely."[21] Many people feel that this is detrimental to real communication and feel that Esperanto would be a solution.[22] To test its precision, a French newspaper once summoned leading linguists. They were given French technical and literary tests and told to translate them. They were translated into six different languages: Esperanto, Russian, German, English, Spanish, and Italian. They then translated the translations back into French to see which language was most precise and accurate. Esperanto translated best from and back into French, and the second French version was virtually identical with the original.[23]

Preceding Esperanto was the language of Volapuk, invented in 1879 by a German, Johann Martin Scheyer. Scheyer, himself, spoke over seventy languages and was considered a linguistics genius. He created Volapuk from English, French, German, and the Romance Languages and it was the first artificial medium to enjoy mass appeal.[24]

It became the rage of Europe between 1879–1889. Volapuk societies were formed and even the American Philosophical Society, founded by Benjamin Franklin, considered it. Because of the difficulty of the grammar the Philosophical Society abandoned the idea. In 1889, the difficulty of the language and its complex rules caused Volapuk's collapse. At an international conference of Volapuk, speakers and enthusiasts found it too hard to understand and too cumbersome to use effectively. Volapuk was, however, very instrumental in helping Zamenhof launch Esperanto, which was far easier to understand.[25]

After Esperanto was recognized, a splinter group was formed by an American linguist, Dr. Alexander Gode. Dr. Gode believed in the ideas of Esperanto but his aims with his artificial language were more modest. He created Interlingua from French, Italian, Spanish, English, German, and Russian and made no real attempt to promote it as a spoken language.[26] His primary objective was to secure acceptance of the language as a medium of scientific and scholarly written communication.[27] "It has done quite well in the dozen years of its existence, and by now, some twenty journals make use of Interlingua, mostly for summaries."

Many other systems of artificial language have been proposed without much success. In the nineteenth century a man named Sodre invented Solresol, based on the musical scale. Later, scholars devised a method of language based on a numerical code called Translingua Script. Zoning and machine language have also been proposed without success to date.[28] Another school of thought discredits artificial languages altogether, and prefers to take their languages "straight." A large number of natural languages have been advocated as world auxiliaries, but only French and English have any real chance of acceptance, because they are actually functioning as auxiliaries in almost every continent.[29] It is interesting to note what occurred in 1960 at the bitterly anti-Western Bandung Conference, to which the United States and Britain were not invited. India and Pakistan, which had hoped to establish Hindi and Urdu as their number one tongues, had to communicate in English because it was familiar to the largest number of delegates.[30]

"The trouble with artifical languages is that, although arousing tremendous enthusiasm among their devotees, they do not attract enough mass support to achieve their objectives."[31] There are three major problems which probably account, to a great extent, for the lack of support in the area of a world language. These problems arise in connection with natural languages:

1. If a natural tongue were selected for international use, it would have to have an official, standard form; this will tend to differentiate it from the language spoken by its native speakers.
2. No natural language is fully phonetized, with precise correspondence between spoken and written form. If a natural language were selected, it would have to be given precise phonetic correspondence between speech and writing; this would differentiate the language still further from the one spoken locally.
3. Most important of all, natural languages are viewed, rightly or wrongly, as the vehicles of national cultures, points of view, and ideologies. This means that a Russian or Chinese, who will willingly learn English as a foreign tongue, will balk at accepting it as a fully international medium; an American will in like manner, reject the international use of Russian or Chinese.[32]

Esperanto, as an example of·a constructed language, would escape these drawbacks since it is fully phonetized and standardized.[33] It is also "neutral" in the sense that it doesn't belong to any particular nation.[34]

The drawbacks of constructed tongues are largely imaginary. The most common criticism is that they do not have "grass roots" and a "cultural" background. The true grass roots and cultural background of such constructed tongues as Esperanto lie in the fact that they are drawn from all the cultures that go into their construction.[35]

It is considered an anachronism, by many linguists, that in this progressive day and age we do not have a blended, constructed means of international communication.[36] Mario Pei offers an interesting example concerning the charge of "artificiality" often leveled at constructed languages:

A horse is "natural," an automobile is "artificial." For purposes of present-day travel under present-day conditions, no one seriously questions the superiority of an "artificial" automobile.[37]

It is logical to assume that a world auxiliary tongue would be useful and beneficial for international communication, but the fact remains that none has ever achieved complete acceptance. Until our culture is one which will *or is able to,* accept this concept we will probably remain in the position we are in currently; with French and English used, with interpreters, and with misunderstanding occurring because of the constant fluctuation in the natural tongue.

Footnotes

[1]Janet Rankin Aiken, "Why not Esperanto?," *The Bookman,* (Jan., 1931), p. 491.
[2]Ivy Kellerman Reed, *Esperanto Grammar* (Netuchen, New Jersey, Scarecrow Press, 1968), p. 8.

[3]Paul A. Eschholz, Alfred Rosa, and Virginia A. Clark, *Language Awareness* (New York, St. Martin's Press, 1974), p. 222.

[4]George A. Connor, "A Neutral Tongue," *Saturday Review Literary*, (Oct., 1943), p. 9.

[5]Eschholz, Rosa, and Clark, *op. cit.*, p. 221.

[6]Connor, *op. cit.*, p. 9.

[7]Reed, *op. cit.*, p. 11.

[8]Stanley S. Jacobs, "The Tongue that Unites," *Coronet*, (Nov., 1958), p. 156.

[9]Eschholz, Rosa, and Clark, *op. cit.*, p. 222.

[10]Jacobs, *op. cit.*, p. 154.

[11]Reed, *op. cit.*, p. 12.

[12]Jacobs, *op. cit.*, p. 156.

[13]*Ibid.*, p. 158.

[14]*Ibid.*

[15]Eschholz, Rosa, and Clark, *op. cit.*, p. 222.

[16]Jacobs, *op. cit.*, p. 9.

[17]Connor, *op. cit.*, p. 9.

[18]Eschholz, Rosa, and Clark, *op. cit.*, p. 222.

[19]Henry W. Hetzel, "The World Language, English or Esperanto?", *Education* (Jan. 1931), p. 627.

[20]Jacobs, *op. cit.*, p. 154.

[21]Hetzel, *op. cit.*, p. 624.

[22]Reed, *op. cit.*, p. 10.

[23]Jacobs, *op. cit.*, p. 158.

[24]Eschholz, Rosa, and Clark, *op. cit.*, p. 220.

[25]Aiken, *op. cit.*, p. 489.

[26]Eschholz, Rosa, and Clark, *op. cit.*, p. 223.

[27]*Ibid.*, p. 224.

[28]*Ibid.*, pp. 226–227.

[29]*Ibid.*, p. 225.

[30]*Ibid.*

[31]*Ibid.*, p. 224.

[32]Reed, *op. cit.*, pp. 8–9.

[33]Jacobs, *op. cit.*, p. 154.

[34]Reed, *op. cit.*, p. 9.

[35]*Ibid.*

[36]Hetzel, *op. cit.*, p. 628.

[37]Reed, *op. cit.*, p. 9.

AVOIDING FOOTNOTES, EVEN FOR DIRECT QUOTATIONS

Scholars in many fields of study, especially the sciences, use no source footnotes, even though they quote from sources. Instead, they use the bibliography to provide the source information, after supplying key information in the texts of their compositions, often in parentheses. The key information that must be included is the last name of the person who originally wrote the book or article in which the quotation appears and the date of publication of that source. A reader can then find the original quotation by checking the bibliography to find the full reference for a book, journal, magazine, or newspaper published by that author on that date. Furthermore, source material that has been paraphrased by a writer can be acknowledged in the same way. The following essay illustrates this concept.

READING SELECTION

Just What I Choose It to Mean?
Some Translation Problems
by Verner Bickley

> "When I use a word," Humpty Dumpty said in rather a scornful tone, "it means just what I choose it to mean—neither more nor less."
> "The question is," said Alice, "whether you *can* make words mean different things."
> "The question is," said Humpty Dumpty, "which is to be master—that's all."
>
> —Lewis Carroll
> *Through the Looking Glass*

Despite Humpty Dumpty's statement, an important function of language is to communicate thought and it can serve this function adequately only if there is a general measure of agreement upon the meaning of words. The problem is that languages are dynamic and the fact that they change, as do the cultures of which they are part, hampers successful translation, whether it be intralingual, intersemiotic or interlingual.

Intralingual translation, the process of rewording something within the same language, is of particular concern to those interested in legal processes and to diplomats and employees of international organizations.

Words cause problems for lawyers because they change their meanings over time and have emotive functions that express affective attitudes or arouse such attitudes in others, and because of the special care that must be taken to interpret their special meanings in wills and contracts. A case in point is quoted by Glanville Williams (1945) where the testator, who had lived with an unmarried woman and had four children by her, died leaving her certain property "during her widowhood." It was held that the gift had failed, because a woman who had not been married could not be anyone's *widow.*

Handbooks of diplomatic etiquette caution against the misplaced use of humor even when the language employed is a common international language such as English. I can vouch from my own experience that such caution is necessary. At a diplomatic reception held in Jakarta in 1963, I asked a senior attache from a certain South American country whether or not his wife had accompanied him to his Indonesian post. "No," said he, without a trace of humor in his expression, "I killed her before I left." I looked in vain for the twinkle in the eye. Was it possible? I shall never know the answer.

Richard Hoggart (1974), a former Assistant Director-General of UNESCO, has noted that when in doubt more and more formal politeness is the order of the day, because national styles differ and are easily misunderstood. Wooliness, says Hoggart, has sometimes to be resorted to so as to help keep the organization (in this case, UNESCO itself) still talking.

Intersemiotic translation involves the translation of a message from one kind of symbolic system to another, for example, when the meanings of flags used at sea were rendered as verbal messages. F. F. Weeks (1980) observes that, for a non-English speaking person, the understanding of a flag signal involved (1) the placing of an alphabetical

From *English Around the World,* May, 1981 pp. 1, 5, 8.

CITING AUTHORITY

meaning to each flag and (2) translating the received message into the speakers' own language. Such translation was relatively easy since it could be done at a very leisurely pace. With the introduction of the VHF radio transmitter, communication at sea has become much quicker but, in present circumstances, can lead and *has* led to disasters because of language difficulties.

The sinking in 1967 of the Danish ship "Elsa Priess" in the North Sea was directly attributable to a failure in VHF communications. Weeks describes another, less serious incident that occurred in Swedish waters.

"Vessel A (20,000 tons) had a pilot on board and was on a North-Westerly course. She collided with B (5,000 tons) coming from a crossing channel from starboard. Both channels were in the archipelago and were comparatively narrow. Visibility was limited by the mainland and the islands between the channels. The vessels sighted each other about 4.5 minutes before the collision at a distance of 0.6 M. Both were then about 0.6 M from the point of collision and made relatively high speed considering the visibility. Just after A had sighted B, A's pilot called B and spoke to B's Master. According to A's version, the conversation was as follows:

A. If you can see me, take it easy because I can't stop.
B. Yes, I can see you. You are welcome.

According to B, the conversation was like this:

A. Now you have to watch out because here we come.
B. Yes, I can see you. All right.

Weeks points out that both ships were found to be at blame for the collision which "is hardly surprising, considering the ambiguous nature of their conversation."

A major problem is that few native English-speaking officers speak any foreign language and ships' crews include a large and increasing proportion of non-native English speakers, even though English remains the official International language of the sea.

Sea-to-sea and sea-to-shore communication problems are often those which occur in *interlingual translation,* the interpretation of one language by the verbal signs of another. It is, however, sometimes impossible to find an equivalent meaning in some languages. In English the word *therefore* indicates some kind of logical conclusion whereas the meaning given to it by Cantonese speakers of English is "in the light of this experience."

Misunderstandings caused by inadequate interlingual translation and interpretation can be wry or serious. For example, the definition of the Japanese expression "kekkon sodansho" (public marriage matchmaker's office) in one popular dictionary was given as "public love maker's office" and the head of such an organization was referred to as a "public lover maker." The Far Eastern Economic Review reported recently (October 17, 1980) that a group of Australian academics being conducted round the Imperial Palace in Peking were shown the women's quarters with the words: "This is where the emperor kept his cucumbers." According to All-Language Services Inc., (1978) a mistranslation of a business agreement concluded with the U.S.S.R., converted "Hydraulic ram" into "wet male sheep." The description of a bid by an American firm to build metal fencing for an Iranian excavation site included the line (translated) "We are the leading manufacturer and safest receiver of stolen merchandise." In an American shipping firm's proposal to an Arabic firm, the phrase "dummy load" was changed to "false pregnancy." *Clipper* Magazine (September, 1979) pointed out that when General Motors marketed the Nova in Latin America, executives could not understand why the car was not selling well—until someone discovered that "no va" in Spanish means "doesn't go." The magazine also noted that the Parker Pen Company was not amused to find that an advertisement in Latin America had been mistranslated, and that it indicated that a particular Parker pen "had contraceptive benefits." Stanley Rundle (1946) refers to the following advertisement which appeared in 1915 in the personal column of the London Times: "Jack F. G. If you are not in khaki by the 20th, I shall cut you dead. Ethel M." This was rendered in the Cologne Gazette as " . . . I will hack you to death" (hacke dich zu Tode).

In a pamphlet published in 1960, Bertil Malmberg wondered if the differences in semantic structure and the differences in connotations between the words of different languages were not just as dangerous for the future as the atomic bomb. Certainly, it is not difficult to find numerous instances of the ways in which mistranslations sparked off international disputes, or at least created problems in international relations. A serious gaffe was the mistranslation of Nikita Khruschev's comment to a group of "Western" ambassadors in 1956. The report that he had said "We will bury you" reinforced Cold War attitudes—perhaps unnecessarily since it was the consensus of United Nations translators that Khruschev actually declared "Because our system is better than yours, we will *survive* you."

Two frequently quoted incidents involved former President Jimmy Carter. During a luncheon with President José Portillo in Mexico City, the President referred to his love for jogging. "As a matter of fact, I first acquired my habit of running here," he said, "I discovered that I was afflicted with Montezuma's revenge." Only one Mexican newspaper *Uno Más Uno* quoted Carter's words, but it did not translate "Montezuma's revenge" for its Mexican readers.

During the President's visit to Poland in 1977, it was reported naively in the American Press that many Poles thought that he had made vulgar and insulting remarks to them upon his arrival. It is unlikely that the mistranslation by the American interpreter of the President's "I have come to learn your opinions and understand your desires for the future" as "I desire the Poles carnally" was accepted by Polish listeners as anything other than an unfortunate mistake. Perhaps the most serious consequence was the revelation of the interpreter's ineptitude and therefore the inadequate preparations for the visit made by the President's advisers.

The President's interpreter was a professional free-lance who used Russian syntax and archaic Polish idioms. The problems he encountered occurred because of his inability to express for the Polish language community the experiences that were rooted in his own American language community. The problem is not an unfamiliar one in the interpreter's profession. As an interpretation problem it is linguistic in nature but in so far as it arises out of differing community experiences, it is also a cultural problem. To understand a communicative act in a homogenous language community, the individual needs to know the context of situation of which that act is a part. To understand a

communicative act in a language community different from his own, the individual also
needs to be familiar with the cultural patterns most closely related to that act in its
particular context.

References

Hoggart, R., *On Culture and Communication*, Oxford University Press, 1972.
Malmberg, B., *Linguistic Barriers to Communication in the Modern World*, Ibadan University Press, 1960.
Rundle, S., *Language as a Social and Political Factor in Europe*, Faber and Faber, London, 1946.
Weeks, F. F., *Communications at Sea* (unpublished manuscript).
Williams, G., "Language and the Law," in the *Law Quarterly Review*, London, Vol. 61, 1945.

In the third paragraph, there is a reference to "Glanville Williams (1945)."
In the list of references, the last entry is

Williams, G., "Language and the Law" in the *Law Quarterly Review*" London, Vol. 61, 1945.

This is the source of the author's information about the legal definition of
"widowhood."

In paragraph five, the author paraphrases Richard Hoggart and gives a date,
1975. In the list of references, we find

Hoggart, R., *On Culture and Communication*, Oxford University Press, 1972.

What are the full sources of the information in paragraph 7 about the ship
collision and of the quotations in paragraph 11?

SUMMARY

Reading other people's statements about a subject can help a writer in two
important ways. In the first place, it can add to the writer's understanding of
the subject by providing him or her with additional facts, figures, examples,
descriptions, etc. Secondly, references to the ideas of experts add credibility to
the writer's own ideas. It is essential for a writer to acknowledge, through correct footnotes and/or bibliographic entries, that she or he has borrowed a
phrase, a sentence, or an idea from someone else's work. Using someone else's
work without proper acknowledgement is both rude and dishonest. The best
writers in the world give credit where it is due; their example is a good one
for neophyte writers to follow.

Epilogue

This book is full of advice on how to write well in English words, phrases, clauses, sentences, paragraphs, and themes. One of the greatest authors in English literature was not a native speaker of the language, and yet he gave would-be writers the best and briefest advice ever given. Joseph Conrad, who was born and raised in Poland, who spoke no English until his late teens, who learned English as a sailor on British ships, and who loved to read, explained his responsibility as a writer: "My task which I am trying to achieve is, by the power of the written word, to make you hear, to make you feel—it is, before all, to make you *see*. That—and no more, and it is everything."

Index